Black Sons to Mothers

COUNTERPOINTS

Studies in the
Postmodern Theory of Education

Joe L. Kincheloe and Shirley R. Steinberg
General Editors

Vol. 107

PETER LANG
New York • Washington, D.C./Baltimore • Boston • Bern
Frankfurt am Main • Berlin • Brussels • Vienna • Canterbury

Black Sons to Mothers

Compliments, Critiques, and Challenges for Cultural Workers in Education

EDITED BY
M. Christopher Brown II
and James Earl Davis

PETER LANG
New York • Washington, D.C./Baltimore • Boston • Bern
Frankfurt am Main • Berlin • Brussels • Vienna • Canterbury

Library of Congress Cataloging-in-Publication Data

Black sons to mothers: compliments, critiques, and challenges for cultural workers in education / edited by M. Christopher Brown II, James Earl Davis.
p. cm. — (Counterpoints; v. 107)
Includes bibliographical references.
1. Afro-American young men—Education—Social aspects. 2. Afro-American young men—Family relationships. 3. Mothers and sons—United States. 4. Home and school—United States. I. Brown, M. Christopher. II. Davis, James Earl. III. Series: Counterpoints (New York, N.Y.); vol. 107.
LC2731.B53 371.829'6073—dc21 99-013961
ISBN 0-8204-4292-5
ISSN 1058-1634

Die Deutsche Bibliothek-CIP-Einheitsaufnahme

Black sons to mothers: compliments, critiques, and challenges for cultural workers in education / ed. by M. Christopher Brown II and James Earl Davis.
–New York; Washington, D.C./Baltimore; Boston; Bern; Frankfurt am Main; Berlin; Brussels; Vienna; Canterbury: Lang.
(Counterpoints; Vol. 107)
ISBN 0-8204-4292-5

Cover design by Lisa Dillon

To our dear mothers, Jannie Lee Brown,
and Minnie Briggs Davis, and
to all of the birth mothers, adopted mothers,
godmothers, church mothers,
community mothers, school house mothers,
extended families, neighbors,
coaches, aunts, uncles, cousins, friends,
teachers, and other cultural workers
who contribute to the education and
development of African American boys/men.

Ubuntu: I am because you exist.
—South Africa

Acknowledgments

This book would not have been possible without the help of so many of our friends. There are numerous colleagues around the country who have aided in conceptualization, author selection, and editing. We thank each of you. We are particularly thankful to Joe Kincheloe and Shirley Steinberg, who believed in this project from the beginning. We are also grateful to Christopher Myers, Jacqueline Pavlovic, and the production staff of Peter Lang Publishing who provided all of the time and support needed to complete this project. While we, the editors, are responsible for all errors, gaps, and inconsistencies, this volume represents a collective effort on the part of a group of authors with whom it has been a pleasure to work. Without their collective effort, this book could not have been put together.

We would like to thank the soon-to-be famous poet and storyteller, Shirley M. Washington, for the use of her poem "They Call Her." Shirley's poem sets the tone and pace for the chapters which follow. Special thanks are extended to Debra Gough who prepared the manuscript for publication. Additionally, we thank Ms. Eileen Ahearn and the James Baldwin Estate for permission to reprint "A Talk to Teachers." We would also like to thank D. Kamili Anderson and the *Journal of Negro Education* for permission to reprint a version of Vernon C. Polite's "The Method in the Madness: African American Males, Avoidance Schooling, and Chaos Theory"; and David Gillborn of the journal *Race, Ethnicity and Education* for permission to reprint a version of C. Keith Harrison's "Themes that Thread through Society: Racism and Athletic Manifestation in the African American Community."

Table of Contents

They call her strong black Woman.
They call her the backbone of the race.
They call her . . .

When they need a baby fed, a house cleaned, a belly filled, a fevered brow soothed—
They call her.
When don't they call her? When they need someone to praise . . .
someone to love . . . someone to make happy.

When Egypt was a great kingdom during the time of Pharaoh . . .
They called her.
When the race was bought and sold like animals . . .
They called her.
When they sold her baby and told her to nurse theirs at her still filled breast . . .
They called her.

But it is a new day dawning; full of promises and a strange hope, that her baby is now a man—a woman—without fear of anyone except God.

But still we call her.

Momma, momma. We call her.
Mother, mother. We call her.
Mom, mom. We call her.

Still she answers.
Still she is patient, gentle, and understanding.
She is old and tired now.
Her hair is white with the years of strain, toil, and trouble.
Her back is bent, yet still unbroken is her Spirit.
Sometimes her eyes fill with centuries of unshed tears,
As she looks back over the years—and yet it goes on.

They still call her.
You still call her.

Momma, momma.
Mammy, mammy.
Mother, mother.

AND STILL SHE ANSWERS.

Shirley M. Washington, ***THEY CALL HER***

Chapter One

To Be or Not to Be a Mother: Introducing the Conversation

M. Christopher Brown II and James Earl Davis

> At my old school there is at least one teacher who loves me. She is the teacher who "knew me before I was born" and bought my first baby clothes. It is she who makes life bearable.
>
> —Alice Walker, *In Search of Our Mothers' Gardens*

Our Conversation

It was in the Fall Semester of 1998 that we met to put together this volume. We were both somewhat disoriented as a result of recent relocations. James had just begun a sabbatical at the University of Michigan in the Institute for Research on Women and Gender. Similarly, Christopher was in the initial weeks of a professorship at the University of Illinois at Urbana-Champaign. As has been the case in our other research initiatives and/or work sessions, we spent the first several hours exploring the social events and professional dynamics occurring in our lives. Although we had seen each other just a few weeks earlier, there was a chatty excitement about our conversation.

As conversation shifted from our individual "soap operas," we began to focus on why we had commissioned the participation of our colleagues and friends for this book, *Black Sons to Mothers: Compliments, Critiques, and Challenges for Cultural Workers in Education*. We spent the next hour attempting to position their and our voices within the larger academic debate on black education, the culture wars, and social change. Since Chris is a social reconstructionist and James is a progressive, we agreed that the text must focus on the voices, discourses, and narratives that reveal and/or illuminate the educational relationship between students (particularly black males) and their teachers.

The conversation explored Robin Kelley's *Yo' Mama's Disfunktional!* (1997), which we had both recently completed reading. We dialogued about the simplicity of Kelley's thesis: social control has a low correlation with the development of black urban youth. Reading from the text, Chris quoted: "Rather than try[ing] to change the person through rigid regimentation . . . , we need to change . . . the built environment, the economy, and the racist discourse that dominates popular perceptions of black youth" (p. 76). The time had come to stop talking and start working. We needed to write words that would implode existing constructions of black males as menaces to society, as well as perceptions of teachers as babysitters. We needed to write about black boys/men and cultural workers as participants in a proactive (not reactive) educational system. We needed to move our conversation from private diatribe to public discourse.

Inasmuch as the discourse on black men and their role performance is steeped in the hegemonic rhetoric of traditional notions of masculinity, it fails to sensibly represent the diverse complexity of black boys'/men's lives and relations (Harper, 1996). Black boys/men are sons, fathers, friends, colleagues, husbands, lovers, and even "mothers." It was therefore incumbent upon us to rethink the cultural places where black boys'/men's identities are shaped and where the politics of manhood are informed and enforced. As such, each contributor in this volume committed himself to exploring the lives—both personal and professional—of black boys/men in ways that would acknowledge the multiplicity of the black male subject in relation to "mothering" and identity.

Mother/Cultural Worker/Educator: A New Etymology

The investigation of gender and its effects on schooling experiences and achievement has been an important area of scholarly and political concern (Adler, Kless & Adler, 1992; Kessler, et al., 1985; Wexler, 1988). Without question, schooling contexts are important sources for gender construction and development (Polite & Davis, 1998). In most of this work, gender is viewed from a social constructivist perspective, in which the qualities of masculinity/femininity are culturally attributed and predefine: for both students and teachers (Connell, 1993; Thomas, 1990). For the purposes of this book, the gendered construction of teaching is not only redefined, but left to individual interpretation.

Teachers are charged with formally overseeing the transference of cultural knowledge, traditions, and values to their students. However, this is merely the beginning of their duties. They are also responsible for nurturing and protecting both the student and her/his intellectual curiosity (Brown, forthcoming; Brown, Davis, & McClendon, 1999). Teachers are mothers, and the act of mothering is a form of cultural work. We can therefore claim singularity among mothering/cultural work/educating. Moreover, we can declare that teaching is a form of cultural work (Freire, 1998).

Mothering/cultural work/educating is particularly interesting given the existing narratives of black women as mothers and teachers in U.S. society. The historic and cultural persistence of black mothers through slavery and other social degradations laid the foundation for a maternal focus on child development and cultural enrichment. At the same time as the focus on maternal roles and functions was created, the patriarchal epistemology and ontology of Western society cemented the perception of mothering as feminine and/or related to the gonad-deficient gender. This rigidification intentionally failed to acknowledge the major role that men and "fathers" could play in intellectual development and social preparation. Consequently, it limited any meaningful discourse on the role of males in the traditional mothering space (Collins, 1995).

The logic of our argument utilizes the following syllogism. First, there is no such thing as a mother without children. Second, teachers have a responsibility to be mothers/cultural workers/ educators. Therefore, all educators have children. The question is "How do we make meaning of the educator-'child' relationship?"

The mother/cultural worker/educator is a member of the student/"child"/ learner's world through fictive kinship (Oppong, 1973; James, 1993; McRoy, 1990). Fictive kin are nonbiological friends, neighbors, or persons who assist in performing family roles and/or care-giving. Fictive mothers perform these roles. Given the above understanding of the nurturing and developmental role that educators perform, it is necessary to focus sociologically and anthropologically on how this fictive mothering emerges.

According to Patricia Hill Collins (1987), there is a "generalized ethic of care" by which black women feel accountable to all the black children in the community and interact with them as if they were their own. There is an intentionally nonbifurcated recognition of all children as "mine" rather than "theirs." Often referred to as the "other" mothers (Troester, 1994), these women are responsible for educating "all of their children" about the traditions and culture of a specific community (Reagon, 1988). While the concept of the fictive mother was originally a historical and cultural survival mechanism, it remains a cornerstone of cultural work on race, particularly for African Americans. What remains is the interest and willingness of teachers to enter the cultural space of "mothering."

Summarily, the word "mother" is more than a noun. It is a verb. A verb which means to give life to, to nurture and protect, and/or to assist in the development of a person. Everyone involved in the life of a learner (from the classroom teacher to the minister to the rap artist to the school bus driver) has the potential to mother. As such, the word "mother" is etymologically semantic. Humpty Dumpty said: "When I use a word, it means just what I choose it to mean—neither more nor less." This is how we feel about the terms "mother/cultural worker/educator." These words mean just what we choose them to mean—neither more nor less.

The Responsibilities of Mothering/Cultural Work/Educating

The confluence of social and political mandates, ideologies, and alleged pathologies is most profound as it relates to home and schooling. And according to the literature, mothers are the primary teachers (Chodorow, 1978; Collins, 1987; Comer & Poussaint, 1992; King & Mitchell, 1995). However, the contexts, conflicts, and concessions of schooling and mothering have received little intellectual analysis and/or interrogation. Yet if we had to list the most influential relationships in our lives, mothers and schoolteachers would be at the top of the list.

The interest of the editors and contributors in investigating the nexus between education and familial ties is grounded in "our" shared experiences of being mothered and educated in communities where these lines are blurred and congruent. Further, our focus is driven by the consequences—social, economic and cultural—of mothering and educational experiences.

All too many African American students (as well as members of other marginalized groups) are educated in classrooms whose curricular content ignores if not nullifies their existence. The relationship between these students and society is often ahistorical, repressive, and stereotypical (Hall, 1997; Castenell & Pinar, 1993). As a result, these students become grotesque spectacles who detract from the corpus of information, rather than patron stakeholders who are seamlessly woven into the fabric of information. Ancillary and peripheral notions of these black boys/men place them outside the anthology of social and cultural knowledge. Because the experiences of black boys/men are not perceived as necessary within the educational setting, the personhood of these students is often devalued, ignored, and displaced.

The marginalization and sorting of the schooling process therefore forces mothers/cultural workers/teachers to recontextualize what is currently known or believed about black boys/men. This book is that recontextualization. In each chapter, the research subject of extrapolation is the oppressed and/or marginalized population of black boys/men or a black boy/man. In other words, the research on white boys/men is not being applied to black boys/men, but the research on black boys/men is being applied to all students. Additionally, in an unusual reversal, the black boy/man is not being discussed in relationship to a dysfunction or pathology. The black male student is at the center of a discourse that is not about "at-riskness" or "special education." Thus, the text is able to offer a complex and higher-ordered understanding not only of schooling and cultural work, but of black boys/men as well.

In Nah Dove's recent work, *Afrikan Mothers: Bearers of Culture, Makers of Social Change* (1998), she explores the efforts of mothers of African descent to situate their children in school environments that both acknowledge and value the unique positionality of children from the African diaspora. The truth is that many parents will not have the option of immersion schools, Afrocentric academies, and/or African-centered magnet schools. Additionally, these initiatives often divorce the non–black, brown, or other teacher from their responsibility to educate all children. If school is the anteroom for the stage of life, many black and brown youth are being grossly unrehearsed, under–costumed, and ill–prepared.

In short, mothers/cultural workers/educators are central to preparing youth for their roles in a global society. In order to carry out their charge, mothers/cultural workers/educators must believe that they can assist in building a new social order (Counts, 1932). They must believe that everything they do can impact and improve the quality of life for someone, somewhere, somehow. Mothers/cultural workers/educators must declare that everyone can learn, and that their role is to assist individuals in their academic and intellectual development. Likewise, mothers/cultural workers/educators must know the individuals charged to their care. It is necessary for this knowledge to be free from prejudice, bias, and deficit–model constructions of individual identity premised on race, class, gender, sexual identity, or theological persuasion. Finally, mothers/cultural workers/educators must sacrifice their time, talent, and resources to aid in developing the lives and experiences of their children—daughters and sons.

Black Sons Speak to/as Mothers

Without question, the black boy/man/male has enticed the U.S.'s societal and intellectual imagination (Akbar, 1991; Comer & Poussaint, 1992; Hare & Hare, 1985; Kunjufu, 1988; Madhubuti, 1990). Sadly, too much of the enticement has resulted in pathological discourses on dysfuctionality. There is the still–current statistic about more black boys/men being involved in the penal system than in higher education. In fact, "In 1991, there were 136,000 black males aged 18–24 in prison, and fully 378,000 black males of the same age in college. The Sentencing Group's statement is misleading: comparing black male prisoners of all ages to the overwhelmingly young college population gives a very false perception" (Chideya, 1995, p. 197). The statistic is erroneous. Similarly, most pseudopathologies can be easily debunked. The traditional educational research focus has been on the educational "problems" of black males rather than their "successes." These narrow and deficit-model queries obscure the diversity and complexity of how black males operate and maneuver within educational settings. Invariably, social science constructions of black boys/men in schools have remained unidimensional and static.

Current discussions, particularly those presented in the popular media about the "plight of black males," have captured the interest of many politicians, educators, and social commentators. However, too little is truly understood about educating black males. The meanings of black boys'/men's lives, and the relationships that undergird these meanings, remain elusive because their personal space is overshadowed by the scholarly dispositions and expectations of educational researchers. Hence, the personal and communal dynamics of black males in school remain unexplored, misunderstood, and silenced. Although there has been substantial discussion of the alleged plight of black boys/men, only modest attempts have been made to connect their lives to meaningful sources of influence and support, such as their teachers and mothers. In this book we take considerable intellectual risks in crossing the border between the personal and the scholarly in order to allow current and potential cultural workers insight into the real lives and lived experiences of "black sons."

The pages of this book provide a critical site in which to explore the meanings and connections of black boys'/men's lives. Hence the text offers literary, scholarly, and personal space within which to interrogate the seemingly elusive intersection of race and gender. Each chapter will be offered in one of two voices—one in which boys/men speak to mothers as cultural workers and/or one which represents a boys'/man's transformation into the cultural space of mothering. The book's intent is to question black boys'/men's constructions as sons (cultural offspring), and to engage in the project of representing mothering as cultural work and black boys'/men's roles in and ties to this work. The words Black/black, White/white, African American, Caucasian, African descent, and European background are all used interchangeably.

Part 1 of the book focuses on the sociology of education and the politics of schooling. Each of the chapters provides the reader with information that forces both a recontextualization and a reconsideration of the terms "mother," cultural worker, education, schooling, and masculinity. William Eric Perkins offers a history of the black family in the United States. His focus is on how social scientists and academics have intentionally constructed a doctrine of pathology around the black family in general, and the black male in particular. He anchors his chapter in the life and legacy of Malcolm X. Eric utilizes Malcolm's life history to reposition the discourse on how masculinity and manhood are encouraged, reinforced, and cemented.

The next two chapters deconstruct and reconstruct the definitions of mothering and manhood. Edward Underwood narrates his personal experiences with life, death, and rebirth. He explains how the death of his wife forced him into "mothering." This personal narrative is buttressed with childhood accounts of his parents and contemporary experiences with his daughter. Similarly, James Earl Davis utilizes conversations with his mother to explore how manhood and gender are (re)produced. James attempts to examine the complex relationship between black boys/men and their mothers. Although this chapter remains an intellectual presentation, the voice of the author is ever present and overarching.

In part 2, the book shifts to specific educational concerns that are burned into the societal consciousness regarding black boys/men and schooling—violence, sports, and intellectual inferiority. The chapters highlight myriad aspects of the educational endeavor. Garrett Duncan offers a refreshing look at how everyday pedagogies inform the development of black youth. Underscoring the white supremacist sociopolitical milieu that often goes unnoticed in U.S. society, especially in schools, Garrett recounts numerous instances of prejudice in the schooling experiences of black boys/men. His argument problematizes violence in a new and thought-provoking way. He asserts that the issue is not with student-to-student violence, but with the school-to-student violence which continually assaults black boys/men throughout the educational process.

The issue of "school violence" is extended by Karl Bell in his chapter on race and teaching. Karl, like Garrett, suggests that modern schooling has the potential to victimize black boys/men both intentionally and unintentionally. Karl, however, posits that this victimization might be limited by the presence of mother-like teachers. Similarly addressing racism in schooling, C. Keith Harrison interrogates the nexus between sport and education. His contention is that sport performs a unique role in the construction of social perceptions of black boys/men. According to Keith, this construction contributes to the belief that black males are physical entities rather than intellectual beings. Part 2 closes with a reprint of social critic James Baldwin's article, "The Negro Child—His Self-Image," which originally appeared in *The Saturday Review* in December 1963.

Constructive criticisms and recommendations regarding the educational future of black boys/men, as well as other learners, are presented in part 3. Christopher Span details the experiences of black males in Milwaukee's immersion schools. After summarizing the history of Milwaukee's immersion schools and the immediate effects of such schooling, Christopher advances a philosophical argument for the educational value of schooling centered around the African diaspora. Tyrone Howard borrows Christopher's social context in order to pose questions on how black boys/men should be educated in U.S. schools. Unlike Christopher, Tyrone does not select Afrocentric schooling as a response to "miseducation." Tyrone affirms the usefulness of multiculturalism, especially if it is reconceptualized. He offers design principles which can enhance teaching and learning across and within racial contexts.

Part 3 concludes with two chapters exploring often-ignored populations of black boys/men. Michael Mobley devotes his chapter to discussing the sociocultural and psychological dynamics between black gay males (and/or gay black males) and schooling. Additionally, he develops a model for working with these black boys/men in educational settings. Vernon Polite's chapter examines the contexts of schooling among black male students, particularly as they relate to school avoidance. Drawing upon elements of chaos theory, Vernon problematizes the systematic methods of schooling avoidance behaviors.

The book concludes—or should we say commences—with part 4. Part 4 presents a lone chapter by M. Christopher Brown II—"The Good Reverend Doctor." This final chapter issues a call for educators to engage in radical cultural work. Christopher argues that being a "prophet of power" is the nirvana of educational practice. After detailing the relationship between empowerment and education, he invites teachers to answer the call to radical cultural work.

Closing Thoughts

On December 27, 1997, we were both in attendance at a ceremony called "Living the Dream." The program was part roast, part tribute, part reception, and part "This Is Your Life" program for "DR." M. Christopher Brown II (recently minted Ph.D.). There were a host of speakers and well-wishers, one of whom admonished the audience about what it requires to support black boys/men in the school system. Dollie Brown, a now retired public school guidance counselor, borrowed from the strength of our mother (Chris's biologically and James's fictively) to offer this necessary advice. (Note: The name "Jannie Brown" has been replaced with "mother)".

> So many times we don't have a [mother]. What has happened to our lost children? Many of our doctors, many of our lawyers, many of our preachers have been miscalculated because some educator did not understand the behavior that moves man. . . . They didn't understand. And as a result of that, many of our children have fallen through the cracks. They have fallen because there was no [mother] to come to their rescue and challenge the system in a bold manner. . . .
>
> Let me tell you one thing, and I plead with you tonight. I am getting ready to leave the school system soon. You be there! Be there for your children!
>
> So many times we don't understand children. . . . So with our frail understanding we diagnose the case wrong. . . . We have to provide ways for our children that bring out the very best in them.

The following pages are a series of analytical investigations rather than one holistic linear argument. Join each of the contributors in engaging and interrogating mothering/cultural work/educating as both an educational practice and an intellectual/sociopolitical positionality. Like black boys'/men's multifaceted experiences—lived and imagined—this book reflects various modes of inquiry and presentation, including traditional scholarship and personal narrative. You alone must ultimately decide whether you desire "to be or not to be a mother." Education is the responsibility of mothers—the true cultural workers in education.

Again, welcome to our conversation.

References

Akbar, N. (1991). *Visions for black men*. Nashville, TN: Winston-Derek.

Blount, M., & Cunningham, G.P. (1996). *Representing black men*. New York: Routledge.

Brown, M. C. (forthcoming). Involvement with students: How much can I give? In M. Garcia (Ed.), *Microcosms of diversity: Succeeding in an academic career as faculty of color*. Westport, CT: Greenwood Press.

Brown, M. C., Davis, G. L., & McClendon, S. A. (1999). Mentoring graduate students of color: Myths, missions, models, and modes. *Peabody Journal of Education, 74*, 105–118.

Castenell, L. A., & Pinar, W. F. (Eds.). (1993). *Understanding curriculum as racial text: Representations of identity and difference in education*. Albany: State University of New York Press.

Chideya, F. (1995). *Don't believe the hype: Fighting cultural misinformation about African-Americans*. New York: Plume/Penguin.

Chodorow, N. (1978). *The reproduction of mothering: Psychoanalysis and the sociology of gender*. Berkeley, CA: University of California Press.

Collins, P. H. (1987). The meaning of motherhood in black culture and black mother/daughter relationships. *Sage: A Scholarly Journal of Black Women*, 4(2), 2–10.

Collins, P. H. (1990). *Black feminist thought: Knowledge, consciousness and the politics of empowerment*. New York: Routledge.

Comer, J. P., & Poussaint, A. F. (1992). *Raising black children: Two leading psychiatrists confront the educational, social, and emotional problems facing black children*. New York: Plume/Penguin.

Counts, G. S. (1932). *Dare the school build a new social order:* New York: John Day.

Dove, N. (1998). *Afrikan mothers: Bearers of culture, makers of social change*. Albany: State University of New York Press.

Freire, P. (1998). *Teachers as cultural workers: Letters to those who dare to teach*. Boulder, CO: Westview Press.

Hall, P. M. (Ed.). (1997). *Race, ethnicity, and multiculturalism: Policy and practice*. New York: Garland.

Hare, N., & Hare, J. (1985). *Bringing the black boy to manhood: The passage*. San Francisco: Black Think Tank.

Harper, P. B. (1996). *Are we not men: Masculine anxiety and the problem of African-American identity*. New York: Oxford University Press.

Hopkins, R. (1997). *Educating black males*. Albany: State University of New York Press.

Hunter, A. G., & Davis, J. E. (1994). Hidden voices of black men: The meaning, structure, and complexity of manhood. *Journal of Black Studies, 25*(1), 20–40.

James, S. M. (1993). Mothering: A possible black feminist link to social transformation: In S. M. James & A. Busia (Eds.), *Theorizing Black feminisms: The visionary pragmatism of black women*. New York: Routledge.

Kelley, R. D. G. (1997). *Yo' mama's disfunktional: Fighting the culture wars in urban America*. Boston: Beacon Press.

King, J., & Mitchell, C. (1995). *Black mothers to sons: Juxtaposing African American literature with social practice*. New York: Peter Lang.

Kunjufu, J. (1988). *To be popular or smart: The black peer group*. Chicago: African American Images.

Madhubuti, H. R. (1990). *Black men: Obsolete, single, dangerous: Afrikan American families in transition: Essays in discovery, solution and hope*. Chicago: Third World Press.

McRoy, R. G. (1990). A historical overview of black families. In S. M. L. Logan, E. M. Freeman, & R. G. macro, *Social work practice with black families*. New York: Longman.

Oppong, C. (1973). *Growing up in Dagbon*. Tema, Ghana. Ghana Publishing.

Reagon, B. J. (1989). African diaspora: The making of cultural workers. In R. Terborg-Penn, S. Harley, & A. B. Rushing (Eds.), *Women in Africa and the African Diaspora*. Washington, DC: Howard University Press.

Troester, R. R. (1984). Turbulence and tenderness: Mothers, daughters, and "othermothers." *Sage: A Scholarly Journal of Black Women, 1*(2), 13–17.

Walker, A. (1983). *In search of our mothers' gardens: womanist prose*. New York: Harcourt Brace Jovanovich.

Part One

Compliments on Mothering

Chapter Two

Matriarchy, Malcolm X, and Masculinity: A Historical Essay

William Eric Perkins

> They seem to require less sleep. A Black after hard labour through the day will be induced by the slightest amusements to sit up till midnight or later, though knowing he must be out with the first dawn of the morning. . . . They are more ardent after their female? but love seems with them to be more an eager desire, than a tender delicate mixture of sentiment and sensation. Their griefs are transient. . . . In general, their existence appears to participate more of sensation than reflection. . . . Their love is ardent, but it kindles the senses only, not the imagination.
>
> —Thomas Jefferson

Masculine Pathologies

For more than two centuries, this image of black manhood, carefully articulated by Thomas Jefferson, has been the dominant image. Before analyzing the content of various representations and the connotations of their multiple meanings, a brief review of some of some of the social science literature on African American males and masculinity will be useful.

Much of the literature on African American fatherhood and masculinity comes out of examining the role of men in the family during slavery. E. Franklin Frazier (1948), whose work firmly established the "pathological" model of African American society and culture, set the tone. He argued that familial disintegration was "due to the natural impulses of the Negro which, acquired through natural selection during his long residence in Africa, broke through all forms of social control of sex conduct" (p. 245). The removal of sanctions on African American males and females under slavery would have had a profound effect on their relationships, since "when the sexual impulses of the male were no longer controlled by African customs and mores, they became subject only to the periodic urge of sexual hunger. Under such circumstances the males, as is generally true, seized up the woman who happened to be at hand and with whom they had been thrown into closest contact" (p. 19).

Drawing on another source, Frazier argued that the family which had developed during slavery was "a natural organization," a consequence of adaptation to the slave system. Part of the development of this "natural organization" was the emergent dominance of the "matriarchy," the form of family organization that encouraged illegitimacy and consequent instability. This form of "natural organization" was carried forward into emancipation and urban migration, with dire consequences. The domination of the matriarchy, especially among the lower classes, meant that children would not enjoy the security, affectional as well as economic, which children in the upper class enjoy. The absence of the male from the matriarchy had a devastating consequence for young boys, because it meant that there was no adult role model or image of the values which should shape their personalities. Men were needed in the family to serve as disciplinarians so that children, especially young males, would be provided with a routine and regimen that curbed potentially impulsive behavior. Frazier believed that the failure to exercise discipline, the province of the male, accounted for the large amount of juvenile delinquency and crime among Negroes.

In a similar vein, Hortense Powdermaker (1966), in her study of post-bellum African American culture, written during the 1940s, argued that the matriarch was critical in the development of African American religion since black people derived their security from a female figure, rather than a male, creating an image of God based on the female attribute of benevolence, rather than the male attribute of dominance.

Black psychologist Kenneth Clark (1967) built on this model, arguing that the black urban matriarchy produced antisocial behavior. Growing up without a strong black male role model tied to a stable relationship, young black men took the position that it was "unmanly" to form and maintain stable and monogamous relationships; that the nature of masculinity was in fact promiscuity. Masculinity, Clark argued, was thought to be measured by the number of sexual conquests a young man could count. Young black women then used sexuality, sex, and pregnancy to capture a prospective mate, to "hook" him, and to affirm an inner-city version of a stable relationship.

Abraham Kardiner and Lionel Ovesey (1951), who were Freudians, argued that African American women of the lower classes were well-indoctrinated with Victorian morality (chastity and abstinence) and if reared by "white standards" they would develop similar patterns of sexuality. For young black males, however, the dominance of the matriarchy predisposed them to negative ideas about females: "if the male comes from a female-dominated household, the relation with the mother is one of frustrated dependency and hostility. This was not conducive to good relations with the female" (p. xix). Sexual intimacy thus became unimportant, fostering an indifference that resulted in a lack of commitment to a potential companion. Sexual indifference coupled with chronic joblessness prevented the black male from exercising the traditional male sex role. Kardiner and Ovesey's interpretation of black male sexuality reinforced the traditional view of black male emasculation, echoing sentiments articulated by many, including W. E. B. DuBois in *The Souls of Black Folk*. Emasculation occurred in the bedroom, where the woman stripped him of his masculinity. Neither white men nor the "system" accounted for this emasculation; black women did. If the role of male authority was to be restored to the household, black men would have to be employed, for employment would restore the "natural order."

The Kardiner and Ovesey thesis informed what would become the most important theory of the crisis facing African America. Daniel Patrick Moynihan's 1965 report, *The Negro Family: The Case for National Action*, had as its central thesis that the federal government must intervene in rebuilding the paternal role in African American families. For Moynihan, the "tangle of pathology" was directly related to the weak male role in African American households. The dominance of the matriarchy was incompatible with the "patriarchal" structure of American family life. Moynihan believed that if the state propped up the position of the black male, young black people would have proper role models, and this would foster socialization into mainstream values—personal responsibility, hard work, deferred gratification, and self-control. The Moynihan model, couched in terms of the racial liberalism of the 1960s, was one which extended the role of the regulatory state into private life. The "rehabilitation" of the black male would put the black community on a more equitable course to compete for the benefits of the "great society." The elevation of black patriarchy to preeminence would strengthen black families. In asserting the importance of this role, Moynihan stated that "the very essence of the male animal, from the bantam rooster to the four-star general, is to strut" (p. 4). The Moynihan thesis paved the way for the theory that emphasizing the importance of employment for black men would lead to familial health being repaired and the centuries of damage ameliorated.

While there were many critics of the Moynihan report, few questioned the wisdom of his argument concerning the relationship between patriarchal authority and employment. Sociologist Hylan Lewis criticized the "slavery-specific" hypothesis which argued that the source of much of the pathology of black America was the familial disorganization bred during slavery with the establishment of the matriarchy. Lewis cautioned that "Negro-white differentials in family structure diminish when controlled for income and . . . differences by income are more striking than differences by color. . . . Since a much larger proportion of Negroes than of whites are on the lowest income levels, what looks like statistically significant differences between Negroes and whites may actually be differences between socioeconomic levels" (Lewis, 1967a, pp. 314, 353).

In a further article, Lewis wrote, in line with Moynihan, that "the answer to the problem of family disorganization is not one of inculcating marriage and family values in young couples; there is ample evidence that they exist. The critical test is to find ways and means for the young adult male to meet the economic maintenance demands of marriage and family life" (Lewis, 1967b, pp. 158). This pathological model of the African American male has been the dominant trend in the social science literature, a model that was eventually challenged, with overwhelming evidence, by the late Herbert Gutman. As he noted,

> The capacity of the emancipated slaves to adapt to the general emancipation is evidence of their earlier adaptation to enslavement. The capacity of early-twentieth-century southern black migrants to adapt to

> the northern city in 1905 and 1925 is evidence of the adaptive capacities of Afro-Americans living in the rural and urban South between 1880 and 1900. Their household arrangements were not without "problems." A vast and painful record documents the economic and social—as well as the psychological—costs extracted from poor rural and urban blacks between the general emancipation and the Great Depression. But that record is not evidence that the black family crumbled or that a "pathological" culture thrived. . . . Not surprisingly, the rate of family breakup (measured by male presence) increased between 1965 and 1970. But that "rate" had little if any connection to "a tangle of pathology" rooted in "deep-seated structural distortions in the life of Negro Americans." Poor migrant blacks responded to the devastating pressure of rural enclosure and urban employment in diverse but little studied ways. (Gutman, 1976, pp. 465–66)

Gutman's assessment, and his demolition of the "pathology" model of African American family life, centered on amassing a mountain of evidence to show that black households in slavery, freedom, and urban America conformed to the nuclear family form, in which resident males exercised traditional fatherhood roles. While he did look at other forms of household organization (such as the extended family and the nonresident male), he did not include these in his study, since he chose to challenge the conventional wisdom on African American household organization. Rather than systematic breakdown and the "tangle of pathology," most African Americans, both during and after slavery, lived in two-parent nuclear families.

A Man in the House

Sociologist Carol Stack's studies (1974) show how extensive networks of "kin and friend" devise ways of dealing with deprivation, but she too invokes the economist interpretations of much of the literature, arguing that "the single most important factor affecting male/female relationships is work," and while her work is a pioneering look at African American household organization, including the roles of nonresident males, it does not avoid the trap of the economist interpretation, reducing the complexities of African American household organization to holding and maintaining a job.

The role of men in these extended households could best be viewed as a combination of traditional and counter-normative roles. They were either absolutely dominant family figures or shared that role with their wives. The roles of younger men within these extended households might be entirely different. The intergenerational gap between older resident males and younger nonresident males did not mean that young male children did not or do not have the opportunity to observe masculine roles.

Thus, the internal structure (the organization of the household independent of socioeconomic forces) of organized kinship in the African American community still retains a curious combination of alternative gender roles, as Staples noted. This retentive structure has seldom been looked at on its own terms, without being informed by the prejudices developed by years of what Albert Murray called the "fakelore of black pathology." Raymond T. Smith (1996), in his studies of West Indian kinship, draws a number of important conclusions about household structure that have a direct bearing on our understanding of male/female roles within African American households. For example, he notes:

> The aspect of Caribbean society that has attracted the attention of feminist theorists has been the matrifocal family, in which women are salient in domestic affairs and men, in the station of husband-father, are marginal to the close bonds between mothers, children, and daughters' children. (Smith, 1996, p. 79)

The entire family functions, in the memorable words of George Lamming (1953), as "my mother who fathered me." This particular model of looking at African American familial roles poses a distinctive counterpoint to the traditional model of the middle-class, patriarchal family invoked by scholars from Frazier through Gutman. This model can be quite helpful in understanding male roles. In another important, but neglected, work, Elizabeth Bott's study (1957) of British working class families, the author develops the concept of "segregated conjugal roles," in which men and women engage in separate spheres of activity within the organized family, and separate interactions outside the family with kin and friends. Bott posits that the "women and their children formed an important group, helping one another in household tasks and child care, and providing aid in crisis. . . . Within the network of relatives, there was thus a nucleus composed of the grandmother, her daughters, her daughters'

daughters; the relationships of the women were sufficiently intense to warrant the term 'organized group' " (p. 69).

These alternative theoretical models offer us important clues as to how scholars and practitioners might develop new ways of examining African American male and female roles. These studies indicate that organized kinship does not have to fit the traditional nuclear family mold. Let us now examine how male roles have been examined in what I call the "ghetto studies" school of scholarship, which grounded itself in "culture of poverty" theory. The culture of poverty theorists took their cue from Oscar Lewis, whose studies of lower-class culture in Latin America set the tone for studies of North American inner cities. In one study, he argued that "most of the characters in this volume are badly damaged human beings" (Lewis, 1961, p. xxx). When culture of poverty theory began to take root in American social science during the 1960s (during a wave of civil insurrection), the cornerstone of the theory, linking itself to Moynihan's "tangle of pathology," was the pathological or deficit model of behavior. Lower-class and working poor African Americans were "incomplete" carriers of culture, as reflected in the lack of paternal responsibility taken by African American males. While there were some who openly challenged this interpretation of African American culture and society (Lewis, 1967; Liebow, 1967), they were still wedded to normative conceptions of African American masculinity that focused on the male role as breadwinner and disciplinarian. They argued that the "underclass" and working poor were quite receptive to so-called "mainstream" values, but it was the racial discrimination and the scarcity of economic opportunity that prevented them from adopting these.

David Schulz's study (1964) developed a typology of African American males' roles within African American households, carefully breaking each of them down. There is the boyfriend, most often but not exclusively nonresident, who contracts with his female companion a set of standardized obligations; there is the biological father, who may not cohabit with the children's mother, but who has also contracted a set of standardized obligations; there is the supportive companion, with whom the female may be in a conjugal relationship, but who is more often a male friend; and of course the ubiquitous pimp, whose paternal role, summoned in the vernacular by such terms as "daddy" or "big daddy," brutally exploits his female stable. This last role surfaced as a category for analysis in the late '60s, and was a hallmark of the "blaxploitation" film era. Schulz's typology would inform a whole generation of social science scholarship on black men, but like the work of his peers and predecessors, it was informed by the pathological or deficit model of black male behavior.

In an important but overlooked article, Robert Staples (1986) offers the classical typology of how black men have been viewed—as stud, athlete, and criminal. Black men are in frequent conflict with the "normative" view of the male—autonomous, master of one's environment, and of course, "head" of the household. Staples argues, persuasively, that there is an inherent conflict between "normative expectations," black men fulfilling their role as head of household, and the ways in which those "normative expectations" have been proscribed by countervailing socioeconomic forces such as labor market discrimination, low-paying jobs, and criminal justice stigmatization.

What have been the sources for these dramatic shifts in conceptions of the male roles? There can be no doubt that deindustrialization, job losses, and the globalization of the economy have had a dramatic impact on African American working-class and underclass households (Wilson, 1987, 1997; Anderson, 1978, 1990; Malveaux, 1989; Dunier, 1992; and Larson, 1988). These authors have examined the relationships between the erosion of the American manufacturing base, declining educational performance, and growing workplace skills deficits as major factors contributing to changing male (and as a result female) roles. What they all have in common is that their work reflects the continuing "economist" interpretation of African American household structure, arguing that policy initiatives should focus on job production and the elimination of workplace skills deficits. This in turn would lead to the rehabilitation of black male authority as the center, once again, of the household. While some of this holds true, this point of view overlooks the cultural components of black masculinity, and the ways these cultural components have been molded and shaped by various forms of popular culture. While some of these authors are sensitive to these components (Dunier, 1992, for example), they have not fully analyzed their impact on black men in general and on young black men in particular. Dunier's ethnographic study of a group of older men at Valois' Restaurant on Chicago's South Side is a prime example of how the two modes—economist and cultural—might be fused in looking at black masculinity. Much of his analysis focuses on how older black working-class men look at "respectability," and how this respectability is constructed in black working-class culture. This is important as an advance in the literature, as well as in its implications for how we might formulate more responsive social policies that meet the challenges these men see to the core of their manhood.

The second major source of changing male roles has been the exponential growth in the number of unmarried mothers since World War Two. The number of unmarried mothers tripled between 1940 and 1957. The growth in numbers of unmarried mothers in turn led in an increase in welfare dependency for African Americans. Dramatic changes, initiated in the 1950s and continuing through the mid-1990s, altered gender roles. As welfare dependency expanded, there were also dramatic changes in the age-structure of African American households. While the birthrate declined among older, better-educated, middle class African Americans, the birthrate among younger age cohorts has risen, and has only recently stabilized. The result—a disproportionate increase in the number of births to unmarried black women.

This distinct demographic pattern has had a profound impact not merely on gender roles but on the ways in which young African Americans view manhood, motherhood, and masculinity. Phyllis Harrison-Ross and Barbara Wyden (1973) have noted that the ongoing absence (nonresidence would be a far more accurate term) of men from many lower-income households contributes to maladaptive child-raising patterns, resulting in what we often call children "raising themselves" on the street. These new family formations, created by deindustrialization and immigration, have led to what Christopher Jencks (1989) called the "reproductive underclass." Even though there has been a decline in teenage pregnancy, there has been a startling increase in unmarried mothers, and this has important, though largely unexamined, consequences for gender roles and behaviors. While one cannot ignore these demographic patterns, it is important to note that the populations we study do not view themselves through this particular kind of lens. Laura Carper (1967), in an extraordinary work, cautioned students of lower-class culture about the dangers of pathological and deficit models. She states that "Pathology is in the eye of the beholder. If one eliminates the positive function of a cultural constellation, if one ignores the meaning personal relations have to the people involved, if one, in short uses science to depersonalize, what emerges is pathology" (pp. 472–73). While the social sciences have contributed to the stigmatization and stereotyping of black men, particularly in their role as fathers, another school of thought has challenged many of these theories, contributing to alternative conceptions of African American masculinity and fatherhood.

Malcolm X Is a "Real" Man

The African American cultural nationalists have devoted a considerable amount of writing to the subject of black masculinity. Much of this literature has taken its cue from the role that Malcolm X played in his life and the transformation of that role to iconographic status on his death. Nowhere was this sentiment better expressed than in Ossie Davis' moving eulogy at Malcolm's funeral:

> Many will ask what Harlem finds to honor in this stormy, controversial and bold young captain and smile. Many will turn away—away from this man, for he is not a man but a demon, a monster, an enemy of the black man—and we will smile. They say he is of hate—a fanatic, a racist who can only bring evil to the struggle: And we will answer and say to them. Did you ever talk to Brother Malcolm? Did you ever have him smile at you? Did you ever really listen to him? Did he ever do a mean thing? Was he associated with violence or any public disturbance? For if you did you would know him. And you would know why we must honor him. Malcolm was our manhood, our living, black manhood giving his meaning to our people. And in honoring him, we honor the best in ourselves (Davis, 1965).

Malcolm's saintly status in African American and American popular culture centers on what it means to be a man—indeed, a role model. But what actually lies behind this iconography? Malcolm's journey to respectability was first and foremost accompanied by an astonishing personal transformation, from petty street criminal to the Nation of Islam's inner sanctum of power. This personal transformation was marked by Malcolm's redefinition of his manhood—from hustler, womanizer, and addict, to patriarch of his household. Malcolm, unlike the other canonized saint, Martin Luther King, Jr., believed that a monogamous relationship was the key to both personal and familial stability. Malcolm's personal transformation was secured by his exorcism of all vice, with one exception, as he frequently told audiences—his coffee. This dimension of Malcolm's personal transformation is reprised brilliantly by Denzel Washington in Spike Lee's otherwise flawed film, *Malcolm X*. This emphasis on monogamy as the key to both stable and healthy relationships was the cornerstone of the Nation of Islam's strategy of redeeming the lower classes, since so many "ghetto-specific behaviors" revolved around sexual promiscuity and out-of-wedlock births; without a monogamous relationship, gender roles became confused and children were at risk. Though the Nation of Islam has been, and continues to be, demonized by the mainstream media, its success in stimulating and supporting stable, monogamous relationships among its members is well worth further examination.

The Nation of Islam revived patriarchy as the foundation for the nuclear family, making the male the sole arbiter of familial power. To that extent, the male's familial role was a mirror image of the conventional, white, middle-class suburban family. The man was breadwinner, disciplinarian, protector, and patriarch all rolled into one; the woman was mother and homemaker. Malcolm was the quintessential expression of the familial patriarch, vividly expressed in the photograph of him brandishing a semiautomatic rifle following the firebombing of his Queens, New York, home. He was, as he told reporters, "protecting" his family. But Malcolm's, and the Nation's, sense of masculinity was more than the role of patriarch. If we take Noel Cazenave's finding (1981) that most black men believe that the essence of fatherhood is responsibility, then Malcolm embodied that—as breadwinner, provider, confidant, and even, in martyrdom, betrayed by a Muslim Brutus, as Caesar. In this astonishing personal transformation, Malcolm "fessed up" to the sins of his past life, accepting full responsibility and all the consequences including his prison years (Malcolm X, 1963).

Though Malcolm underestimated his own inner strength and conviction in this astonishing transformation, it is testimony to Muhammad's powerful role as mentor and shepherd. When accusations were leveled at Muhammad for his infidelity and proclivity for teenage girls, Malcolm, model father and husband, defiantly left the Nation of Islam, and despite death threats and firebombing continued to use his moral sword to remind his followers of the righteousness of monogamy. Malcolm, the man, was also the warrior, and this is perhaps the quality of masculinity so many young, black men identify within him—because they see themselves. Frequently accused of advocating violence, Malcolm challenged his accusers by reminding them all of their constitutional right to self-defense and to bear arms. His warrior spirit was wise and prudent, not reckless and undirected like that of so many of the young warriors of today. Malcolm loved talking, talking to teach, and it was his uncanny ability to "make it plain" that led, and continues to lead, many to follow his ideas: for example, his way with words, with the vernacular English of the masses, has been a powerful influence on hiphop lyricists. Malcolm's status as "our shining black prince" is contained in one of his most frequently used adages, "no sell out," and it was this slogan that became one of the foundations of the hiphop underground.

If Malcolm embodied the essence of "our black manhood" (in Ossie Davis' words) in life, the images crafted of him in death were larger than that life. In his passage to martyrdom, Malcolm has become symbolic of what black masculinity can and must be. This remarkable passage, from demonized villain to saint, has been marked by Malcolm's construction as icon. Streets, college campuses, and children have been named after him. There is a growing movement afoot to preserve and rehabilitate the Audubon Ballroom, where he was assassinated, as the Malcolm X Memorial Museum. There has been a wave of documentaries and docudramas, even preceding Spike Lee's cinematic biography. In 1986, writers Anthony and Thulani Davis staged an opera, *X*, which focused on Malcolm's life. It premiered at the New York City Opera and was characterized by a dark, nontonal palette and complex, shifting rhythmic patterns with a poignant lyricism, containing all of the musical forms accompanying Malcolm's rise and fall. The year 1990 saw the release of the docudrama *Malcolm X—El Hajj Malik-el-Shabazz,* with Morgan Freeman playing Malcolm, and Yolanda King (Dr. Martin Luther King's daughter) playing Betty Shabazz. In 1992, Dan Rather, anchor of the CBS Evening News, produced and narrated a revisionist interpretation of Malcolm, called *The Real Malcolm X.* Rather was astounded at how Malcolm had taken symbolic hold of African America's popular memory. The most important of the documentaries is Henry Hampton's (known for his *Eyes on the Prize*) *Make It Plain,* an indepth examination that was shown on public television in 1994. In 1994, John Akomfrah, of the Black Audio Film Collective in England, released his rarely seen (in the U.S.) documentary, *Seven Songs for Malcolm X,* which includes a rare interview with Betty Shabazz. Trumpeter Terrence Blanchard released a double compact disk set in 1993, *Malcolm X,* which is a biographical musical journey through Malcolm's life and times. There was also a 1995 documentary on the assassination, *Brother Minister,* a two-hour portrait of the forces behind the assassination.

By far the most important media event surrounding Malcolm was Spike Lee's 1992 autobiography, *Malcolm X,* which rehabilitated Malcolm's legacy for the American mainstream. Criticized vehemently by old-guard black nationalists and the black left for its watering down of Malcolm's militancy, the film nevertheless provided "generation black" with its first glimpse of the power that Malcolm had wielded over another generation. The first part of the film, critics charged, spent too much time on Malcolm's criminal background, his interracial romances, and his abuse of women, without setting that phase of his life in the larger context of his transformation. Critics also felt the film portrayed Malcolm's racial fundamentalism—his belief in the superiority of "the Asiatic Black Man" as he had been taught by Elijah Muhammad—as not the real Malcolm X. In fact, there was great debate on Malcolm's ideological integrity. He did not become the "pseudointegrationist" the film and certain Marxist groups have made him out to be. Lee's film, however, does manage to give us a look at Malcolm the man, the husband, and the father, and, of course, Malcolm the patriarch. The film, marketed in typical Lee fashion, also brought the image of Malcolm to the mass market. There were Malcolm tee-shirts, hats, trinkets, medallions, buttons, posters, a swirling array of commodities graced with Malcolm's image, but with little of his legacy to guide and direct us. While Malcolm's widow, the late Betty Shabazz, supported this marketing blitz, the campaign did little to resurrect the importance of the Malcolm legacy—the "no sell-out," uncompromising, black nationalist militancy that governed his life and work. The image makers and the media moguls, however, have done much to rehabilitate and resurrect Malcolm for "generation black" and its descendants as an image and symbol of uncompromising black manhood and personal responsibility. If there is a legacy of Malcolm, it is just that: a man must accept responsibility, for himself, his family, and his community.

Black Men and Masculinity

So how were these revised notions of masculinity adapted by subsequent generations of cultural nationalists (those activists who argue that the major battleground for African Americans is on the culture and values front)? While there is a large literature of this type, I will focus on three of the most important (Akbar, 1991; Ali, 1990; and Madhubuti, 1990).

Akbar's work might best be called an Afrocentric discourse on African American masculinity. Akbar calls for the overthrowing of the Western model of male socialization, replacing it with an Afrocentric model. Akbar argues that African Americans must cultivate a vision for black men containing "the ancient and pre-European African experience, the experience of the American holocaust (slavery), the consequences of white supremacy and racism, and the contemporary European American socialization, with regard to the impact of each of these experiences on the African American reality" (p. ix). Akbar marshals much of the traditional Afrocentric narrative—ancient African and Kemetic (ancient Egyptian) wisdom, the blackness of the biblical prophets, and contemporary male role models who should be counted as heroes. He identifies personal attributes he thinks should become universal values in defining black manhood—the "courage" of Martin Luther King, Jr.; the "defiance" of Elijah Muhammad; the "economic strategy" of Booker T. Washington; the "uncompromising integrity" of Paul Robeson; the views of Cheikh Anta Diop (this Senegalese historian is considered the godfather of Afrocentrism); and the "use of scholarship for self-definition" (pp. 63–87). Akbar's work, like much of the Afrocentrists' work, is blatantly ideological, grinding its ax against both the Western and the classical canon. It is part theology, part mythology, part folk wisdom, and part motivational writing, which is really what this school of thinking is most concerned with (Perkins, 1997).

One of the most popular works in this genre is that of Haki Madhubuti (1990). For him, the examination of the situation of black men and the solutions to that situation must be grounded in a new cultural revolution. As one of the critical architects of the 1960s Black Arts Movement (as Don L. Lee), Madhubuti invokes the legacy of Elijah Muhammad, Malcolm X, and the Nation of Islam. Only "knowledge of self" can change and transmute the plight of the African American male. He reminds his audience that African American "culture, as a force for survival and development, is given very little attention in the education of our young" (p. 5). He goes on to argue that the African American condition is dominated both by a culture of survival and by one of dependency, and that in order to change this condition a revolutionary culture, centered on the reconstruction of the African American family, must be African America's top priority.

The last work I will consider in this genre has been by far the most popular, approaching near best-seller status in the African American community. Shahrazad Ali's *The Blackwoman's Guide to Understanding the Black Man* (1990) is a complement to her controversial *The Blackman's Guide to Understanding the Blackwoman.* As a follower of the Nation of Islam, Ali's works have been designed to provoke discussion in the African American community on the current state of gender roles, and how black men and women have been "brainwashed" by white society and thus damaged. As such, it follows in a line that most cultural nationalists have articulated, from nineteenth-century proto-nationalists straight through to the Nation of Islam. It is written in an almost conversational style, making it all the more popular with the mass African American audience. Central to the development of her arguments, as in the previously mentioned writers' works, is the role that culture plays in socialization. Ali asks:

> What is culture? Some say culture is a system of preserving historical social ideas, traditions, memorabilia and basic principles by which a people live. Culture contain rites, qualifying tests and other values passed from one generation to the next who are emotionally connected by nationality, including skin color. Culture serves the purpose of functioning as a moral compass to direct and monitor people to keep them on the right track to preserve their ideas. Using this definition it is plain to see that the Blackman is not earnestly trying to adopt his Black culture. In fact, he is far from it. His definition of culture is a smorgasbord of unharmonious ideas and practices that so far have only inspired a few Black men to wear African clothes, a kente cloth scarf, fezzes, ethnic jewelry or slogan t-shirts. (pp. 22–23)

Despite the flawed writing and confused conceptualization (split infinitives; and what are "qualifying tests" in a cultural context), her work has struck a resonant chord with the mass audience, and has precipitated her appearance on all of the major television talk shows. In building her argument, Ali notes that the "Blackman" has three required accomplishments in order to have a meaningful life: knowledge of "self" (the Nation of Islam cornerstone); the ability "to do for self" (one of the Nation's key building blocks); and the ability to be a good son, brother, husband, and father (p. 153).

Ali's analysis of African American male/female relationships illustrates how two trends have intersected in the discourse on black masculinity: the social science "tangle of pathology," the black family that is deficient because of the absent male; and the "culturalist"/Nation of Islam emphasis on personal transformation. Especially important in her analysis is her take on teenage males. As she states, "[this] background partly reveal[s] the circumstances that have led up to producing nearly two generations of young Black males who are disinterested, ill-mannered, obnoxious, scholastically ignorant and foul-mouthed, culturally unaware, lethargic, irresponsible, ill-motivated, and lazy. They are the perfect example of a reason the Blackman ought to insist on resegregation" (p. 189).

They are, in the words of rap artists 3rd Bass, a "Product of the Environment." Ali takes no prisoners in arguing that teenage males' socialization in hiphop culture is the reason for the negative behaviors she outlines. She notes that part of the problem is that the codes and rituals of the street have made them "gangbangers" (gang members or street criminals), unlike the warriors who were raised and nurtured in the Civil Rights and Black Power movements. They have so little culturally to bond them to the past as it becomes the prelude to the future. Here Ali, like all of the other generations removed from today's, demonstrates little understanding of the positive force that youth culture can produce, and in some specific instances is producing, on the culture industry. While she is absolutely correct in castigating these warriors of the street for their bravado and sexual irresponsibility, she, like so many of the "movement" generation and their predecessors, want a return to that age of innocence when a mythical version of African American family values prevailed and men ruled the roost. These members of the African American intelligentsia invoke knowledge as therapy, as the balm that will heal the wounds of the African American male.

A Concluding Thought

Much of the literature that I have reviewed has been molded by negative images of African American masculinity and matriarchal structures. This pseudo-"social science" literature has played a major role in societal constructions of the African American male. As such, it is no wonder that they are—we are—looked upon with disdain and revulsion when we enter schoolhouses, college classrooms, and places of employment. The extent to which cultural workers can build a new literature base will correlate strongly with the future experiences of African American males in school and society.

References

All lyrics have been taken from the web site, Original Hiphop Lyrics, at http://www.ohla.com/

Akbar, N. (1991). *Visions for black men.* Nashville: Winston-Derek.

Ali, S. (1990). *The blackwoman's guide to understanding the blackman.* Philadelphia: Civilized Publications.

Amber, J. (1998). I Need Love. *The Source, 100,* 156–57.

Anderson, E. (1978). *A place on the corner.* Chicago: University of Chicago Press.

Anderson, E. (1990). *Streetwise: Race, class, and change in an urban community.* Chicago: University of Chicago Press.

Anderson, E. (1994, May). The code of the streets. *Atlantic Monthly.*

Bogle, D. (1974). *Toms, coons, mulattos, mammies, and bucks.* New York: Bantam.

Bott, E. (1957). *Family and social network.* London: Tavistock.

Carper, L. (1967). The Negro family and the Moynihan Report. In L. Rainwater & W. Yancey (Eds.), *The Moynihan Report and the politics of controversy* (pp. 472–73). Cambridge: MIT Press.

Cazenave, N.A. (1981). Black men in America? The quest for manhood. In H. P. McAdoo (Ed.), *Black families.* Beverly Hills: Sage.

Christon, L. (1989, December 10). The world according to the Cos. *The Los Angeles Times Calendar,* 6, 62–65.

Clark, K. (1965). *Dark ghetto? Dilemmas of social power.* New York: Harper & Row.

Coker, C. H. (1998). Under my thumb. *XXL.* 2, 150.

Davis, O. (1965). Our shining black prince. Eulogy for Malcolm X.

Duneier, M. (1992). *Slim's table? Race, respectability, and masculinity.* Chicago: University of Chicago Press.

Franklin, D. L. (1997). *Ensuring inequality: The structural transformation of the African American family.* New York: Oxford University Press.

Frazier, E. F. (1948). *The Negro family in the United States.* Chicago: University of Chicago Press.

Guerrero, E. (1994). The black man on our screens and the empty space in representation. In T. Golden (Ed.), *The black male: Representations of masculinity in contemporary American art*. New York: The Whitney Museum.

Goffman, E. (1963). *Stigma: Notes on the management of a spoiled identity*. Englewood Cliffs, NJ: Prentice-Hall.

Gutman, H. G. (1976). *The black family in slavery and freedom, 1750–1925*. New York: Vintage.

Jencks, C. (1989). What is the underclass and is it growing? *Focus, 12*.

Lewis, H. (1967a). The changing negro family. In L. Rainwater & S. Yancey (Eds.), *The Moynihan Report and the politics of controversy* (p. 156). Cambridge: MIT Press.

Lewis, H. (1967b). Culture, class, and family life among Negroes. In A. Ross & H. Hill (Eds.), *Employment, race, and poverty*. New York: Harper & Row.

Liebow, E. (1967). *Tally's corner: A study of negro streetcorner men*. Boston: Little, Brown.

Madhubuti, H. (1990). *Black men? Obsolete, single, dangerous.* Chicago: Third World Press.

Majors, R., & Billson, J. M. (1992). *Cool pose: The dilemmas of black manhood in America*. New York: Simon & Schuster.

Malcolm X (1963, February). The Playboy interview. *Playboy*.

Martin, E., & Martin, J. M. (1978). *The black extended family*. Chicago: University of Chicago Press.

MEE Productions. (1994). *Reaching the hiphop generation*. Philadelphia: MEE Productions.

Moynihan, D. P. (1967). The Negro family: A case for National Action. In L. Rainwater & S. Yancey (Eds.), *The Moynihan Report and the politics of controversy*. Cambridge: MIT Press. (Reprinted from *The Negro Family: A Case for National Action*, by D. P. Moynihan, 1965, Washington? Government Printing Office.)

Perkins, W. E. (1994). "It all comes down to money": The Political Economy of Hiphop. Unpublished manuscript.

Perkins, W. E. (Ed.). (1996). *Droppin' science: Critical essays on rap music and hiphop culture*. Philadelphia: Temple University Press.

Perkins, W. E. (1997). Bridges on the I-way: Multicultural resources on line, The Bernal-Lefkowitz debate. *The Multicultural Review, 5*(1), 99–101.

Rose, T. (1994). Rap music and the demonization of young black males. In T. Golden (Ed.), *The black male: Representations of masculinity in contemporary American art*. New York: The Whitney Museum.

Schulz, D. (1964). *Growing up black: Patterns of ghetto socialization*. Englewood Cliffs, NJ: Prentice-Hall.

Smith, R. T. (1996). *The matrifocal family*. New York: Routledge.

Stack, C. (1974). *All our kin: Survival strategies in a black community*. New York: Harper & Row.

Staples, R. (1977). The myth of the impotent black male. In *The black male in America* (p. 138). Chicago: Nelson Hall.

Staples, R. (1986). Black masculinity, hypersexuality, and sexual aggression. In R. Staples (Ed.), *The black family* (57–63). Belmont, CA: Wadsworth.

Thompson, R. F. (1998). An aesthetic of the cool. In B. Beckley with D. Shapiro (Eds.), *Uncontrollable beauty*. New York: Hayworth Press.

Van Deburg, W. L. (1998). *Black Camelot: African-American culture heroes in their times, 1960–1980*. Chicago: University of Chicago Press.

Willis, A. (1997). A womanist turn on the hip-hop theme: Leslie Harris' *Just another girl on the IRT*. In J. Andrews & A. Andrews (Eds.), *Language, rhythm, and sound: Black popular cultures into the twenty-first century*. Pittsburgh: University of Pittsburgh Press.

Chapter Three

From Son to Mother: Intellectualizing the Personal

Edward Underwood

> African American families are matriarchal, unstable, pathological and most live below the poverty line. As a result of this human condition, African American children do poorly in school, often drop out, and most end up in the juvenile justice system and ultimately in prison, if they are males and pregnant and on welfare rolls if they are females. Furthermore, history has shown that African American families have been matriarchal over a long period of time mainly because female and male relationships are dysfunctional and this has resulted in a vicious cycle of pathology, deviance, and irresponsible sex in the African American community.
>
> —Moynihan, *Negro Family*

Introduction

The above-mentioned themes of deficit-worth, social pathology, and cultural victimization are characteristic of most of the social science research on African American families and are often reported in the news media as research facts. However, many of the widely published views of the African American family have resulted in a great deal of misunderstanding about the "holistic" function of family in the African American community and the true conditions that exist. Much of the research on this topic, especially during the 1970s and 1980s, has discounted or failed to understand the full impact of racism, classism, sexism, back to back recessions, double-digit inflation, the shift from high-paying manufacturing jobs to low-paying service jobs, and the increase in competition from legal and illegal immigrants on the social, political, economic, and mental health of African American families.

In 1987, the William Monroe Trotter Institute initiated a project entitled "The Assessment of the Status of African Americans." The report states that policy makers employ a conventional perspective on research within a framework that has the following deficiencies:

(1) It reflects a superficial treatment of black families. Black families are not considered to be an important unit of focus, and thus are omitted entirely or treated peripherally;

(2) It accepts uncritically the assumptions of the "deficit model," which attributes most of the problems of black families to internal deficiencies or pathologies;

(3) It fails to incorporate numerous new research findings and programmatic insights produced over the past two decades concerning black families—many of which contradict basic tenets of the deficit model; and

(4) It fails to focus on positive policies, programs, services, self-help efforts, and coping strategies that are successful in strengthening the functioning of black families.

In addition to the findings of the Trotter Institute, African American fathers are generally portrayed as absent from the home and irresponsible or are simply the forgotten parent. Conventional research has focused on the role of the single-female household theme to the virtual exclusion of the role the father plays in the family. In particular, the research almost always focuses on a single mother having to raise her children, especially boys, to adulthood. There is very little research on the growing circumstance of the single African American male as head of the household, and even less on the phenomenon of single African males raising their daughters, or what I call "fathers as mothers" or "sons to mothers."

A Personal Context

The following narrative is not the result of scientific research on the subject, but my personal story of being a single African American male raising a daughter. The value or utility of my experience lies in the fact that my voice, I believe, represents an important story that is becoming common to many African American males around the country, but not commonly known by the general public. African American males who subscribe to the belief that family is important, and that sacrifices must and will be made for the good and welfare of family, are not researched but "anecdoted." Career and job success for many in our society is the top priority for measuring success. It is paramount because success at work equates to "position," money, and prestige in the general society. Reaching a high position has not for me been the motivation which has served as my guide, inspiration, and desire. The one thing most important to me, by which I have measured my success, has been the safety, emotional and physical well-being, and nurturing of my daughter.

At an early age my daughter, Amber, had to deal with the powerful felt absence of her mother due to death. My career and other personal and professional goals were secondary to a primary goal. Fame, fortune, and career were only important for the material items and comfort they could give my child. I knew I had only one chance with my daughter and the growing-up process, and failure was not an option. In order to understand my transformation from son to mother, it is important to know about my own upbringing, and how the seeds were planted in me as a child to handle and master this unique role.

Preparation for Motherhood

My immediate family was what sociologists called a nuclear family—father, mother, and children in the home. My father was a hardworking railroad man, with a job considered by many, in the African American and white community alike, as a good job for a black man. Working on the rails carried with it the benefit of free rail travel around the country, and it was this benefit which allowed us to take family summer vacations and give the false impression to my friends that my family was "in the money." Nevertheless, my father worked forty-seven years on this job, and he often called the first forty years hard, back-breaking labor. His one wish for me, which he expressed on numerous occasions, was for me to get a college education and pursue a professional career. "Get an education," he would say, "and avoid the rails," he would warn. What he never talked about and on which I can only speculate was the on-the-job racism and humiliation he faced for forty years from whites. This racism and humiliation had to be more frustrating to this strong, God-fearing African American man than any of the physical requirements of the job. Not until his death did I fully understand the depth of his love for me, and the tremendous positive impact his relationship with me had on my life. Although work and second jobs would often prevent him from attending my little league games and school functions and activities, he had a way of demonstrating his love for me through "our little father and son chats." I can still hear his deep baritone voice in my head today, advising me to "get an education because no one, once that has been obtained, can take it away from you." Older and wiser, I now realize that my father was a giant among men. He took an elementary education and conquered a world that had been set up to ensure his failure.

My mother was an independent businesswoman with a steady income. She was a cosmetologist with a beauty "shop" in the basement of our home. I can vividly recall as a child being awakened by the smell of hair burning through a hot-comb, and wondering if I would survive the smell or the unending gossiping that went on between the ladies in the shop, as they waited patiently for their time on the "chair." I always marveled at the genuine pleasure and sisterhood the women that visited my mother's shop seemed to enjoy during their visit. It seems as though they were able, for the few hours they were there, to get away from the troubles, whatever they were, in their lives and just enjoy being women.

My two sisters, both older than I, seemed to rally around the goals of making their younger brother the fall guy for anything that went wrong, and making sure that I shared equally in the housework—washing dishes, cleaning the bathroom, washing clothes, and ironing. I can remember at an early age protesting to my mother that "such work" was girls' work and no young masculine male should be subjected to such cruelties. I quickly learned from my mother that my views of "such work" were not to be tolerated in our house. She quickly informed me that there was no such thing as girls' work or boys' work and I needed to get my head straight. In order to make sure I understood the message, I was given two whole weeks of doing "such work" by myself to the delight of my sisters. From that encounter with my mother and sisters, I begin to understand, although I didn't know it at the time, the meaning of sexism and the disparity of opportunity for girls and boys. During my high school years, I began to observe the myriad dynamics between males and females in my school, in the community at large, and particularly in the Baptist church.

From the day I came out of the womb, I was convinced there were only three places in the whole wide world—home, school, and church. Church was a place we would go to on Sunday morning and return from sometime before school on Monday. Sunday's regimen consisted of Sunday school, morning service, afternoon service, "Baptist Training Union," and evening service, with meals somewhere in between. As a child, church for me at first was a test of my endurance and not a place for spiritual growth and uplift. It was like a required course that was mandatory in the Underwood family curriculum of life. A course that had to be repeated until one left the fold. However, when I was twelve years of age, the church took on a new dimension of meaning in my life. The Bible verses were no longer just something to read, nor were the hymns just words to sing. I begin to see a correlation between my young life and the wisdom of my elders based on the biblical teachings. I began to see the relationship between what was taught at church, concerning right and wrong and a belief in God, and the day-to-day patterns of family relations at home. I saw how my parents used their faith in God to survive in the cruel and inhumane system of segregation in which we lived. More importantly, I began to understand the moral fabric of my parents and how they used it to impact my own life and perspectives.

Of course, I believe that "God created heaven and earth," that "God so loved the world that He gave His only begotten Son," and that "God answers prayer" and does what "He promised." My mother constantly reminded me to have faith in God, and if I had the "faith as a grain of a mustard seed," God would move mountains for me. "Faith," she said "is the confidence that you can go boldly to the throne of grace and find and obtain mercy and find grace to help in time of need" (Heb. 4:16). Take the words of Hebrews 11:1 with you always—"Faith is the substance of things hoped for, the evidence and assurance of things not seen." Always she admonished, "remain steadfast in faith in the face of trials and tribulations." "If you have faith," she said, "the Lord will be your light and salvation; whom should you fear? The Lord will be the strength of your life; of whom shall you be afraid?" (Ps. 27:1. Little did I realize how her sage advice would stay with me and provide a source of strength later in my life. In retrospect, my family and the values we had concerning honesty, hard work, education, and belief in God were not significantly different from what I observed in almost every household in my immediate neighborhood.

The Beginning of Motherhood

On top of the world and the view is fine: this describes my euphoria at being married to a beautiful and talented woman—Rosa—and the father of a daughter named Amber. Like most professional families, we set our personal and professional goals and worked jointly to provide for the needs of the family and of Amber in particular. A new home in a racially mixed neighborhood was purchased, and plans for Amber's collegiate future were made. Church was on Sunday and the mad rat race for success took up the other days of the week, with community organizations and commitments worked into the mix. Life on a personal level was like a bowl of cherries, and everything else was really secondary. Everything was going according to our personal plan, and there was no stopping us now. Then without warning our perfectly planned world was turned upside down. Our bowl of cherries was now the pits. Overnight, events occurred that would forever change my life and the life of Amber. Rosa was diagnosed with an incurable illness and given less than a year to live. Shot through the heart is the only way I can describe how I felt when I received the news. It left me feeling numb, helpless, and lost. As I tried to handle my grief, I was also consumed with fear, sorrow, and befuddlement on how to broach the subject of Rosa's death with Amber.

Death and Dying

Death to me was something that happened when you were old, or as the result of an accident, or if you were the victim of a crime. It had never really occurred to me that life was so fragile and could be taken away in an instant. Besides, I had always been taught in church that God was a just God, and it only seemed logical to me that a just God would not allow an eleven-year-old girl to suffer the pain of losing her mother at such an early age. Furthermore, Rosa and I had a perfect, loving marriage. A just God surely would not ruin that type of relationship. To say that I questioned my faith—the foundation my life was built upon—is putting it lightly.

Soon afterwards, the reality of our situation set in. Rosa, one night as we tried to comprehend everything, said to me, "Ed, you must now prepare Amber for my death. She must know from your strength how to handle adversity and know that she is safe and in good hands with you. You must become both mother and father to her. I know you can do it and I know you will. I can face my own death because I believe in my heart that you will always be there for my Amber. I know you are questioning your faith at this time, but you must always believe and accept the wisdom of God!"

The first talk Amber and I had about her mother's illness was the beginning brick on the pavement of building the road to open communication. As I explained the situation to her, I could literally see the pain and suffering building up in her heart. "Is mom really going to die?" she asked. At that moment I wanted to say anything but yes, so I said, "The doctors believe that her illness will be fatal. However, I still believe in miracles and the power of prayer. Doctors are well-trained, Amber, but they are not always right. I still hope and pray for her recovery." "If mom dies, what will happen to me? Who will take care of you, dad?" The questions she raised, "who will take care of you, dad?" suggested to me that Amber was not only concerned about her mother's circumstance and the effect on her, but what would happen to our family. I knew at that very moment that failure to handle Amber's questions with integrity and strength would mean losing her confidence in me and her hope for a safe and secure life.

It was at that every moment that I felt I should now pass on to my daughter the wisdom handed down to me by my mother. "Amber, your mother and I have had a good life together and a perfect relationship. We were able to withstand the storms of bad times in our lives because we both had a firm foundation in religion. It is the same religion that allowed our ancestors to endure slavery, segregated schools, menial jobs, and civil rights abuses. It is the same religion that helped your great-grandmother to raise seven kids when their father died. It was there to help see your grandparents through different times, and it is here for us if we can keep the faith. I don't know why this is happening, but remember these things. God makes the sun rise on the evil and the good person, and He sends the rain to fall on the just and the unjust" (Matt. 5:45). I recounted to her the story of Job and said that although we cannot compare our suffering to Job's, it can give us some understanding of why things happen. "Remember you must not curse God but continue to praise Him."

During and after Rosa's death, Amber and I tried professional counseling to help us deal with our loss. We quickly found our strength to overcome the adversity, not in professional counseling but through a mechanism I had learned from my father as a boy—the evening "chat." Every night before bed, Amber and I would lie down and discuss the events of the day. In short order, we both began to share our fears, hopes, and dreams, and openly discuss Rosa's death. I believe these "chats" opened a line of communication between us that can never be shut down, but at the time it helped to ease our fears about "moving on" to the next stage in our lives.

Thoughts on Schooling

Just about the time we learned about Rosa's illness, we had moved into a new house in a new development. The middle school Amber had previously attended was 50 percent African American and 50 percent European American. She had a solid core of friends, and now she was faced with adjusting to a new school where the racial make-up was less than 5 percent African American and more than 95 percent European American.

"Why can't we move back to our old house? It was nice. . . . and all of my friends live over there. You and mom did not ask me if I wanted to move. I hate this new school." As I listened to Amber bombard me with these very valid questions, in my mind I realized that I was now harvesting the fruits of my own parenting philosophy which encouraged her always to question, especially things she did not understand. I should have known that at some point I would have to deal with the product of the seeds I planted. "First, young lady," I said "let me remind you that I gave my word to you that I would be open and honest with you always and that I expected the same from you. Some decisions made by your mother and I were made in what we believe to be the best interest of the family. Those decisions were made by us and not by you, because we had information and knowledge that in this case only we could process and understand and consider. We are here (in our new home) and we cannot move back to the old house, and this move was for the good of the whole." "I still don't like my school and the white kids are fake," she retorted. "This experience will help you to prepare to function in the real world, and remember Martin Luther King said you should judge people not by the color of their skin but the content of their character," I asserted.

"Yeah? There are some really strange characters at my school, and they don't like black folks anyway, Dad," she declared. "The teachers feel the same way." As I listened intently, I could feel the pain and frustration in her voice. I recognized that this was a situation, if not handled thoughtfully, carefully, and with "mother-wit" (i.e., common sense) could forever alienate her from education and non-African American people in general. As a professional educator, I know that when students and teachers are of different cultures, their difference in values can result in misunderstandings and frustrations on both sides. In order to have a positive school experience, it is necessary for the teacher to have a positive relationship with students, display and impart social skills which appreciate and celebrate diversity, and last but not least provide a quality educational experience. The worst thing a teacher can do is to label my daughter or any student as "disadvantaged" or "at-risk," since labels are counterproductive and harmful, in that they feed prejudice, discrimination, and low expectations. I was determined this would never happen to my daughter.

In the teacher education courses I teach, I always inform my students that as educators their first contact with parents or guardians should be a positive one. It should be a situation in which they are informing the parent of their child's curriculum, or of a good grade on a test, or inviting the parents to participate in some school activity. "When your first contact is related to a problem," I would tell them, "you are setting up an adversarial meeting or relationship." Off to the school with Amber in tow, I went to start what I hoped would not be, but I perceived would be, the start of an adversarial relationship with her teachers. As we sat in the small conference room with her Social Studies, English, Math, and Science teachers, I tried to take the high road as we started our discussion. "Well, you know our school has high standards. We place great demands on our students, and they must keep up on their work," the English teacher said before I could open my mouth. "How many students and teachers of color do you have in this school?" I asked. "We don't see color and I can't answer that question," one teacher responded. "Do you take the learning styles of the students in your classes into consideration when you make your lesson plans?" I inquired. "Why are you asking these questions? . . . they are inappropriate and not important. You need to be concerned with your child's poor performance in Math this quarter," said an obviously agitated male Science teacher. "Well, what are you going to do, Ms. Math teacher, to help Amber in your class?" I asked. "I can't help her," she said, "I have too many students and I must keep on the schedule that the Math curriculum states I must follow." "Bullshit!" I shouted. "Your job is to help students to learn and understand the Math concepts you teach in your classroom. You need to be concerned about all your students, and mine in particular because you are not getting across to her," I said, slamming my fist on the table. "The problem here is not my daughter's ability but the will and commitment of you and the school to insure that her needs are met," giving the Science teacher the facial expression I learned from my mother which clearly meant "don't mess with me or I will have your butt in a platter." "I expect some change on your part that ensures my daughter's success," I said, as I began to leave the room. And then my final words: "I will be back."

As we exited the school. Amber's face bore an expression somewhere between a smile and a frown. "What's on your mind, kid?" "Well dad, I have never seen you that upset before, but I feel good that you were there to take up for me," she responded. "Let me explain something to you Amber; education is the most valuable commodity you can obtain. Excellence in education goes beyond good grades and high test scores. Your school must prepare you to be a rational, reflective, and critical thinker. It should provide truthful knowledge about who you are and how you can become a productive member in society. This can only be accomplished if you and your classmates have respect for your cultural group and other cultural groups. I will not leave it up to the school to provide your total education. I must do some things as your father." "Like what?" she asked. "I must ensure that you know your cultural history, for example. It is impossible for you to meet others in the world on an equal footing if you are illiterate or lack respect for your own culture. Discrimination and racism are still the evil twins in our society, and I must make sure you can handle, survive, and thrive from the many negative conditions they throw your way. In other words, I want to guarantee that you are not a victim of miseducation." This school conference proved significant, as Amber realized that not only was the school going to be held accountable, but she was also responsible for her academic success. I remember closing our conversation that day with the words my father gave to me. He said, "Once you get a good education, no one can take it from you."

Whatever You Do . . . Do Something You Love

The school conference and our conversation afterwards served as the vehicle which allowed Amber to explore many topics related to school and life in general with me. She appeared to feel comfortable in broaching just about any subject, including school matters, hobbies, boys, disputes with friends, drugs, gangs, and even sex. However, the one concern from early middle school to early high school, for her, was what vocation or profession she should consider. "When the students are asked what they want to be in life," Amber declared, "they always say a doctor, lawyer, or something of that nature, but I always say I don't know. What should I do, and what if I choose something, spend all those years studying, and then I don't like it? School teachers put all this pressure on you by saying you need to take this class so you can take this class—boy, it is all so confusing."

"Don't worry about it," I said. "Just enjoy being a kid; you have the rest of your life to be an adult. . . . Don't worry about what your profession will be, you can always do more than one thing or change your career. I know many successful people who have started in one career and later switched to another. However, when you decide, pick something you like and dedicate yourself to being the best." Amber replied, "Thanks, Dad, for the message but I am still lost." "Well," I responded, "if you don't know where you are going, any road will take you there. Pick something you love to do, and find out if it can be turned into a career." Several months went by before Amber broached the subject with me again.

She said, "Dad, you remember that little talk we had about what I should do professionally with my life? . . . Well, I have been doing some serious thinking and what I love is my music. I have been playing the flute since grade school, and I love it. In order for me to improve my playing, I want to take private lessons and I need a new flute. Do we have the money so I can do that?"

As I told her we could manage the money matters, I tried to hide my shock concerning her choice of music. I guess I thought she would decide to be a doctor or lawyer, or something, but music? How will she ever be self-reliant and take care of herself after I die? Perhaps it's just a phase, and she will outgrow it. I knew that this was just a phase of growing up.

Throughout her middle school years, Amber took her private lessons, and success soon followed: first chair flute player in the high school symphonic band, a "one" rating at state competition, selection to the all-state high school band, and many more awards for achievement. I did not fully understand the depth of her commitment to music until she asked my opinion on an essay she had written for a class.

Amber's Essay

When I pick up my flute from my flute stand and prepare to play Suite Antique, movement one, Prelude, composed by John Rutter, it's like picking up a story of my mother's life with mine. As I play the first few slow measures of the piece it reminds me of her beautiful, colorful and cheerful face. Her character shines through the music and reminds me of the summers we spent together.

As I hit the E natural and start to play at box A, it starts a new chapter of our lives. I can see the gymnastic classes, the girl scouts' cookie order forms, the smell of the fresh rice crispy treats she used to make. When I turn the page not knowing what is ahead of me, and taking a gasp for air, I glance and see the change of the notes moving all over the page. It's like looking into the future not knowing what it is until you get right upon the measure.

When I come to the eighth notes and sixteenth notes, it tended to get louder and then moderately louder. These particular measures remind me of the roller coaster ride that my family has been through and the trauma we experienced when we found out that my mother had cancer.

When I carefully go through the runs and reached a ritard, I know I need to slow down, life needs to slowdown. I take each note very

> carefully and seriously until I reached the end of the measure. At box D, I am at tempo again just like the beginning but a little different. I looked at this tempo a little differently than I did at the beginning. Every precious movement was special now. I was getting to the end of the story and it was getting compelling.
>
> I approached box E delicately. I knew what was ahead for me and now I still sing the E natural to close the book of my mother's life. The last six measures are hard for me . . . I take a gasp of air to complete the story. Each note symbolically leads to the last breath my mother would take in this life!
>
> I cherish the few short years I had with my mother but my music helps to lighten the burden. I feel that God has blessed me with a strong man in my life who will be my mother and father. This experience has left a significant impact and special meaning on my family and me.

Reading her words caused tears to come to my eyes, as I finally realized the profound strength my daughter possessed, and how she had used music as a therapeutic agent and means of expression. I knew at that moment that Amber had a drive and a resilience that would guarantee her success and happiness in any walk of life. Upon graduation from high school, she was offered many college scholarships to continue her love for music. Today, Amber is a college sophomore majoring in Music Performance/ Music Education at one of the top music schools in the country.

Gender Does Not Determine Motherhood

Looking back over the past ten years, I have learned that motherhood is not necessarily determined by gender. Nevertheless, a great deal of the research on African American families has focused on their characteristics and structure while overlooking the concept of family functioning. "One-parent families are arbitrarily assumed to be broken and unstable while two parent families are arbitrarily assumed to be intact and stable, without providing for any independent assessment of the stability or cohesion of each family" (Hill, 1989, p.7). Focusing on these characteristics often results in describing the titular head of the clan, and not how well the family functions as a unit in handling life situations and events. In African American families, roles are often flexible, with a support system to help adjust, meet, and cope with life demands. This support system has often been described as the extended family concept or system. The African American male has multiple cultural roles to play.

As any parent/teacher/educator/mother can attest, child rearing is a difficult job, even in the best of circumstances. Given my experience over the past ten years, as both mother and father to Amber, we were able to survive, stabilize, and maintain a healthy family unit. Five factors identified by Hill (1989) as a common thread for strong family life are strong kinship bonds, strong work orientation, adaptability of family roles, strong achievement orientation, and strong religious orientation. We knew we had the support of relatives, friends, and church, which served as a safety net for our psychic, emotional, and spiritual well-being, plus stable employment to provide for our material needs. Primary care-giving, mentoring, modeling, nurturing, and assessing were probably the most important responsibilities for me as a mother. From this, I believe that Amber, by her own admission, has had a happy and well-rounded childhood. She will be successful in her life endeavors, in part, because her father was able to move from being a son to being a mother.

References

Hill, R. (Ed.). (1989). *Research on the African American family? A holistic perspective Vol. II*. Boston: William M. Trotter Institute.

Moynihan, D. P. (1965). *The Negro family: A case for national action*. Washington: Government Printing Office.

Chapter Four

Mothering for Manhood: The (Re)Production of a Black Son's Gendered Self

James Earl Davis

> Glorifying the strong Black mother represents Black Men's attempts to replace negative white male interpretations with Black male ones. But no matter how sincere, externally defined definitions of Black womanhood—even those offered by sympathetic African American men—are bound to come with their own set of problems.
>
> —Patricia Hill Collins, *Black Feminist Thought*

The words of Patricia Hill Collins provide both challenge and encouragement for me. I am challenged to reflect more broadly and extend my thinking beyond any well-intentioned (no matter how sincere) effort to defend, protect, or honor black women and mothers. To be clear, my representation of black women, particularly that of my mother, is a personal one framed by my own gendered experience. I am aware that the views of black men on these issues have traditionally not come under the same critical scrutiny as those of white males or even under the scrutiny of white feminists. In light of a growing black feminist critique, I am also encouraged to put forth a personal reading on motherhood, because of a disappearing reluctance to critique and challenge the work of black men. Indeed, I benefit from a shattered silence of black feminist voices that hold my analysis accountable, both theoretically and culturally.

The complexities in constructions of black manhood have rarely been examined, especially the perspective of black men who focused upon their mothers. Although there has been substantial discussion about the plight of African American men, only modest attempts have been made to connect men's lives and experiences to maternal sources of influence. In this chapter, I focus on the role of mothering and my personal gender development. While my experiences with my mother may not reflect the generalized experiences of most black males, the purpose of this work is illustrative rather than prescriptive. Exploring and presenting my personal narrative offers a compelling juxtaposition to a grand narrative in the black community that describes the role of black women, often mothers, as being complicit in the "crisis of black males." Drawing on work from a range of literatures in the social sciences and humanities, I place reflection of my cultural life and my mother's at the center of an analysis that tries to shed some light on the production of black manhood. I have developed this chapter around three interconnected issues: a mother's educational history and experience; a son's masculinized social and educational development; and the ways in which a mother brokers her son's development toward manhood.

Making Gender, Making Manhood

The cultural lives of black boys/men are often marginalized by the deviant-centered media hype and the obsession with negative social constructions of black males. But how are these lives played out in the history of survival in African American communities? During the last five years alone, our understanding of the contemporary black male condition has been enhanced by intellectual and practical work highlighted in recent volumes about African American men (Majors & Gordan, 1994; McCall, 1994; Mincy, 1994; Belton, 1995; Boyd & Allen, 1995; Blount & Cunningham, 1996). This body of work covers the spectrum from quantitative data-driven social science research to insightful theoretical offerings of literary criticism. Although varied in content, theory, and methodological approaches, this work shares in the broader objective of broadening the discourse about the lives of black men in America. Recently added to this growing repertoire in black male studies is *Sacred Bond? Black Men and Their Mothers* (Brown, 1998). Written by broadcast journalist Keith Michael Brown, with photographs by Adger Cowans, this collection of stories about black men and mother-son relationships is both compelling and challenging. With integrity and sincerity, Brown weaves an impressive tapestry of black males' lives shaped by mothers whose love and sacrifice nurtured and sustained them. In an example of his mother's valor, strength, and understanding as she faces the death of a son, Brown reflects on his brother's death.

> At that moment, I saw my mother's strength and I understood the depth of her love for us, her three sons. And I painfully understood the depth of my mother's suffering—one-third of everything she and my father had worked and lived for was taken from them. My mother, the first woman in our blue-collar community to send her sons off to college and to watch each one of them graduate, had now become another "first": the first to lose a child to the AIDS virus. But she never bowed in defeat. (1998, x)

While I may be challenged by the ever present archetype of the strong black woman, I cannot deny the profound space created by personal renderings of such experiences and connections black men have with their mothers. Personal narratives, at the risk of constructing black womanhood too narrowly and away from women's own voices, provide a compelling discourse for exploring how black men make meaning of their lives through their mothers.

Our thinking about the gender-role socialization of black manhood has been influenced by work on the lifestyles and experiences of urban and low-income males (Cowman, 1989). According to Callahan and Hunter (1996), the literature of the twentieth century has incorporated one of three theoretical approaches: the culture of poverty approach, traditional white masculinity models, and the cultural deficit approach. The culture of poverty approach is based on the idea that black male gender roles are the products of a culture that has been disadvantaged by the history of slavery, oppression, and disenfranchisement. The denial of manhood because of racism is the major tenet of traditional white masculinity models. The theoretical approach asserts that black men *can* perform the traditional male role, but are unable to do so due to the lack of financial and operational means. The cultural deficit approach is based on the assumption that the inability of black men to meet traditional masculine standards has led to alternative avenues to manhood. This development of culturally specific constructions of manhood is often maladaptive and narrowly conceived (Casenave, 1984; Franklin, 1987).

Because perspectives on black masculine development and male role performance are steeped in a traditional hegemonic construction, they fail to elaborate on the variations in the meaning of black manhood that reflect my personal experience (Brod, 1987; Pleck, 1981). For instance, the diversity in the meaning of manhood is hidden by the monolithic notion of manhood that pervades the popular media and culture. A new construction of manhood—one that comes from personalized cultural history in families and schools—is sorely missing from the discourse on the "crisis in black manhood." I try to remedy this omission by presenting a personal narrative that captures the complexity of meaning and variations in manhood connected to issues of schooling and mothering.

A Mother Speaks—A Son Hears

My mother's voice was often overshadowed and rendered silent by my father. However, the death of my father last year, although painful, shifted my mother's positioning in the family. Her voice became clearer and more powerful. I now see my mother in ways that were made invisible by the presence of my father. This does not mean that my mother played an insignificant role in the family. My mother had (and continues to have) a profound influence in the family and on my social development. However, this influence became more visible to me after my father's death. I recently had a conversation with my mother about her life and our relationship. She agreed to have the conversation tape-recorded and was excited to participate in the documentation of her own oral history. I considered it very important, as she did, to provide contextual information about her family and about her educational background. Her story of navigating the historical and personal currents of poverty, race, and gender as a black woman coming of age is one that I have constantly needed to hear.

The fifth of ten children born to a mother and father who were the offspring of slaves in northern Alabama, my mother's early life was very conventional for those constrained by poverty and racial caste. With very meager economic resources, her family survived on farm earnings and occasional "day work" by her mother. The family was very close, and shared in the household and farming responsibilities. My mother enjoyed friendships with her five brothers and often participated in work and play activities, such as possum hunting, that were considered boyish or often assigned to the exclusive domain of males. During the non-farming seasons, when the family was neither planting or harvesting, my mother went to school. Although her schooling was severely crippled by the intensity of the Jim Crow South, the one-room schoolhouse was a very special place.

At the Penny School she reveled in academic work. Her teachers encouraged her to read and write as much as possible, and to learn arithmetic. After Bible recitations, each school day began with Math, followed by English and History. Spelling and grammar contests were frequently used to excite children about words and their usage. There were very few books available to her, at school or at home. Her parents did not have much formal schooling but insisted that their children, especially the girls, go to school when their help was not required at home. The boys in the family participated in school less often and for shorter periods of time, because of the need to do home chores such as hauling wood and caring for the stock animals. Moma's brothers stopped attending school earlier than the girls, to take advantage of job opportunities. The economic effects of the Depression took their toll on the already meager existence of her family. Nevertheless, she continued to attend school when the weather permitted and when she had appropriate clothes to wear (particularly shoes). Moma reflects on the scarcity and importance of school clothes:

> It was important to be dressed right for school. All the school children had to wear underwear—unions and bloomers and cotton stockings. I had one school dress. My mother would buy flowers in a sack and use the flower sack as material to make dresses. I would wear my school dress every day and Moma would wash it on the weekend.

The journey to school was also problematic. The Penny School was about five miles from her family home, and students had to walk. As she describes it, walking was part of the schooling ritual, one she considered a welcome sacrifice:

> We walked at least five miles from the home place to the school house and five miles back every day. I would sometimes walk with a sister and three of my younger brothers to this little old school building. It had a wood and coal heater. We had to first make fire when it was cold and then we gathered for classes. The walking wasn't that bad. It was kind of fun. And on Wednesday, we would walk an additional eight miles or so, to the school at Mt. Carmel to play ball with students at that school. It was very exciting, the whole school would go. We would walk in groves of five or six girls and boys on the right side of the road. The

> teachers and older students would be at the front leading the group. On the next Wednesday, they would walk to our school.

Some bus transportation was provided for white students in this rural school district. My mother recounts an unfortunate encounter with a busload of white schoolchildren that passed her and a friend walking home from school on a lonely dusty country road. From the windows of the bus, the students taunted my mother with racial slurs and childish banter. Moma's throwing arm and aim, as accurate as any of her older brothers', were put to the test. In a very successful effort, my mother sent a rock through one of the bus windows to pierce the head of the most vocal of the white schoolchildren. As shouts of "You are in trouble" and "We will get you for this," rang from the passing bus, my mother and her friend Pauline tore a path through the adjacent cotton field and ran home.

The following day a white official from the school district appeared at the Penny School to identify "two little black girls" who were responsible for this egregious attack on an innocent white girl. My mother and Pauline were questioned about the incident; they not only denied throwing the rock, but also denied even seeing the bus of white students. My mother apparently knew that it would be almost impossible for any of the students to identify her, given the very distinct social lives black and white families lived in their brutally segregated community. She was right. None of the students at Penny's were ever connected to the incident. My mother lived with the secret of that day and often reflected, with some gleeful guilt, about what became of the "innocent" white girl that was hurt by her hand. She asks with much interest, "I wonder if I ever saw her again, cleaned her house, cooked food for her, took care of her children?"

Instructions on Manhood

Of all the stories my mother has shared with me, the school bus incident resonates with me more than any other. The reason why is not really clear to me. I am definitely attracted to the deviance of the moment—the thought of my mild-mannered and soft-spoken mother deliberately striking out to defend herself and her relegated social space on that country road. The act is extremely unlike the woman I have come to know over the years. Yet it is also who she is, and a connection to who I am. Like my mother, I have always been the nice guy. My mother insisted that my brother and I were always well-mannered, well-spoken (particularly to our elders) and polite. "I raised you to be nice boys," she would say. I too, like Robin Kelly, (1995) secretly desire at least on occasion to provoke a sense of threat and fear—to be perceived in a different way, other than as a "good boy." Kelly discloses: "I shouldn't admit this, but I take particular pleasure in putting fear into people on the lookout for black male criminality mainly because those moments are so rare for me. Indeed, my inability to employ black maleness as a weapon is the story of my life" (1995, p. 13). The black maleness that my mother taught was one steeped in civil, kind, orderly, and respectful behavior—both for oneself and for others. She was pretty effective in raising a "good" boy, one that always plays by the rules, is never threatening, and always polite. I am a reflection of her in so many ways. She was very successful, consciously or unconsciously, in reproducing her gentle disposition.

The story about the school bus was occasionally revisited, not only upon my insistence but by her in a way that served as both lesson and warning. While she states her sadness about any harm brought to the white girl and more broadly reflects on the evils of violence, she also teaches about the responsibility for protecting one's self-respect, personal honor, and space. This was part of her training to make sure I would develop into the kind of man she would be proud to call her son. One important thing she wants me to take from the story is the need to protect my space and defend it, aggressively if need be. For her, the walk to and from school was part of schooling. So the insults of students who were provided with transportation was in some ways a call to arms. This same tenacity of ownership and protection of school space was made clear to me early on. My mother insisted that I let nothing interfere with the sacred schooling space. Next to her religious convictions, there was nothing more important to her than education. In some ways, my educational development was a religious conviction. She also saw it as a part of God's work. She states:

> I did all I could to make sure you boys had a good education. If there was anything you needed for school, I would try to get it. I sacrificed my life and things for you. I would give my last. I did have the chance to go to school but I wanted you to go as far as you could. I didn't always understand what you were doing and studying, but I wanted you to do it because you wanted to do it. I thank the Lord for all that He has done for you and your education.

Masculinity in School? Breaking the Code

While the current plight of young black males in school is the focus of much concern, little is known about how the school context affects their educational and social experiences. Because schools are important sites for gendered learning and development, masculine identities and socialization are often produced and reinforced in school environments. In this section, I attempt to frame a personal discussion of how the intersection of gender, race, and mothering are informed and influenced by the school experiences of black males. I draw on both research literature and personal schooling history to sketch a picture of connected lives—one dictated by the school culture of boys, and the other directed by my mother.

The investigation of gender and its effects on schooling experiences and achievement has been an important area of scholarly and policy concern (Adler, Kless & Adler, 1992; Kessler, et al., 1985; Wexler, 1988). In most of this work, gender is viewed from a social constructivist perspective, in which qualities of masculinity/femininity are culturally attributed and defined (Connell, 1993; Thomas, 1990). Without question, schooling contexts are important sources for gender construction and development (Polite & Davis, 1998). The traditional focus on the educational problems of black males obscures the diversity and complexity of how masculinities operate in educational settings. Invariably, constructions of black boys/men in schools are unidimensional and implicitly universal. The issues defining and setting the context for understanding the relationships between black males and education are complex. Associated with each issue are multiple questions and problems facing black boys/men and their families—blood and fictive kin. Although there has been substantial discussion about the precarious status of black males in school, only modest attempts have been made to connect their lives to meaningful sources of influence and support such as their mothers.

Black boys are loved and hated in American schools. They are the heroes and standard bearers of hiphop culture and athleticism in schools. On the other hand, they experience disproportionate levels of punishment and academic marginality there. This juxtaposition of being, as Tony Sewell (1997) says, "the darling of popular youth subculture and the sinner in the classroom" has lead to a range of behaviors, strategies, and constructions within and beyond schooling spaces that frames identities. How do African American boys respond to a context that sees them as "sexy" and as "sexually threatening"? How do they purchase a space in schools that is self-maintained and reproductive? From my schooling experiences, I understand that these are highly normative masculine spaces that are restricting and oppressive. In these spaces, black males construct a meaning of who they are, what they do, and how they are perceived as males. I was not completely exempt from being victimized by male school culture.

One reason commonly mentioned for the alienation and poor academic performance of some black males is that they perceive most schooling activities as feminine and irrelevant to their masculine sense of self and development (Holland, 1989). It is also contended that the increased presence of committed and successful black male adults in educational environments is essential for enhancing black boys'/men's academic and social development, and to counter inappropriate sex-role socialization and maladaptive masculine identity. Research on African American males in school is relatively recent and scant, centering typically on "at-riskness." Little attention is given to how black males construct personal meaning for their lives in and out of school. Discussion about how black boys make sense of their own masculinity and the masculinity of others around them has been noticeably absent.

Out of this "male oppressive" context, a socially responsive subculture centered around masculine expectations and acceptability has emerged. Based on a study of a middle school where I have interviewed black males, and also reflections on my own schooling experiences, I contend that this subculture is distinct from traditional school cultural behaviors of white boys

(Davis, 1998). The difference is attributable to the cultural space that is fashioned by the confluence of a distinct racialized and gendered experience for these students. Black boys clearly understand and embrace the accepted code of conduct. This code is more than a masculinized coping strategy (e.g., Cool Pose) or racialized identity formation (e.g., Black Consciousness). It meticulously crosses borders of race, gender, class and sexuality, while maintaining its solid masculine character. I have found that a masculine code of expectation characterizes much of black boys' social experience in schools. For instance, the code dictates social relationships and interaction styles—primarily between males and females, but also among males. For the most part, friendships between black boys and girls were taboo, unless the friendship was a pretext for sexual positioning or at least for talk of sexualized relations. The non-sexual content of opposite sex friendships is what is problematic for the code. Unfortunately, relationships centered on academic work generally fall victim to the masculine code. Another prominent area of transgression is self-presentation style. The masculine code makes clear the accepted masculine presentational behavior in school, including how boys walk, talk, dress, and carry themselves. One of the most telling parts of the code covers interactions with same-sex peers.

Recently, I have become interested in boys who for a variety of reasons do not always adhere to the masculine code. I refer to these males as "transgressors." These transgressors are unsurprisingly ostracized and socially sanctioned by the black male peer group. Ironically, punishment seems to be the relationship aggression type—most commonly practiced by girls in school and viewed as a more feminine social tactic. But there is always potential for and some evidence of physical aggression by some black males.

I was often a transgressor in many of my school settings. My mother encouraged my transgressions and provided the kind of support that honored and rewarded my transgressions. Moma comments on her support:

> I like having boys better. You were easy to raise. I didn't have trouble with you and your brother. I always wanted the best for you. I would do what I could do to protect you. . . . I didn't want you hanging with the

> wrong crowd of boys who did not mean you any good. I wanted you to do good in school and did what I could to make it easy for you.

With my mother's help. I crossed the sexual/intimate line in same-sex relationships. I must explain that my transgression was not really about sexual acts or intents, but about peer constructions of sexuality that are often based on violations of other planks in the code. The mere act of verbalizing my alternative view on sexuality and relationships, as well as questioning any aspect of the code, resulted in my definite violation of the code. The most severe punishment is reserved for this transgression. Without fail, there came the conclusion that I was gay and thus the ultimate sanctioning—banishment from the "black boyhood" to the exclusive company of black girls or to the social networks of a variety of white student groups. With the constant support of my mother, I wore my social punishments like badges of courage.

A Gendered Educational Journey

A number of competing and sometimes contradictory experiences structured the context for my masculine experiences in school. As a black male, my own experiences, at least in part, inform my thinking about issues of motherhood and manhood. As a young boy, growing up in a poor family in the deep rural South, I ironically had little awareness of how race and gender affected my schooling experiences. I attended an all-black, segregated school until fifth grade, at which time the "deliberate speed" of the *Brown* decision brought desegregation to schools in Alabama.

In the early years, my schooling experiences were very different from those of my peers. Most other young black boys I knew were experiencing school in less positive ways—more disciplinary problems and lower levels of academic performance and engagement. The current construction of the "black male crisis" in education was not prevalent, at least as a policy and intervention imperative. However, the discourse of educational opportunity and quality schooling for all black students, both males and females, dominated most community education concerns. I was repeatedly told by my mother that a high school education was essential for my future success. By graduating from high school, I met most of her schooling demands. As a product of one of the federally funded Trio Programs (Upward Bound), in which my mother had encouraged me to participate, I was prepared for, and almost forced to consider, postsecondary education.

During those early days, I never dreamed that I would complete as much schooling as I have. My father, while maintaining that schooling was important, also thought that too much schooling could be useless at best and maybe dangerous at worst. These ideas were developed in a class context that supported traditional notions of working with the hands. Paradoxically, my family, particularly my mother, was very supportive, for reasons that have become more clear over time, of my decision to attend college. My choice to attend an all-male institution, however, raised some concerns. While my parents, community, and peers supported my decision to attend a historically black college, the composition of the student body at Morehouse created some apprehensions. To some people, the idea that someone would willingly choose an all-male educational environment seemed "inappropriate.? On the contrary, Moma never blinked. She only responded in her usually sage way, "I'm with you. Whatever you want to do, I will support you." And she never failed in her personal obligation to create the best schooling space for me. She made two trips to Atlanta. The first one was to convince the director of housing that her son was a "fine young man, very mannerable and nice, and that it would be really good if he could stay on campus so he could do his work better." I got a room, although officially there was no housing available on campus. Her second visit was to see me graduate.

Although enrolling at Morehouse was contradictory to many expectations of my family and friends, those years made me more reflective of and interested in the intersection between race and gender. My conceptions of masculinity and manhood were challenged and reinforced within this race/gender-exclusive context. My current thinking about the dual status of being black and male continues to be influenced by that experience.

I often had conversations with my mother while I was in graduate school. She always asked about my work, although never fully understanding the real purpose of graduate school. But her limited exposure to higher education never prevented her from providing guidance and advice about my deportment and appearance within an environment that was often very competitive and stressful. She always made sure that I had plenty of underwear, and that I had plenty of jeans (preferably ironed), so that I could wear a different pair each day of the week. I think these directives are connected not only to her own memories of school clothes, but to her experience with our school clothes in elementary school. My mother reflects:

> I remember when you went to elementary school and you and Larry had to wear the same clothes on Monday and Tuesday, and the same thing on Wednesday and Thursday. Friday was a free-for-all. You had to take off your school clothes when you came home after school. When you started going to the white school, I felt you should wear something different every day. So I worked to get you and your brother more clothes for school. I didn't want the white children to think you were any different than them.

Emerging concerns about black males and their relative lack of educational success have been, at least in part, antifeminist. The ensuing debate has by and large constructed black males as victims, often setting their interests against those of black girls. I am very conscious of the potential outcomes of this strategy. However, I will continue to argue that our thinking needs to be refocused and centered on the cultural lives of black males, and relevant narratives such as the one I have provided about my mother. My masculine self is in many ways attributable to her care regarding educational matters in my life. The masculine lives of other black males—that I was either victimized and/or saved by—are unfortunately too often ignored, misunderstood, or rendered invisible.

Concluding Thoughts on Mothering and Manhood

The educational marginalization of African American males in school and society has too often been laid at the feet of black women. The social narrative that black women, particularly mothers, are complicit in the "black males' crisis" maintains much currency in academic writing and popular culture (Kelly, 1997). For instance, poor single mothers bear a disproportionate level of criticism for the unhealthy development of black boys/men (Cottingham, 1989). Also, the overprotectiveness of some black mothers toward their sons is seen as being restrictive or maladaptive to masculine development (Patterson, 1995). In both cases, black males are forced to seek male socialization and explore the meaning of masculinity among their peers. Similarly, this narrative has taken hold in the discourse surrounding the precarious positioning of African American boys in school. Much concern has recently been expressed about the anxiety black males experience in schools that are dominated by women and by a feminine culture. In essence, what it means to be a black male is so marginalized and suppressed at school and at home, that the manhood of black males is developed with great difficulty.

I have tried to argue that there are other ways in which to view relations between black males and their mothers, specifically in relation to schooling. In doing so, I have attempted to examine the complex nature of black manhood from the perspective of a son's relationship with his mother. I have tried to overlay a personal narrative with social science literature on manhood and masculinity. As intended, the product is instructive, but not prescriptive. Obviously, this is not the first analysis of the mother-son relationship; nor will it be the last. The subject explored here is not only of increasing cultural and educational interest, but is framed by a larger critique of the meaning of masculinity and the making of manhood. While my narrative is authentically personal and meaningful to my development and current social positioning, it is also grounded in the familial and communal. Questions are raised, and traditional constructions of mother-son relations and implications for masculine identity are problematized. I desire to strengthen my thinking about these issues in ways that will transcend traditional genres from the social sciences and humanities, while also serving as both a guide and a reflector for understanding the contemporary schooling context of black boys, and challenging masculine anxiety among African Americans. If I have partially fulfilled this intention and offered a minimal contribution to the critique on the cultural lives of black males, then the rendering of my mother's voice remains personally sacred yet publicly relevant.

References

Adler, P. A., Kless, S. J., & Adler, P. (1992). Socialization to gender roles: Popularity among elementary school boys and girls. *Sociology and Education, 65,* 169–87.

Belton, D. (Ed.). (1995). *Speak my name: Black men on masculinity and the American dream.* Boston: Beacon Press.

Blount, M., & Cunningham, G. P. (1996). *Representing black men.* New York: Routledge.

Bowman, P. J. (1989). Research perspectives on black men? Role strain and adaptation across the black adult male life cycle. In R. Jones (Ed.), *Black adult development and aging.* Berkeley, CA: Cobb & Henry.

Boyd, H., & Allen, R. L. (1996). *Brotherman: The odyssey of black men in America.* New York: Random House.

Brod, H. (Ed.). (1987). *The making of masculinities: The new men's studies.* Boston: Allen & Unwin.

Brown, K. M. (1998). *Sacred bond? Black men and their mothers.* Boston: Little, Brown.

Callahan, M. R., & Hunter, A. G. (1996). *On race and manhood: Retrospective and current views on self, family, and community.* Paper presented at the Annual Conference of the National Council of Family Relations.

Casenave, N. A. (1984). Race, socioeconomic status, and age: The social context of American masculinity. *Sex Roles, 11,* 639–56.

Collins, P. H. (1987). The meaning of motherhood in black culture and black mother/daughter relationships. *Sage: A Scholarly Journal of Black Women,* 4(2), 2–10.

Collins, P. H. (1990). *Black feminist thought: Knowledge, consciousness, and the politics of empowerment.* New York: Routledge.

Connell, R. W. (1993). Disruptions: Improper masculinities and schooling. In L. Weis & M. Fine (Eds.), *Beyond silenced voices: Class, race, and gender in United States schools.* Albany: State University of New York Press.

Connell. R. W. (1995). *Masculinities.* Berkeley: University of California Press.

Davis, J. E. (1998). *Black males' construction of transgressive sexualities in middle school.* Paper presented at the Annual Meeting of the Australian Association for Research in Education, Adelaide, Australia.

Franklin, C. W. (1984). *The changing definition of masculinity.* New York: Plenum Press.

Franklin, C. W. (1987). Surviving the institutional decimation of black males? Causes, consequences, and intervention. In H. Brod (Ed.), *The making of masculinities: The new men's studies.* Boston: Allen & Unwin.

Hunter, A. G., & Davis, J. E. (1994). Hidden voices of black men: The meaning, structure, and complexity of manhood. *Journal of Black Studies, 25*(1), 20–40.

Kelley, R. D. G. (1997). *Yo' mama's disfunktional: Fighting the culture wars in urban America.* Boston: Beacon Press.

Kelly, R. (1995). Confessions of a nice Negro, or why I shaved my head. In D. Belton (Ed.), *Speak my name: Black men on masculinity and the American dream.* Boston: Beacon Press.

Kessler, S., Ashenden, D. J., Connell, R. W., & Dowsett, G. W. (1985). Gender relations in secondary schooling. *Sociology of Education, 58,* 34–48.

McCall, N. (1995). *Makes me want to holler: A young black man in America.* New York: Vintage.

Mincy, R. (1994). *Nurturing young black males? Challenges to agencies, programs and social policy.* Washington, DC: Urban Institute.

Pleck, J. (1981). *The myth of masculinity.* Cambridge, MA: MIT Press.

Polite, V., & Davis, J. E. (1994). Pedagogical and contextual issues affecting African American males in school and society. Special Issue, *Journal of Negro Education, 63*(4).

Sanders, E. T., & Reed, P. L. (1990). An investigation of the possible effects of an immersion as compared to a traditional program for African-American males. *Urban Education, 30,* 93–112.

Sewell, T. (1997). *Teacher attitude: Who's afraid of the big black boys?* Paper presented at the Annual Meeting of the American Educational Research Association, Chicago, IL.

Thomas, K. (1990). *Gender and the subject of higher education.* London: Open University Press.

Wexler, P. (1988). Symbolic economy of identify and denial of labor: Studies in high school. In L. Weis (Ed.), *Class, race, and gender in American education.* Albany: State University of New York Press.

Part Two

Critical Commentary for Cultural Workers

Chapter Five

School Violence, Black Masculinities, and a Mother's Love: Reflections on (In)Formal Urban Pedagogies

Garrett Albert Duncan

> Not economically rich—but culturally wealthy, not politically powerful—but socially conscious, not mainstream educated—but armed with the knowledge, commitment and determination that only a mother can possess.
>
> —Madres del Este de Los Angeles-Santa Isabel

Introduction

Most critical black educators, researchers, and cultural workers have long made distinctions between schooling and education, the former being potentially a subordinating process, and the latter, one that is implicitly liberating. Within this pedagogical perspective is an understanding of learning as a process that begins long before children ever enter formal educational settings. The pedagogies of the various informal contexts that shape young minds and bodies are mostly indirect and subtle and, moreover, are as much affective and intuitive as they are cognitive and effective. Further, such pedagogies are often mediated via cultural tools that are shaped by the white supremacist sociopolitical milieu of the United States, a place within which black people know that we are normal, like everyone else, and at the same time, understand that this society looks upon us as abnormal.

Informal, everyday pedagogies that inform the development of black children and youth reflect a double-consciousness that is necessary to survive and thrive in a white supremacist world. For example, it was my mother who, very early in my life, taught me, in a sing-song voice, that the "blacker the berry, the sweeter the juice." Anticipating the color prejudice that her blue-black man-child would encounter in a racist world, even among his own people, she began instilling in me from the outset the truth of my own beauty and the power and worthiness of my being. She made a conscious decision to challenge the negative cultural artifacts that supersaturated the social milieus of my childhood and youth.

Many of those cultural artifacts still persist today. Indeed, as James Baldwin (1963) warned his nephew during the early 1960s, the period of my childhood: "Know whence you came. If you know whence you came, there is really no limit to where you can go. The details and symbols of your life have been deliberately constructed to make you believe what white people say about you. Please try to remember that what they believe, as well as what they do and cause you to endure, does not testify to your inferiority but to their inhumanity and fear" (p. 22).

At the same time, my mother also exercised the wisdom to teach me that there are many shades of black, and to affirm and love, but not to take pride in, the accidental circumstances of my birth. During my preschool years, whenever she overheard me teasing my younger siblings with the poem she had taught me, my mother would call out from some remote location in the house, "Yes, the blacker the berry the sweeter the juice, but when it gets to your color, it ain't no more use!"—and my younger, butter-colored sister Veronica would repeat, "Yeah, it ain't no more use!" The colorism that I have encountered frequently throughout my life has never been tolerated among the children in my mother's house, despite my stepfather's habit of calling black people "boots" and his insistence that he was not black, but rather Portuguese, an unfortunate lie that the youngest of my siblings, David, would later in his life internalize in an extreme and hurtful way.

Thus, instead of sending mixed signals to me about my beauty and worthiness, my mother was adept in fostering in me a capacity to engage the ambiguities and contradictions that are prominent in all aspects of North American life, including our conceptions of masculinities, love, and violence. My mother, like black mothers throughout the nation, has much to offer educators and cultural workers, many of whom are black mothers themselves, who seek to eradicate systemic violence in society, including that which underlies many of the pedagogies in urban schools. In what follows, I draw upon the lessons I learned from my mother during my childhood and youth about violence and masculinities, to consider how they may inform urban pedagogies that are humane, culturally relevant, and socially responsible.

Mr. Rubberband Man

I don't recall the boys' name. And while the specific circumstances surrounding the incident have faded with time, the central lesson remains a permanent part of my memory bank, a part with which I mediate my understanding of violence and certain dimensions of my own masculinities as a black man. I was in the first grade, at Brookfield Elementary School on the east side of Oakland, during the mid-1960s. The boy, a classmate, had been ill for quite some time; he may not have been ill, but injured, because I do remember his right arm being in a sling upon his much celebrated return to class. My teacher and classmates alike made such a big fuss that day. I don't remember the exact words, just images, mostly smiling faces and adoring gazes. I do recall, though—quite vividly, in fact—how struck I was with the boys' demeanor: he was extremely gracious, so humble that he seemed embarrassed that so much attention was being directed his way. There was almost an angelic quality to his character. Thus, my action was that much more callous and deplorable.

For no particular reason, except perhaps jealousy, I pulled a rubber band from my pocket, took aim and fired, point blank, at the space where his right ear met his head. I felt sick, even before the rubber band popped, burning, against the side of the boys' head. To make matters worse, he began to cry, a low whimper at first that soon became a sorrow-inducing sob, so much so that even other students began to cry. His tears seemed to flow less from the physical pain that I had inflicted upon him and more from the senselessness and undeservedness of it all. And our teacher was completely outraged. I had done what I did in plain sight—there was no reason for what had happened or even any need to explain why I had done it. My action was completely indefensible.

As it was nearing the end of the school day, rather than sending me to the office to be punished by the vice principal, my teacher sent me home with a slip and a warning to not return the following day without my mother's signature on it. Naturally, I returned to class the next day without my mother's signature on the slip. While I could read neither the slip's fine print nor the additional comments that my teacher had written, I knew from witnessing the experiences of Dominique, my oldest sister, that a note brought home or a call from school generally meant that I was going to get my behind whipped, and good. Moreover, given what I had done, I knew that this would be a special whipping, not with the usual black leather belt but probably with a switch from the peach tree in the backyard or even an extension cord. Why endure certain pain, I reasoned, especially since I had by now taken the high road and forgiven myself for the unfortunate circumstances of the previous day? However, upon entering the classroom the following day I could sense that my classmates had a longer memory than I did, so I avoided all eye contact with them. This did not work, however, with my teacher.

"Garrett," she summoned me to her desk, "do you have the note that I gave you to take home yesterday?"

"Yes, Mrs. —. Here it is," I replied, presenting to my teacher, a white woman, perhaps in her late thirties, the now crumpled piece of yellow paper that I had been sent home with the day before.

After a few moments of studying the slip, the teacher, obviously perplexed, asked me, "Where is your mother's signature? Did you give this to her?"

"Well, no," I answered, amazed at my own truthfulness under the circumstances.

"And why not?" she demanded.

"Well," I thought for a moment. "Because she didn't come home last night," I said, impressed with how fast I came up with that one. "My mother doesn't always come home at night," I continued to explain, completely unaware of the myth of black permissiveness to which my words, even at such a young age, responded.

"Oh, really?" replied Mrs. — "Well, this is fine, I guess," she said, as she placed the note in the drawer of her desk. "You can go to your seat," she said to me, with that teacher's smile that always made me feel warm and happy to be in her class. Other than a few dirty looks from my peers, the day went along rather well for me. When Mrs.— dismissed class at the end of the day, I ran along to my baby-sitter's house, happily, pretty much having forgotten the events of the previous day.

"Ooooooh, you in trou--ble!!" sang my four-year-old sister Veronica, greeting me at the door of our baby-sitter's house. "You in trouble!" she repeated, as the Reverend Williams, an old black man in his sixties, came to the door to tell her to quit making all the noise.

"Boy, come in here and get you something to eat," he said to me, holding the screen door open. Obviously, Veronica didn't know what she was talking about, for, as I looked around, the only thing I saw was Mrs. Williams, who nodded over to a plate on the table, where there was a snack waiting for me. It wasn't unusual for Mrs. Williams to speak with gestures and, further, there was the food—how could I be in trouble? But something wasn't completely right, however. I caught Mrs. Williams more than once shaking her head, while looking at me, not so much like she was mad or disgusted, but rather like she was sad and disappointed. I would soon find out that not only was I not in the clear, but there was a reason for Mrs. Williams' look.

The whipping I got when my mother came home from work that afternoon stands out in my mind. I had never before and have perhaps never since seen my mother so upset over something I had done. Initially, it seemed as though most of her emotions were directed at my comments to the teacher that "my mother doesn't always come home at night."

"Boy, why would you tell your teacher that I don't come home at night?" my mother asked me in disbelief, not quite in anger but rather in distress. "I work all day to help keep food on the table and clothes on your back, and you go out and tell people that I stay out all night, like I'm fast or something? What is wrong with you, boy?" I knew immediately what my mother was talking about and sensed why she was so upset. While it would be a number of years before I understood the racialized undertones of my comment, when my mother mentioned "fast," even at that age I knew that it had to do with messing around, like the white third-grade teacher who taught at my school, the one with the bright red hair who, on weekends, rode around my neighborhood in an open convertible with the Reverend and Mrs. Williams' teenage son.

However, as my mother began to whip me, she also started crying. Oddly, she barely mentioned what I had done to the boy. Perhaps this is why I remember, almost to a word, what she said to me as she whipped me:

"Boy, I know we live in a crazy world but I'll be damned if I let it make you a monster!" I will kill you myself before I let this happen!" she said, as much to herself as to me.

A Crazy Schoolboy

This theme would emerge several times during my life. It came up when, at twelve, I struck the only female that I have ever hit in my life. Veronica had been teasing me about something, and after having tired of my complaints to her, my mother told me that if my sister kept it up I should "pop her in the mouth." My sister kept teasing me but, having overheard my mother, covered her mouth, pointing out to me in a muffled voice "You can't hit me—I got my mouth covered!" So I hit her in her eye. In this instance, my mother was upset not only because I had hit my little sister, but also that I had used her words as my justification. Similar to the incident years before, she whipped me while, at the same time, warning me that she would "be damned" before she would allow me to strike another female—girl or woman—again.

When I was in the eighth grade and a group of my buddies decided that they wanted to jump me, my mother intervened on my behalf. My friends, not having seen me fight since the fourth grade, a year after we had moved from Oakland to Hayward, wanted to test my mettle. Part of this had to do also with the recent arrival at Rancho Arroyo Junior High School of Lil' Jimmy, whose father, Big Jimmy, had dated my mother after she had divorced my stepfather a year earlier. Lil' Jimmy had just relocated from Los Angeles where, he bragged, he was a Baby Crip. Initially, we had been ace boon coons but, distance developed between us when he began telling all the guys that his father was screwing my mother. However, I held off confronting him because, one, I suspected that I was going to be ambushed by the entire group and, two, my mother had already warned me upon entering junior high school that she would not tolerate me fighting. However, as Lil' Jimmy kept running his mouth and the tensions increased, I warned my mother about the pressure my friends were putting on me, but without sharing with her the rumor that Lil' Jimmy was spreading. At that point, it was inevitable, I thought, that I was going to have to fight.

My mother, however, averted the confrontation between me and my friends. I remember riding my bike to school one morning, only to be passed on the road by that familiar maroon '68 four-door Chevy Impala with the white vinyl top. Before I arrived at the campus, my mother would pass me again, this time in the opposite direction, without so much as glancing at me. *'Oh hell,'* I thought, *"I cannot believe that Moms would do this to me. Why would she go up there to tell the guys to stop messing with me? Now I'm really going to have to fight."* I had already begun to visualize Lamont, with his quick left jab, taking the first swing at my right eye. I could see the guys calling me a "chump" for telling my mother on them. It was going to be a long day. When I finally arrived at school, I locked my bike to a rack and figured that I might as well go over to the boys and get it started. Not that I was going to throw the first punch or anything; I just did not plan on hiding from the fellows all day. I walked over to the front walkway area where the group was assembled. The first bell was to ring in a few minutes, so there was a good possibility that the fight would be interrupted before I got beaten to a pulp. However, once I arrived on the scene, the guys began acting really weird.

"Hey man, what's up?" said Lil' Jimmy, like he was nervous or something.

"Nothing. What's up with you?" I asked.

"Nothing," replied Lil' Jimmy. Soon, we were all engaged in conversation, lying about what we had had for dinner the previous night and bagging on other students' cars as they were dropped off by their parents for school. The day went along without even the slightest sign that there had ever been tensions between me and the boys. As I rode home that day, still paranoid that I was going to get jumped, I could not imagine what my mother had said to the fellows that made them change their minds about wanting to fight me.

"Moms, what did you say to Lil' Jimmy and them?" I asked when I arrived home.

"Nothing. Now go do your work," she replied, with a hint of irritation that suggested that she was trying to avoid a confrontation.

"Moms, did you threaten them or something?" I pressed, still trying to imagine what she could have possibly said to get them off my back.

"Naw, boy. If you really want to know, I'll tell you what I told them. I told them that you told me that they had been on your back lately. Well, I said 'you know he's crazy and he takes karate—the only reason why he hasn't gone off on you is because I won't let him.' However, I told them I didn't know if I could stop you any more. If they wanted to keep messing with you, they couldn't say I didn't warn them. I basically told them to do what they wanted to do, just don't blame me. They know how you are!"

I did not know whether to laugh or to scream. On the one hand, I had been taking karate, had been for two years, but couldn't advance beyond the two yellow bands on my white belt—the asphalt knuckle push-ups were holding me up. Yet, on the other hand, what if the fellows had called my mother's bluff? I asked my mother this—and what was all that stuff about me being "crazy"? I demanded.

"Garrett, you *are* weird sometimes—you and your moods. And you know this. Now leave me alone so I can get dinner ready. And I better not hear about you fighting at school. Do you hear me talking to you boy? Boy!!!" she called after me. I had already stomped out of the room. What does she mean, "me and my moods"?

Mommy Will Knock You Out

Even during my high school years, my mother would intervene when it came to me and fighting. For instance, after I picked a fight with Gary Smith and he kicked my butt, my mother gave away the tickets to the third game of the World Series between my favorite Oakland A's and the Cincinnati Reds that she had planned to surprise me with. Before calling Dean Cagle at Mt. Eden High School to arrange a meeting between me, him, and Gary the following day, she also told me that "I would whip your ass too, but it looks as though Gary did a pretty good job of it already!" Her last intervention came during my senior year, after I had confronted a group of girls, known as the Hair Bears, after they had threatened Veronica. I recall vividly how out of nowhere came my mother, parting the crowd of at least fifty students who had encircled me and the girls. "Garrett, get in your car and go home," she ordered. I didn't think twice about it; I was not embarrassed in the slightest, either. And no one in the crowd said a single word to me as I turned and walked away. Walking through the crowd, I could hear students murmuring, "Yeah, Mrs. Jackson don't play—she don't take *no* mess!"

My mother's zero tolerance for violence when it came to me and my siblings never compromised her sense of responsibility to us when we were threatened or at risk of being violated, whether in the streets or at school. I truly believe that my mother would have thrown down on Lil' Jimmy, Lamont, Marvin, and the rest of my buddies if they hadn't backed down. In fact, she probably had a belt tucked away on her person, to use in a way a girl named Cassandra's grandmother had when I was a middle school teacher. Cassandra's grandmother made a belt appear out of nowhere to whip her granddaughter's behind, right in my classroom during a prep period, for cutting up in school.

Similarly, my mother's determination was impressed upon me soon after our family moved from Oakland to Hayward, a move she hoped would gain her children access to schools that were better than the ones we were leaving. It was early Fall and I had just been excused from my third-grade class and had walked across the courtyard to wait for my sister. As was generally the case, Veronica was still in her classroom preparing to be dismissed for the day. Only two or three students remained in her classroom, and I waited outside, watching through the large plate glass window as my sister, a first-grader, rushed to get her crayons into her cardboard pencil box. She appeared quite agitated and nervous. As I continued watching, her teacher, a white woman in her forties, walked up to my sister and slapped her, open palm, right across the face. I could not believe my eyes. My sister's chubby light-complexioned cheeks reddened, and her eyes began to well with tears. However, she pressed her lips tightly together and forced herself not to cry. Trying too hard to move fast enough to satisfy her teacher only made my sister's task more difficult.

"I said 'hurry up,' slow poke. You are so slow!" screamed the teacher at my sister. As I continued to watch, absolutely mortified, the teacher snatched the box from my sister's tiny hands and shoved it into the opening of her desk. Then she angrily dismissed my sister who, with her head down, walked out of the classroom, hurt and humiliated. She joined me in the corridor and we turned, without looking at one another, and together walked out of the school onto the sidewalk and headed home in silence.

We had barely walked through the front doorway when my mother looked at my sister and asked, "What's wrong?" My sister, who still had her lips pressed together, afraid to speak, could only make unintelligible noises before she finally broke out in tears. My mother turned sharply and looked at me.

"Her teacher slapped her, Mommy," I volunteered immediately, more to let her know that I hadn't done anything to my sister than to provide the information she was seeking.

"Garrett, did you *see* the teacher hit Veronica?" my mother asked, slowly and in a very serious tone.

"Yes, Mommy. I saw her teacher slap her in the face. She slapped Ronnie because it took her too long to put her things away. I was standing outside and saw her through the window," I assured my mother. Without the slightest hesitation, my mother calmly went over to the phone, where she called Johnnie, our neighbor across the street, to see if she could keep my sister a while. After getting that situated, she instructed me to go with her, back to the school. However, instead of taking the car, we walked, retracing the trek that my sister and I had made less than twenty minutes ago. We arrived at the school in what seemed to be only a matter of minutes. My mother walked right past the main office to my sister's classroom. Mrs. Garcia, Veronica's teacher, had just dropped her keys into a gigantic knit bag, when she looked up and saw my mother marching straight toward her. She immediately began searching for her keys, which had apparently become lost among all the things that first-grade teachers carry in those big bags. My mother walked right up to her.

"I told you that if you ever put your hands on my daughter again, I would put my hands on you," said my mother, as she swung and hit Mrs. Garcia squarely in the face with her fist. My mother struck her with a force that sent Mrs. Garcia hurling backwards, and her glasses and the papers in her bag flying around the corridor. It then dawned on me that Mrs. Garcia was much larger than my mother, who stood at 5'5" and weighed no more than 125 pounds. Also, my mother hit Mrs. Garcia with her left hand because her "good" hand was encased in a plaster cast due to tendinitis.

"You bastard!!" moaned Mrs. Garcia, who had gotten up and was searching for her glasses. I recall thinking at that moment that Mrs. Garcia had it all wrong? *men* are bastards and women are *bitches*.

"I had planned to get you only once, but you had to go and call me out of my name!" my mother said, while dropping Mrs. Garcia a second time. Searching for her glasses again, Mrs. Garcia remained on her hands and knees and was conspicuously quiet this time around. "Garrett, gather up the papers and put them in her bag!" my mother ordered.

"Awww, Mommy!!" I complained. Dang, I thought, I can't believe my mother. This woman slapped my sister and called *her* a bastard, and she's concerned about *my* manners? I also recall, though, appreciating my mother's focus; she had clear objectives and was very much on task. She knew exactly what it was that she had to do and did it—no more and no less.

"Boy, do what I said and hurry up!" snapped my mother. Under the circumstances, who was I to argue with her? After I had collected the papers, I gave them to Mrs. Garcia, who remained sitting on the concrete, propped against her classroom door, sobbing. As my mother and I turned to walk away, I noticed the school secretary peering through the office curtains and the principal, apparently standing on his toes, peeking out of one of the windows that lined the top of the office wall facing the courtyard. My mother went to the glass double doors of the main office, only to find them locked and the curtains drawn. However, before turning to walk away, my mother called through the doors? "In case you don't recognize me, I'm Marie Jackson, Garrett Duncan's and Veronica Jackson's mother and I live at fifty-eight two thirty-three Eden Avenue."

When the police officers arrived at our house minutes later, I overheard my mother say, "Yes, I hit her, and if you put your hands on one of my children I will hit you, too!" The officers, two young white men, were extremely considerate and understanding. In fact, I would learn later, they suggested that my mother file a complaint against Mrs. Garcia. Later, it would come out that the teacher had terrorized the children of Loren A. Eden Elementary School for several years and, in at least one case, had even left the imprints of her fingers on the tanned face of a boy named Brad, our neighbor Johnnie's young son. However, due either to intimidation or to malign neglect, the principal had ignored parents' complaints over the years. Needless to say, Mrs. Garcia was removed from class, and her teaching credential was revoked by the State of California.

Schooling = Violence?

I have shared the above story a number of times with colleagues and students, mainly to recast violence as characteristic of dominant institutions as opposed to subjugated communities. The story also gives insight into what informs my militancy, passion, and drive as a cultural worker in particular and as a black man in general. My mother's actions that day were expressive of the love that she has, not only for her own children but for anyone subjected to unfair and violent treatment by those in relative positions of power. And while her actions seemed to be at variance with her expectations of nonviolence for her children, they were completely consistent with a nuanced understanding of violence and her willingness to engage the ambiguities and contradictions of this society. Clearly, as my mother understood, "Violence is initiated by those who oppress, who exploit, who fail to recognize others as persons—not by those who are oppressed, exploited, and unrecognized" (Freire, 1993, p. 37). Paulo Freire continues:

> For the oppressors, however, it is always the oppressed (whom they obviously never call "the oppressed" but—depending on whether they are [citizens] or not—"those people" or "the blind and envious masses" or "savages" or "natives" or "subversives") who are disaffected, who are "violent," "barbaric," "wicked," or "ferocious" when they react to the violence of the oppressors. (p. 38)

Urban schools are directly implicated in the initiation of violence. In many ways they are places where black children and youth are confronted with the problem of being "beyond love," that is, subject to a society that "is prepared to offer neither entrée into the economic system nor love and concern. They are excluded both from the economy and from networks of love" (Delgado, 1995, p. 47). In fact, at the tender age of five, my sister Veronica was quite cognizant of her status in school, and sought reentry within the boundaries of a classroom community where she would no longer be "beyond love." Recently, I asked my mother about her recollections of the events that led to her confrontation with Mrs. Garcia. She informed me that she "knew that something was wrong. Veronica would always claim that she was sick and as soon as everyone was at school, she would jump out of bed and play with David [who was three years old at the time]. Also, she would always ask if she could bring Mrs. Garcia flowers. When I would ask why, she would say 'so she will like me.'"

In many ways, my sister's experience reveals the concrete and psychological dimensions of systemic violence that play out in urban schools. Juanita Ross Epp and Ailsa M. Watkinson (1997) define systemic violence as:

> any institutionalized practice or procedure that adversely impacts on disadvantaged individuals or groups by burdening them psychologically, mentally, culturally, spiritually, economically, or physically. It includes practices and procedures that prevent students from learning, thus harming them. This may take the form of conventional policies and practices that foster a climate of violence, or practices that appear to be neutral but result in discriminatory effects. Systemic violence may not be immediately noticeable but can be found woven into the educational fabric. (pp. xi, xv)

In the classroom, systemic violence is observable in attitudes that result in lowered expectations for black children. A rather poignant example of the way in which systemic violence impairs black children is demonstrated in *The Autobiography of Malcolm X* (Haley, 1965). In this particular scene, fifteen-year-old Malcolm Little was asked by his English teacher what career he planned to pursue upon graduation. Malcolm, who was a superb student by all accounts—high marks, excellent work habits, and outstanding citizenship—replied, "I've been thinking I'd like to be a lawyer" (p. 37). In stark contrast to the supportive and encouraging advice that Malcolm's teacher gave to his academically mediocre white peers, the teacher, a Mr. Ostrowski, gave Malcolm the following counsel:

> Malcolm, one of life's first needs is for us to be realistic. Don't misunderstand me, now. We all here like you, you know that. But you've got to be realistic about being a nigger. A lawyer—that's no realistic goal for a nigger. You need to think about something that you can be. You're good with your hands—making things. Everybody admires your carpentry shop work. Why don't you plan on carpentry? People like you as a person—you'd get all kinds of work. (Haley, 1965, p. 37)

Reflecting upon this incident later, Malcolm X said that it was to become the first major turning point of his life. Systemic violence also works in subtle ways to influence the manner in which teachers and schools organize the curriculum and instruction for black children. An example of how this plays out in later life is found in Haki Madhubuti's (1990) collection of essays, *Black Men: Obsolete, Single, Dangerous.* In his essay "Not Knowing and Not Wanting to Know," Madhubuti describes his early education as a form of training that proved to be more discouraging than challenging. He recalls: "The major piece of information I absorbed after twelve years of public education was that I was a problem, inferior, ineducable and a victim" (p. ii). Having been conditioned to see himself through the eyes of a victim, Madhubuti began to see himself in a different light when he was introduced to other ways of living.

In particular, he points to an occasion when, on his birthday, his mother bought him a gift, "a blue plastic airplane with blue wheels, a blue propeller and a blue string on the front of the plane so that one could pull it across the floor" (p. iii). Madhubuti was delighted to receive the blue plastic airplane. The following week, however, while accompanying his mother and sister to an affluent neighborhood where his mother did domestic labor for the rich white residents, he quickly noticed differences in the way the people in *that* community lived. Differences were especially apparent in the resources that the community made available to its youths. For example, when Madhubuti saw a toy airplane—unassembled, with wooden parts, instructions, glue, and an *engine* to make it fly—in a craft shop, as opposed to a five-and-dime shop, he reflected on the meaning of his schooling and its significance within the broader social order. He observed at this point that:

> This small slice of life is an example of the development—quite early —of two different consciousnesses. In my case and that of other poor youths, we would buy the plane already assembled, take it home and hope it rolled on the floor as if it was a car or truck rather than a plane. In Dearborn, the family would invest in a learning toy, and the child would put it together. Through the process, the child would learn work ethics and science and math principles. And, as a result of all that, the plane would fly. I was learning to be a consumer who depended on others to build the plane for me. The child in Dearborn made an investment, worked on it and, through his labor and brain power, produced a plane that flew. Translating this to the larger world, I was being taught to buy and to use my body from the neck down, while the white upper class boy was being taught, very early, to prepare himself to build things and run things, using the neck up. Two different worlds: my world—depending on and working for others, and his world—controlling his own destiny. (p. iii)

Social scientists have written also on the way urban public schools prevent black children from learning. Researchers describe the structural biases in the institutional context of schooling that lead to the overrepresentation of black males, especially, in programs for students who are educable mentally retarded, trainable mentally retarded, and severely emotionally disturbed, and their underrepresentation in gifted and higher academic tracks.

As it relates to interactions in the classroom, researchers have observed that language, among other factors, plays significant roles in how teachers perceive and treat black children. Beth Harry and Mary Anderson (1994) have identified studies showing that teachers view the social languages, conversational patterns, and narrative styles of black students as aggressive, hostile, and threatening. Teachers' perceptions play powerful roles in their decisions to refer students for special education assessment or to prevent them from advancing into courses that are more challenging and interesting than lower-track courses. As it stands now, large numbers of black students, especially boys, are being warehoused in special education programs that no longer serve their original purpose of providing necessary services to students who require resources unavailable in regular classes. Consequently, the vast majority of special education programs in which black students are concentrated have been reduced to incarceration centers that emphasize behavior management over academic development. The same may also be said for the experience of many black students who are assigned to regular classes that, more often than not, have inadequate resources and ill-prepared teachers (Calabrese, 1988; Darling-Hammond, 1995).

Systemic violence in the classroom plays out for black males in ways that are different than for black females. For example, Sandra Ross and Jeffrey Jackson (1991) found that teachers perceive nonsubmissive black males as threatening and at risk for academic failure, whereas the issue of submission does not affect their perceptions of and expectations for black females. In my view, these differences are manifested in the relationships between black males and white females who are most likely their teachers or who most likely trained their teachers (for excellent discussions on profiles of the teaching force in United States schools and the culture of teacher education programs, see Delpit, 1995; Grant, 1989; Ladson-Billings, 1994). Thus, black males are generally expected to adopt behaviors that do not affront the sensibilities of white women. In speaking of the "sensibilities" of white women, I must pause here to indicate that I am speaking of white womanhood as constructed within a white supremacist, patriarchal society, especially one in which teaching is viewed as (white) women's work. I speak also in a context of a brutal historical record in the United States that includes over a century of lynching black men, including Emmit Till and Yusef Hawkins, for their alleged sexual transgressions against white women, and many highly publicized cases in which black men have been falsely accused of attacking white women.

In the classroom, while muted, these prescriptions are observable in the amount of energy that teachers exert trying to subdue and control both the spirits and the bodies of black boys. This is seen in the way that they are penalized for the way they speak, walk, sit, stand, pose, touch, gesture, exhibit facial and visual behaviors (e.g., rolling of eyes, making eye contact, gazing, glaring, and staring), dress, and interact in other nonverbal ways. While I do not intend to imply that all behaviors exhibited by black boys are appropriate and that none of them need to be addressed, studies show that black males bear the brunt of school suspensions and expulsions (Meier, Stewart, & England, 1990) and that teachers condemn behaviors in black students that they praise in others (Ladson-Billings, 1994). These practices mirror those in the criminal justice system where black males are unfairly and disproportionately targeted for prosecution and are given prison sentences that are 30 percent longer than those given to white men who commit the same offenses (Olson, 1996; Virgo, 1996).

Researchers also report that teachers exhibit certain practices with their most difficult pupils that they do not exhibit with their achieving students (see, for example, Moody & Moody, 1989). While, for the most part, these practices are not specific to the treatment of black boys, they do result in greater educational consequences for this group. Generally speaking, though, understanding the conditions that black students encounter in schools helps us to recast concepts such as "self-esteem" and "motivation" in contextual terms. In other words, children and youth often exhibit what observers call low self-esteem or a lack of motivation in hostile contexts. Moreover, these contexts have an impact on the general well-being of black children and youth. Janice Hale-Benson (1989) captures this sentiment in her statement that "black children do not enter school disadvantaged, but they emerge from school disadvantaged" (p. 84).

Conclusion

In his final book, *Teachers as Cultural Workers: Letters to Those Who Dare to Teach*, Paulo Freire (1998) states that "though one should never oppose the nurturing aspect of teaching, one should never reduce teaching to merely a feel-good process, particularly to a paternalistic nurturing that takes the form of parental coddling" (p. 4). Freire also provides a definition of love that is a response in part to the authoritarianism that informs conservative approaches to pedagogy, but mainly to the permissiveness that underlies much of the liberal response to urban education. These two orientations reflect competing forms of detachment in human relationships, a problem that is fundamentally moral (Ward, 1995), and they foster conditions that place black children and youth at risk and beyond love in urban schools in a white supremacist society. In terms of permissiveness in public schools, I have come across educators who not only affirm, but defend, certain practices of black children that would not be tolerated in most homes. For example, a white female counselor related an episode in her school where a middle school student repeatedly called her and other females bitches after being removed from an after school dance. She told me that she affirmed the boys' behavior, observing that it was an aspect of his "culture." In another case, a white female student teacher in a suburban high school argued in a college seminar that her black students' frequent use of the word "nigger" in her class was simply an expression of their "postmodernity." In both situations, and others like them, when I challenged the educators to understand how they, in fact, were sustaining conditions that undermined the humanity of black students and that could contribute directly to placing them at risk for violence, I was rebuffed and told that I was "conservative," and an oppressor of black children and youths.

Freire's words must be placed within a larger historical context in which members and institutions of the dominant society have consistently undermined the full participation of black communities in the education of their children and youth. This was evident in the establishment of the Freedman's Bureau and Rosenwald Fund earlier and the usurpation of multicultural education by white liberal educators recently. Indeed, in reference to the latter trend, Freire supported the establishment of African-centered academies within public school districts, assailing multicultural education as an "invention of the dominant society" (Freire, 1992). Even the dearth of black teachers in urban schools can be, in part, linked to the distorted goals of desegregation laws that resulted in a shift from educational justice for black children to a policy that mainly favored privileged white communities.

Therefore, white teachers, who comprise the majority of those who teach in urban public schools, would do well to consider the words of James Baldwin: "As long as you think that you are white, there is no hope for you—as long as you think you are white, I will have to think that I'm Black." Baldwin is talking about a relationship, in this case an unholy alliance that informs the construction of white identity in the United States. To the extent that white teachers fail to engage their own identities and their own privilege, and fail to begin to challenge their folkways, habits, customs, and subconscious deeds, even their best intentions will effectively play out in the service of white supremacy. An inability to sustain such a critique underlies the permissiveness of white liberalism and the incapacity of white teachers to distinguish between those forms of black student resistance that challenge systemic violence in schools and promote self-realization, and those forms that mediate systemic violence and arrest the development of humane and ethical human beings.

Black teachers and cultural workers must understand that "assimilation, accommodation, and playing the role of the exotic rebellious other are not the only available options" (hooks, 1990, p. 20). With respect to the last option, those of us who have access to the corridors of power and who choose to not engage the powerful in the interests of black communities commit an unforgivable act, especially when we do so in the name of being "revolutionary." Such a posture is misguided, superficial, and more often than not hypocritical. It ignores the fact that many have suffered to create these avenues for us, and that being in the "master's house" is another front in the battle against white supremacy. Finally, whether or not black teachers and cultural workers accept it, we hold positions of moral and intellectual leadership in our communities. Therefore, to uncritically teach assimilation and accommodation—to teach life as accepting life as it is, is to teach a lie and to affirm the violence that places black children and youth at risk and beyond love. And, as Tashi warns us in *Possessing the Secret of Joy*, "If you lie to yourself about your own pain, you will be killed by those who will claim you enjoyed it" (Walker, 1992, p. 108) or by our children who will bring us to judgment for our misdeeds.

References

Baldwin, J. (1963). *The fire next time.* New York: The Dial Press.

Brown, C. (1965). *Manchild in the promised land.* New York: Signet.

Calabrese, R. (1988). The structure of schooling and minority dropout rates. *The Clearing House, 61,* 325–28.

Darling-Hammond, L. (1995). Teacher knowledge and student learning: Implications for literacy development. In V. Gadsden & D. Wagner (Eds.), *Literacy among African-American youth: Issues in learning, teaching, and schooling* (pp. 177–200). Cresskill, NJ: Hampton Press.

Delgado, R. (1995). *The Rodrigo chronicles: Conversations about America and race.* New York: New York University Press.

Delpit, L. (1995). *Other people's children: Cultural conflict in the classroom.* New York: The New Press.

Epp, J., & Watkinson, A. (Eds.). (1997). *Systemic violence in education: Promise broken.* Albany: State University of New York Press.

Freire, P. (1992, July 16). *Interview and dialogue.* A video produced by the Educational Television Network for the Center for Educational Studies, The Claremont Graduate School, Claremont, California.

Freire, P. (1993). *Pedagogy of the oppressed* (Rev. ed.; M. Ramos, Trans.). New York: Continuum.

Freire, P. (1998). *Teachers as cultural workers: Letters to those who dare to teach.* Boulder, CO: Westview Press.

Grant, C. (1989, June). Urban teachers: Their new colleagues and curriculum. *Phi Delta Kappan,* 764–70.

Hale-Benson, J. (1989). The learning environment and academic success. In G. Berry & J. Asamen (Eds.), *Black students: Psychosocial issues and academic achievement* (pp. 83–97). Newbury Park, CA: Corwin Press.

Haley, A. (1965). *The autobiography of Malcolm X.* New York: Grove Press.

Harry, B., & Anderson, M. (1994). The disproportionate placement of African American males in special education programs: A critique of the process. *Journal of Negro Education, 63*(4), 602–19.

hooks, b. (1990). *Yearning: Race, gender, and cultural politics.* Boston, MA: South End Press.

Ladson-Billings, G. (1994). *The dreamkeepers: Successful teachers of African American children.* San Francisco: Jossey-Bass.

Madhubuti, H. (1990). *Black men: Obsolete, single, dangerous; The Afrikan American family in transition: Essays in discovery, solution, and hope.* Chicago: Third World Press.

Moody, C., & Moody, C. (1989). Elements of effective Black schools. In W. Smith & E. Chunn (Eds.), *Black education: A quest for equity and excellence* (pp. 176–86). New Brunswick, NJ: Transaction.

Olson, J. (1996). Gardens of the law: The role of prison in capitalist society. In E. Rosenblatt (Ed.), *Criminal injustice: Confronting the prison crisis* (pp. 40–46). Boston: South End Press.

Ross, S., & Jackson, J. (1991). Teachers' expectations for Black male's and Black females' academic achievement. *Personality and Social Psychology Bulletin,* 17(1), 78–82.

Thorsen, K., Miles, W., & Dempsey, D. K. (Producers), & Thorsen, K. (Director). (1990). *James Baldwin: The price of the ticket* [Film]. (Video may be purchased at California Newsreel, 149 Ninth Street/420, San Francisco, CA: 94103)

Virgo, S. (1996). The criminalization of poverty. In E. Rosenblatt (Ed.), *Criminal injustice: Confronting the prison crisis* (pp. 47–60). Boston: South End Press.

Walker, A. (1992). *Possessing the secret of joy.* New York: Pocket Star Books.

Ward, J.V. (1995). Cultivating a morality of care in African American adolescents: A culture-based model of violence prevention. *Harvard Educational Review, 65*(2), 175–88.

Chapter Six

Education 101: Thoughts on Teaching and Race

Karl Bell

Introduction

Where have all the mother-like teachers gone?

In this generation of welfare reform, homelessness, and hopelessness this question rings true for far too many people. Recently I began teaching a freshman seminar class, and the pressure to be just and fair has started to mount. I am aware of many of the challenges my students will face. These challenges will not be much different from those that I faced several years ago at the same institution. However, I am faced with the daunting question of what to do to address each student's challenges, concerns, and quandaries. Many of my white students are dealing with the anxiety and uncertainty that comes with having a black instructor. I fully understand that they struggle to identify with certain concepts that are presented in class. These concepts are not hard to understand because they are complex in nature, but because they are presented from the "black" perspective. These students are from rural cities in northwest Missouri, and have never experienced a black instructor, much less one who espouses mother wit. I am certainly aware that there is a fear of rejection and a high level of stress that exists in these students. Just as sons desire acceptance from their mothers, students desire acceptance from instructors. A teacher who would ignore a student because of the student's race is unfit to teach. I am well aware of my obligation to these students, but my experiences have created a reluctance to open myself to them fully.

Teaching Education 101

The reluctance to open myself fully was created by the white instructors who were responsible for my education. All too many of those instructors neglected their obligation to me. This negligence created, and continues to create, an underlying resentment toward my white students, who would benefit from the knowledge I possess, and the opportunities for advancement I might provide. I often wish that I could commit my time and effort solely to the continued development of my African American students. This however was the position of those instructors who were responsible for my own education, and two wrongs don't make a right. I am a victim who teaches the victimizers' children not to victimize.

The educational road I have traveled has not been filled with like travelers. Race has acted as the great divider between myself and others that travel my educational path. Race in education is paramount. Instructors and students cannot avoid the pull that nature has on the soul. Many white students undoubtedly feel more comfortable with an instructor of like heritage. This process is as old as the process of natural selection. I am confident that my African American students feel free to discuss the many ills they may face in a system of higher education that is clearly not committed to their well-being, or their success. Would those students feel as comfortable with a white instructor?

I believe that the current system of education is interwoven with race and racism. This system has the ability to discourage the development of African American students and diminish the accomplishments and contributions of African American people. In all too many instances, the history of the African American is being reduced to Kunte Kinte, the slave ship *Amistad*, and Martin Luther King's "I Have a Dream" speech. Many institutions of higher learning fail to offer courses in African American history, and many choose not to recognize the need to revise the educational curriculum.

Granted, students of color are underrepresented in higher education, and often invisible in or absent from the graduate classrooms in America. I refuse, however, to yield to the positions of power which suggest that this underrepresentation and invisible status is a choice. Many of these students "by virtue of their race, ethnicity, culture, and language are greeted in school with an unwelcome-carpet treatment that steers them away from the classroom and toward the exit door" (Macedo, 1994, p. 1).

Under the current constructions of schooling, racism goes unnoticed by many "well-meaning" agents for change. These agents are high school principals, guidance counselors, teachers, university admission officers, university professors, and the entire educational system itself. "Education remains the primary lever by which the racial situation can be controlled and changed" (Allen, 1988, p. 81). The existence of racism in education reflects the miseducation of society writ large. African American students face a variety of obstacles which impede their progress. "Faced with the smug attitude that 'higher education is not for everyone' and the accompanying behaviors and norms meant to fulfill this prophecy, it is not surprising that Black Americans fare so poorly in the U.S. system of higher education" (Allen, 1988, p. 79).

Opportunities which once existed are beginning to fade. Educational institutions that welcomed African Americans, and provided ample financial assistance, now face a myriad of challenges. African American students face the pressure of "constantly having 'to justify one's right to be on campus'" (Feagin, Vera, & Imani, 1994, p 152). Education for the African American, beyond the high school level, is thought to be a "privilege." While white students continue to exercise the "right" to higher education, African American students are taught to appreciate the little they are "allowed" to have. Any expectation beyond the gift of a high school education for the African American is regarded as greedy and demanding. When African American students pursue higher education, Feagin, Vera, & Imani (1994), argue that teachers attempt "to assimilate black young people in a unidirectional manner to the dominant white perspectives, goals, and culture" (p. 12).

An Old-Time Teacher-Mother

"Elevate your mind, get yourself together." These words were the daily instructions from my high school English teacher. He was well aware that as an African American male, teaching at a predominantly black high school, it was (in part) his responsibility to prepare me to face those who would seek to rob me of myself esteem, pride, and appreciation of my heritage. He also warned of those who would require me to do things twice as well, to receive one-half the credit.

This teacher shared with me the brilliance of the African American writer and taught me to appreciate the writings of James Baldwin, Langston Hughes, and Alice Walker. These lessons were important, for through my appreciation of these African American writers I developed a greater appreciation of, and respect for, myself. This instructor helped to cultivate my appreciation for "Black English," and assisted me in the further development of my appreciation for the history of African Americans. These lessons were instrumental in my development as a young man, and more importantly, as a student with the desire to pursue higher education.

As a graduate student, I find myself searching for my teacher-mother. In too many instances the old-time teacher is lost, and cannot be found. As I walk the halls of educational institutions and complete those courses which are required, I am angered by the blatant disregard for my well-being. To be educated in the academic culture and protocols of higher education, without any instruction on, or even mention of, how these systems operate in historically black colleges, tribal colleges, community colleges, and Hispanic-serving institutions is to be miseducated. If I am to become viable and an active participant in my education, I must value my education and be made aware of the significant contributions that others like me have made. This is imperative to my survival. Teachers and students must speak the same language if a proper education is to be attained.

The presentation of misinformation in any educational institution and the practice of hegemony by teachers is unfortunate. Too many institutions replicate the dominant culture's ignorance of marginalized communities, in an attempt to maintain their own elite status and educational power. As Donaldo Macedo (1994) says:

> This traditional elitist approach to education is inherently alienating in nature. On the one hand, it ignores the life experience, history, culture, and language practices of its students. On the other, it overemphasizes the mastery and understanding of classical literature and the use of great books as the only vehicle that enables one to search for the "Good and True." (p. 63)

Teachers in effect have the ability to create or destroy intellectual life. As such, this skill cannot be haphazardly utilized or handled by the unprepared or disingenuous. The authority to teach must be exercised on the fertile ground of respect and common decency. Teachers must empower their students and encourage them to move forward. As a graduate student, I see the many attempts of instructors to withhold the nourishment that their students desperately need. This lack of nourishment is validated in institutions and cities across the country, and guarantees ignorance. This ignorance is exacerbated by teachers who seek to ignore the important nexus between race and schooling. It could be argued that the calls for curricular and instructional change in schools have been silenced. Teachers are not adequately prepared to actively address the problems which exist in society. This silence encourages the propagation of the status quo. Under this system, the concerns of yellow, red, brown, black, and any other persons of color are ignored. Consequently, these could-be learners are relegated to the comers and alleys where their voices are but cacophonous echoes which fill the dark, void, night air of society.

Race and Education

Institutionalized racism contributes greatly to many of the difficulties that teachers have in addressing the needs of our students even today. The systematic exclusion of the African American student, and of the many contributions African Americans have made to society, are other examples of how students have been bastardized in the educational community. The willingness of teachers (who should be engaged in cultural work) to disregard and discount the contributions that have been made is very disturbing. The indoctrination of African American students by both formal and informal teachers has left them struggling to find themselves in a world of confusion and identity crisis. This identity crisis is as crippling as sudden infant death syndrome. Is the educational community aware of the damage it has caused and will continue to cause by failing to address the relationships between race and education?

The power that teachers wield in our educational institutions is not a mystery. So why should the power of race in educational institutions be a mystery? The power of those whom we charge with the responsibility of teaching is paramount in any educational critique. This power, in many cases, translates directly to what our children learn and how they learn what they learn. In his book *The Miseducation of the Negro* (1933), Carter G. Woodson blames the "oppressor" for the ills of the African American:

> He teaches the Negro that he has no worth-while past, that his race has done nothing significant since the beginning of time, and that there is no evidence that he will ever achieve anything great. . . . If you can thereby determine what he will think, you will not need to worry about what he will do. You will not have to tell him to go to the back door. He will go without being told, and if there is no back door he will have one cut for his special benefit. (p. 192)

Consequently, many African Americans are discouraged in their pursuit of education, and seek avenues to distance themselves, or call for a return to segregated enclaves. Race is inescapable, and I am weary of those who seek to dismiss its importance. African Americans are being systematically removed from educational discourse. Without question, race often guides and directs what teachers presume their students know. One of the great difficulties in our society and in education is the inability to adequately investigate persons who are different, without relying on the social constructions that have been previously formed. Race, and our perception of others based on this single characteristic, is larger than life. The misconceptions surrounding race feed primarily on ignorance and fear. It is imperative that these misconceptions be identified and the barriers which separate one from the other be eliminated.

Race in higher education is often played out in what Paulo Freire calls a pedagogy of exclusion. The majority race is destined to succeed, while the minority race is doomed to failure. In addressing the inequities that African American students face, Russell, Wilson, and Hall (1992) raise a very valid question: "Does skin color still affect educational and occupational opportunities for African American college students today?" (p. 29. The answer to this question is a resounding yes. Teachers must realize the responsibility that rests squarely on the shoulders of educational institutions to alter this trend. Pascarella and Terenzini (1991) explain that educational institutions are responsible for:

> transmitting the intellectual heritage of Western civilization; fostering a high level of verbal and mathematical skills; developing an in-depth

> understanding of social, cultural, and political institutions; facilitating one's ability to think reflectively, analytically, . . . developing one's value structures and moral sensibilities; facilitating personal growth and self-identity; and fostering one's sense of career identity and vocational competence. (p. 1)

Educators who simply close their eyes to the problems that African American students face are a part of the problem, not the solution. Unfortunately, there are teachers who, like many others, turn their backs on African American students due to racism. Racism, while endemic to society, has no place in education.

Multiculturalism and the New Era Teacher-Mother

Inherent in the previous comments is the ideal that African American students will be given an opportunity to succeed, supported and nurtured through their defeats, and ultimately viewed as equals in the college community. Equally inherent are those questions that must be raised about the educational system. Allen (1988) proposes the following:

> It is legitimate to ask whether the nation's colleges and universities can ever hope to offer the genuine promise of equity for disenfranchised citizens. Is it within the capacity of U.S. universities to become permeable institutions, completely accessible to people different in race, sex, ethnicity, age, or financial standing from their traditional students—privileged, young white males? (p. 81)

The demands of African American students are neither unreasonable nor unfounded. They simply represent the basic need of individuals to be comfortable in their environment. It appears most convenient to find someone to blame, or create excuses for the many inequities and barriers that face African American students in education. Are these barriers insurmountable? Do they represent an underlying conspiracy against the African American? Are the teachers of the educational community simply not prepared to educate the American for whom education was once forbidden? Can multiculturalism alone remedy the educational inequities facing African American students?

Many liberal teachers do promote the idea of multiculturalism. But the concept of multiculturalism alone is not enough to rectify centuries of miseducation and missed educational opportunities.

Multiculturalism has become the hiding place for many oppressors who wish to maintain their hegemony. Paulo Freire (1993) states:

> The oppressors who oppress, exploit, and rape by virtue of their power, cannot find in this power the strength to liberate either the oppressed or themselves. Only power that springs from the weakness of the oppressed will be sufficiently strong to free both. Any attempt to soften the power of the oppressor in deference to the weakness of the oppressed almost always manifests itself in the form of false generosity; indeed, the attempt never goes beyond this. (p. 26)

The belief that if one person is successful then all persons can be successful is misplaced. In fact this utopian doctrine serves to further divide and separate the oppressed and disposed. The fallacy in this doctrine is simply that success is an attainable concept. How is success defined? Who defines it? Herein lies a major problem with multiculturalism. Multiculturalism cannot exist when the culture of dominance defines success, prosperity, achievement, and even culture itself. Many fail to realize that true multiculturalism only works when each culture is viewed as equal and necessary. And in order for that to occur, each culture must be an active participant in the process; there can no longer be a racially dominant and a racially subordinate group. Unfortunately, our racist ideology of economic privilege and oppression persists.

However, even with the daunting challenge of creating educational change, teachers can make a difference. Teachers send a clear message to their students. Wisdom and Shaw found that "The white curriculum, the white social environment, the white cultural standards, plus the discovery of hostility . . . and ignorance in the alien world in which they find themselves—is dissatisfaction, bitterness, and the determination to change the system" (p. 100). This is a most critical point of cognitive dissonance that every advocate for true education must reach. That point where to act is an absolute. The determination to change the system is the point of true awareness. It is only from this point of true awareness that higher education can be changed.

This awareness is critical if African Americans in education are to make any real progress; if teachers are to adequately prepare their students for the future, dialogue is important, and action following the "moment of awareness" is imperative. This moment of awareness is not only critical to students, but to the entire corps of teachers who are responsible for their education. It is only through dialogue, which leads to awakening followed by action, that students, particularly African American students, will be understood.

Teachers who are not committed to the development of their students should not be teachers. Teachers are cultural workers who must be willing to answer some very tough questions, especially when the question is race. Who is the African American student? What are his/her needs? Have I prepared all of my students equally for the rigors of life? These questions are formidable questions but must be answered by a new era of teacher-mothers.

A Concluding Query

Where have all the mother-like teachers gone?

References

Allen, W. (1988). The education of black students on white college campuses: What quality experience. In M. T. Nettles (Ed.), *Toward black undergraduate student equality in American higher education*. Westport, CT: Greenwood Press.

Feagin, J. R., Vera, H., & Imani, N. (1996). *The agony of education: Black students at white colleges and universities*. New York: Routledge.

Freire, P. (1993). *Pedagogy of the oppressed* (Rev. ed.; M. Ramos, Trans.). New York: Continuum.

Macedo, D. (1994). *Literacies of power: What Americans are not allowed to know*. Boulder, CO: Westview Press.

McEwen, M. K., Roper, L. D., Bryant, D. R., & Langa, M. J. (1996). *Incorporating the development of African-American students into psychosocial theories of student development*. Boston: Simon & Schuster.

Nettles, M. T. (1988). Factors related to black and white students' college performance. In M. T. Nettles (Ed.), *Toward black undergraduate student equality in American higher education*. Westport, CT: Greenwood Press.

Omi, M., & Winant, H. (1994). *Racial formation in the United States: From the 1960s to the 1990s*. New York: Routledge.

Pascarella, E. T., & Terenzini, P. T. (1991). *How college affects students*. San Francisco: Jossey-Bass.

Russell, K., Wilson, M., & Hall, R. (1992). *Color complex*. New York: Harcourt Brace Jovanovich.

Wisdom, P., & Shaw, K. (1970). Black challenge to higher education. In D. C. Nichols & O. Mills (Eds.), *The campus and the racial crisis*. Washington, DC: American Council on Education.

Woodson, C. G. (1990). *The miseducation of the Negro*. Trenton, NJ: Africa World Press.

Chapter Seven

Brains, Brawn, and Pigskin Balls: Racism and Athletic Manifestation in Society

C. Keith Harrison

> The primary question which now must be asked is what happens to the black athlete between high school and college that seems to totally change how he perceives himself.
>
> —Richard Lapchick, *Race and Sport*

> We must teach our children to dream with their eyes open, the chance of your becoming a Jerry Rice or a Magic Johnson are so slim as to be negligible.
>
> —Harry Edwards, *The African Americans*

> Do you believe in God? Do you believe that everybody is here for a reason? I believe that everyone has a talent and I believe my talent is sports. So when I was born I was naturally an athlete. So it would be pretty dumb for me to go into science.
>
> —Student-athlete, "Negotiating School"

> Don't like scholarships because they hurt me, nothing but a slave to the university, watch me as I run by you, the coach wants to take me higher.
>
> — Rap artist Ice Cube's single "Higher"

Introduction

In the realm of sport in society, one of the areas to escape in-depth philosophic inquiry has been the experiences of the African American male. This particular group has a history of both triumph and tragedy. One's immediate attention is directed at the odds of a sports career coming to reality for most African American male youth. If the odds are slim or none, then why do many African American men place all their attention on sports and not education, or why is there no effort to balance both by the majority of African American men in sport?

This broad question has many implications, and by using Kretchmar's (1994) table in *Practical Philosophy of Sport* on multiple perspectives (academic inquiry through the lenses of History, Physiology, Sociology, and Philosophy) we can reach some philosophic answers. The areas on which I have framed my article center around three perspectives in the context of sport participation by African American men.

(1) What does sport mean to the African American community?

(2) What myths affect African American males in sport?

(3) What does the future entail for African American males in sport?

The purpose of this article is to examine and critically analyze the impact of sport in the African American community. This critique of the social and behavioral outcomes of sport will include philosophical, historical, and sociological inquiry affecting the plight of the African American male in academics and athletics. Data on the perceptions of contemporary African American men participating in sport in higher education will also add support to the conclusion that race and sport are socially constructed in society.

Where Did It All Begin?

When Jack Johnson won the heavyweight boxing title in 1908, African Americans celebrated this triumph, as they instantly perceived sport as "the promised land." This and entertainment were the only areas in which US mainstream society allowed African Americans to excel, as there was and still is a mechanism of social control.

Although some black athletes had achieved fame prior to the Civil War, it was not until the conflict came to an end that large numbers of them would realize national and even international acclaim in a wide range of sports. The newly found freedom following the war and the lasting sporting traditions established during slavery created an atmosphere in which blacks were more readily accepted into horse racing, baseball, and other sports popular during the period (Wiggins, 1993).

Apart from Jack Johnson, other black athletes in this era included Peter Jackson (boxing), Issac Murphy (horse racing), "Major" Taylor (bicycle racing), and "Fleetwood" Walker (baseball). While these and other African American men excelled in sport, the establishment either shunted them aside or pressured them to drop out of their respective sports. The reasons for their elimination from organized sport were varied, including the mainstream culture's belief in black inferiority, the general deterioration of black rights, and the eventual separation of the races (Davis, 1966; Somers, 1972; Lucas & Smith, 1978; Rader, 1983).

This would all change with the integration of baseball by Jackie Robinson (1947), and sport would continue to see an increase in participants of color in the years to follow. What is significant in relation to African Americans in sport is that most African American males in sport have little, if any, historical perspective passed on from their forefathers who paved the way for them to compete today. In a panel discussion (1992) on issues related to the African American male student athlete, Harry Edwards and Arthur Ashe were asked to say whether or not (philosophically and practically) African American men are winners or losers in regard to their experience in sport. Both individuals responded candidly. Ashe: "Over the last 25 years loser, but before that period winner." Edwards: "I think we have both winners and losers and often it is difficult to tell the difference" (Edwards and Ashe, 1992). These statements describe the fate in contemporary society of the African American community and other communities who believe that sport in itself will lead to success. In previous years, as Ashe stated, African American males participated in sport both to achieve a quality education and to compete in athletics. At present in society, this is simply not the case. Pointing to Harry Edwards and his response, the potential outcome of the sporting experience for the African American male is not easily determined, if the goal is simply to play professional ball. But blacks are far more likely than whites (eight to one) to emphasize sports as a means of achieving prestige and economic success, because they perceive more barriers to achievement in other activities.

As African American males have become increasingly successful in a few highly visible sports, young African Americans focus their attention on developing skills in the same sports. This has not only contributed to the high proportion of African American males in certain sports, but it also accounts for their tendency to put all their motivational "eggs" into just a few sport "baskets." Because they have not had the chance to see pay-offs connected with education, they conclude that running and jumping offer the best chances for fame and fortune (Coakley, 1994, p.

264). Putting their total identity and self-esteem into sports results in despair and hopelessness for many.

Not seeing, smelling, hearing, feeling, or even tasting other role models (Harrison, 1996a, 1996b) off the playing fields, many African American youths see little reason to try other vehicles for upward mobility. Unfortunately for these youths, occupational opportunities for runners and jumpers are very limited (Coakley, 1994). In many instances, the idea that sport is the total answer is constantly signaled to young African American boys within their own community. Mothers, sisters, fathers, and friends all wearing sneakers and professional numerical jerseys, and the excessive hours spent on the court and not the classroom, all contribute to a fixation by society as a whole that all the African American male has to do is play ball and the rest will take care of itself.

As Joe Paterno argued vividly in 1983 at the National Collegiate Athletic Association (NCAA) convention, the philosophy must change at all levels for the African American male:

> For fifteen years we have had a race problem. We have raped a generation and a half of young black athletes. We have taken kids and sold them on bouncing a ball and running with a football and that being able to do certain things athletically was going to be an end in itself. We cannot afford to do that to another generation. (quoted in Coakley, 1994, p. 239)

Truth or Dare

One of the more obvious myths affecting African American males is the notion that sport leads to a path of success for many. Without quoting extensive statistics, the average professional sports career is less than four years; about one in 7325 (Lapchick, 1991) will make it to the National Football League (NFL) or National Basketball Association (NBA); and nearly 80 percent of professional athletes will have no money by the end of their careers.[1]

In the broader context of jobs in society, opportunities for African American males even within sports are very limited and controlled. Front office manager, general manager, athletic director, head coach, assistant coach, and other leadership roles in sport are occupied mostly by white American males. This raises the question that if the participants in sport (football, basketball, and baseball) are half or mostly African American, then why are they not represented more equally in leadership roles?

An ethnographic approach leads one toward an answer to this question. "You know those junkyards along the highways in Jersey?" said Larry Doby, former baseball professional with the Cleveland Indians, the first black ever to play in the American League, and now an insurance salesman in Saddle Brook, New Jersey. "Well, they have scrap heaps just like that for athletes—most of them black. Black athletes are cattle. They're raised, fed, sold and killed. . . . Baseball moved me toward the front of the bus, and it let me ride there as long as I could run. And then it told me to get off at the back door" (quoted in Olsen, 1968, p. 168).

In 1987 on the ABC television station's *Nightline*, Al Campanis (vice president for player personnel for the Los Angeles Dodgers at the time) summed up the prevailing philosophy in the sporting world. Ted Koppel asked Campanis on the anniversary of Jackie Robinson's breakthrough (1947) why there were no black managers, general managers, or owners? Is there still that much prejudice in baseball today? Campanis answered:

> I don't believe it's prejudice. I truly believe they may not have some of the necessities to be, let's say, a field manager or perhaps a general manager. They may not have the desire to be in the front office. They're outstanding athletes, very God-gifted and they're wonderful people. . . . They are gifted with great musculature and various other things. They're fleet of foot and that's why there are a lot of black major league ballplayers. Now as far as having the background to become club presidents or presidents of a bank. I don't know. (quoted in Hoose, 1989)

Campanis's observations amounted to a complete record of the subconscious values of those who control major sports in the U.S.A. It was all there—the residue of decades of dugout talk, winter meetings, road meals, hotel lobbies, scouting reports, and banquets (Hoose, 1989). Campanis's statements laid it all bare for examination: blacks can't think. They have no ambition. They don't know how to lead. They have great bodies. They are, as a race, gifted physically but deficient mentally. The philosophy apparently then and now is that blacks do not have the necessary qualities, so why bother to channel them into leading an organization? These traits are only perceived to be possessed by those who control sports, on or off the field.

This, in most cases, is not so for African Americans, women, people of color, or "otherness." Without going too deeply into racial "stacking" in sports, some realities relate to Campanis's comments. While watching a game, any baseball or football fan can easily see racial stereotypes at work. A scorecard and these two principles will help: (1) The nearer a position is to where the ball usually is, the less likely a black will occupy it; and (2) the more responsibility or control involved in a position, the less likely a black will play it (Hoose, 1989). Now, by critically analyzing the media, a connection can be made between the false opportunity of sport for African American men that is visualized through advertising, and the recapitulation and exacerbation of "brawn" but no "brains," and the "natural" athlete notion of African American men.

The historical belief was that African Americans were inferior physically. This idea was disproved totally in 1936 when Jesse Owens dominated the Olympics in track and field. Since 1936, the philosophy, theory, and belief of many in society is that African American athletes are just naturally gifted. However, before critiquing the media, it is important that the race factor be articulated. The following two quotes are from Ted Williams (the only player in major league baseball history to have a 0.400 batting average), a white male, who is considered the best hitter of all time:

> People talk about my great eyesight and reflexes as if those were the reasons for my success. That's bullshit. Do you know how I learned to hit a ball? Practice, dammit. Practice, practice, practice, practice? Trial and error, trial and error, trial and error!

On Eric Davis, an African American male and outstanding player at the time for the Cincinnati Reds, Williams said, "He's a great athlete. He moves well and can run. And those things come from heaven. You don't have to develop it, because it's there" (quoted in Hoose, 1989, p. 51).

This interpretation by Williams is fascinating, considering how different his analysis is on the subject of two great hitters. Is race a factor in who is considered the "natural" athlete? Literature on race and sport suggests that race plays a major role in terms of who gets what type of credit for performance. Despite the lack of compelling scientific evidence to substantiate this notion of athletic superiority, and the lack of evidence to replicate the studies supporting it, the battle over myth and reality continues. Earl Smith (1996) of Wake Forest exposes the falseness of the popular belief that a person, either black or white, can be considered a "natural athlete." Geography, health, genetics, and just plain hard work combine to produce outstanding athletes, from Michael Jordan to André Agassi. Smith also takes to task Martin Kane, the author of a widely read *Sports Illustrated* article entitled, "An assessment that black is best." Kane argues that black athletes have longer legs and arms, narrower hips, and greater arm circumference than white athletes. He also contends that black athletes relax more than whites, and that blacks are superior athletes because they are the descendants of slaves who had to adapt to their harsh environments (Kane, cited in Lapchick, 1991, p. 235). Smith counters that Kane gives little attention to the larger and more important question of differences within the races. For example, Bob Beamon and Carl Lewis are both superstars in the long jump but have completely different body types.

Drew Hyland (1990) synthesizes both sides of this debate in his book, *Philosophy of Sport*. In short, the same two general directions are revealed by Hyland's thesis: sociological explanations, and genetic or physiological explanations. Socioculturally, the accounts are based on the differences that typify the childhood and nurturing of white and black youth. In this context, economics plays a role. Blacks are perceived to have struggled for survival, while whites have had it easy. The theory in this regard would say that the competitive struggle by blacks makes them superior in athletics. Conversely, as Hyland argues, many white youths have it too easy to become great athletes. Or alternatively, blacks, faced with de facto exclusion from many of the standard paths to economic success, recognize early on that athletic success is one of the few available avenues. This validates the "way out of the ghetto" argument (Hyland, 1990). On genetics, as Hyland points out, claims have been made about differences in muscle fiber configuration, and even, at the level of silliness, that blacks have an extra bone in their feet.

The Portrayal of African Americans in Sport by Mass Media[2]

In the context of racial representations in the sports media, the opinions expressed on whether the skills of the African American in sport are "natural" or attained lead me to believe that the media have taken one side. Studies of stereotyping of African American athletes have focused primarily on male athletes. Rainville & McCormick (1977) found that white American players received more praise and less criticism than African American players in NFL commentaries. Media coverage implies that there is a relationship between race and the ability to control one's own performance. Rainville & McCormick (1977) suggest that the NFL announcers they studied believe performances by African Americans are due to uncontrollable external forces, while performances by white Americans are due to controllable internal forces.

Murrell & Curtis (1994) found that the performances of both African American and white American quarterbacks in American football were attributed to internal forces. However, the internal force for white Americans was controllable "hard work" while the internal force for African Americans was uncontrollable "natural ability." The media often reinforce the stereotype that African Americans are "natural athletes."

This stereotype positions white athletes as clearly disadvantaged, relative to black athletes, who are seen as having superior physiology (e.g., Edwards, 1969; Staples & Jones, 1985; Harris, 1993). Many in the media echo commentator Billy Packer's observation, "There just aren't many [whites], to be honest, in terms of pure athletic ability" (quoted in Hoose, 1989, p. 15). The media portrayal of African American athletes depends not only on negative stereotypes, but also on stereotypes that appeal to a white American audience. Much here relies on perceptions of African American athletes as "hip" and "cool." Seiter (1995) studied commercials that feature children and had this to say:

> Most commercials which use African American children today feature a rap theme and/or some reference to sports. The presence of African

> American children in a commercial is used to define the product as "cool," modern, up-to-the-minute. They are set up as more lively, more cool, more fashionable, more with-it than whites. Thus, their presence verifies the product's fashionability. (p. 104)

In general, the message to African American male youth is that sport is the food you should eat, drink, and sleep. Examples of advertising such as "The Dream Team" (primarily African American male basketball players), or "Life is a sport" (parody with innuendo and subliminal meaning that sport is bigger than life), and the various commercials that sell shoes by marketing African American athletes, condone narrow-minded thinking and a neglect of educational pursuits.

The Past and the Future

Historically, Earl Ofari Hutchinson in his recent book, *The Assassination of the Black Male Image* (1996), questions how far the African American male in sport has come since breaking into organized competition. Hutchinson's thesis (in a chapter titled "From Slavery to the Sports Arena") is that comments like those made by Jimmy "the Greek" Snyder in 1988, that blacks dominate major sports because they were "bred to be that way by the slave owner," only bring to the surface what many of the men who make the decisions in the sports profession really think about black athletes.

Hutchinson reminds us that during plantation days, the slave masters would round up their friends and arrange a little sport. They would select two of their biggest, brawniest, blackest men and toss them into a makeshift ring. The masters would guzzle gallons of whiskey and rum, crack jokes, and make big wagers while the two black men beat each other to a pulp. How much and to what degree has this model changed?

In terms of myths and the media, African American males suffer from being perceived, placed, and constructed in a monolithic art form (Hurt, 1996). They also suffer theoretically from the belief systems of those in control of their sporting experience, who view the black athlete as dualistic—not holistic. The inference drawn in this racial context is that they are therefore probably inferior intellectually. This is where sport clichés such as "white men can't jump" (less athletic) come from, and "black men can't think" (not capable of leadership in any field). Few will publicly articulate the latter, but one need only look at the socialization patterns of the African American male in education and sport to find its presence.

The problem with this misguided logic is that it contributes to the self-fulfilling prophecy that black males are more likely to do well in sports than in academia. It also ignores the complex social mechanisms that are responsible for African American male participation and success in sports in the first place. In fact, as stated earlier, this social construction of blacks as naturally superior in sports is a stereotype based on racism. Black youth, however, do not see racism as the underlying factor here. They seem to reason that racism is not a factor so long as they are able to gain respect and recognition through something that they do well or even better than their white peers. They do not conceptualize racism in structural or institutional terms (James, 1995). For most, racism is evident in individual attitudes and actions, something that they can overcome by being good students, and beating whites in sports.

With so much sport on television, scholarship on race/ethnicity and the sport media needs to expand and move beyond current research analysis. Sport media coverage that reinforces the "American dream" has effects on all African Americans. Suggestions that most African Americans have achieved economic success, or that those who have not achieved economic success have moral failings, only reinforce white Americans' image of themselves and their country's social structures and culture as free of racism (Andrews, 1994; Cole & Andrews, 1996; Cole & Denny, 1994). Such messages discourage the pursuit of changes that would benefit people of color, and they help to perpetuate racial inequality.

In the final analysis, the investigation of the statistically enormous black participation in athletics and involvement in the major revenue-producing sports appears intellectually fascinating, potentially important to our understanding of human beings, yet politically delicate and even dangerous (Hyland, 1990).

Qualitative and Ethnographic Data on Race, Sport and Social Construction[3]

In Jan Nederveen Pieterse's *White on Black* (1992), she states that it has often been observed that "race" is not a reality but a social construct. The construct of sport has allowed blacks to manifest themselves on the field, but not off it. The achievements of African American athletes who have challenged "white supremacy" and of African Americans in the Olympics are all breaches in the myth of racial inferiority (Pieterse, 1992). Pieterse eloquently captures the covert and overt manifestation of African-Americans as inferior beings:

> The role of black performers is too complex to show a constant pattern over so long a period, from the "Nigger Minstrels" to Miles Davis, from Bessie Smith to Jessye Norman, but there are some general tendencies. Entertainers do not threaten the status quo but embellish it. Emotive, "feminine" expression by blacks is permitted; conforms to the rhythm myth, the stereotype of musicality. Over the past century or so, and especially since the 1920s, blacks have become musicians, dancers, and buffoons of Atlantic culture, just as gypsies with violins occupy a similar niche—romanticized and marginalized—in central Europe. Also most images of blacks which prevail now in everyday western society are images of entertainers. The imagery of the popular media in which entertainment provides the sole positive role-models for black youth, and social reality, in which entertainment and sport are gilded doors out of the ghetto, together form a vicious circle of stereotyping. (p. 148)

Hence the integration of sport is part of overall black integration. But it is only a limited kind of success. For blacks there is a place in the circus, as gladiators. Their success seems to confirm one of the stereotypes of the black as bestial brute, the "all brawn and no brains" kind of athlete. Besides, new racial myths have been created to "explain" the sports achievements of African Americans. At first the story was that African Americans were inferior to whites in every respect, including physically, and therefore unfit to compete with whites (Pieterse, 1992, p. 149).

Page Smith, in *Killing the Spirit*, seems to agree with Pieterse and her thesis:

> One of the most conspicuous bizarreries of modern academe is the fact that the majority of the big sport athletes and virtually all of the "stars" are black. On every campus I visit I see a little band of black students.

> There are the mammoth black students—basketball forwards and centers, the football tackles, linebackers, and defensive ends—and the small black students—the fleet backs and pass receivers. They mix very little with white students. They are the classic black entertainers. It is for their exploits that arenas of white students shout themselves hoarse. The cultural discontinuity is staggering, the irony beyond articulation. (Smith, 1990, pp. 15–16)

In a study by Harrison (1996), fifty African American male student-athletes at two predominantly white institutions were surveyed. The focus was on their experiences while on athletic scholarships. This was done qualitatively, primarily with open-ended inquiry. Two questions asked by Harrison in the study parallel the theoretical frameworks by Pieterse and Smith, as well as this text as a whole. When reading the responses, it should be kept in mind that the reactions, feelings, and ethos revealed in this particular study parallel the notion of African American male student-athletes buying into exactly the racist myths that so dominate the sports industry. The following is a summary of two of the questions asked, the student-athletes' thematic responses (with author interpretation and clarification in parenthesis), and the percentages of their responses.

(1) Why do you feel that one study revealed that 4 percent of white male student-athletes think that their first paying job will be in professional sports, compared to 51 percent of black male student-athletes (percentages from a study done by Lapchick, 1991)? (Some 90 percent felt that racism and the media play a big role in this perception.) Themes and responses:
—"Whites are taught to balance both, we are taught the easy way out." (Channelization of blacks into labor-oriented endeavors);
—"Blacks are more athletic." (Timeless myth that blacks have more musculature and less cognitive skills, i.e., bell curve rhetoric);
—"Whites have 'the hook up' (good ol' boy network, family, institutional access), we only have sports." (Access and opportunity is perceived to be limited);
—"Whites are geared for minds, blacks for hands." (Internalization of racist myths);

(2) Why do you feel that African American male student-athletes feel isolated on predominantly white campuses? (100 percent felt that the environment of this "white sea" was inhibiting to their performance on and off the field." Themes and responses:

—"Everything is white, only sports for blacks." (Stereotypes internalized by black males);
—"Everyone around us perceives us being there only for our physical talents." (Knowledge of campus construction in higher education at traditionally white institutions);
—"We are like employees on strike with no pay, but must work." (Knowledge of collegiate commercialization, and professionalizing of amateur athletics in higher education);
—"We are not prepared to face the challenge." (Self-doubt of abilities; student-athletes are passed through the system—in many cases beginning at the preschool level);
—"We are told too late to take responsibility." (Exploitation realized by the individual);
—"How do you feel comfortable with people that you can't trust?" (Racism acknowledged).

Conclusion

Clearly, social construction is a major factor in the retention, graduation, and matriculation of the African American male in sport and society. More open-ended studies must be done to assess the needs of this group that fills stadiums and arenas across the country every Fall, Winter, Spring, and Summer. These studies must address not only the perceptions of African American males, but all of society that interacts with these young men. As stated at the beginning of this chapter, we can reach some philosophic answers by critically assessing historical and sociological factors that impact on patterns of sport from the African American community.

In the past, too much time has been spent on physiological arguments for African American male involvement in sport. This inquiry and analysis leaves much to be desired, and perpetuates historical racist beliefs about the ability levels of African Americans in general. The future of the African American male in education and sports appears to be denying more young black people (especially males) academic futures. This problem is not new. The stereotypical myths believed by the institutions and by African American males themselves continue to pervade the psyche of our nation and the world for that matter.

Exclusionary portrayals of African Americans in society impede the growth in understanding of this particular group of people. This manifestation of marginal images has not changed radically, nor have the patterns of African American males in sport over the last few decades.

Endnotes

[1]Interview with intercollegiate athletics representative on Tom Osborne's (coach of the University of Nebraska football program, which is highly successful) lecture to athletic program and kids on education and sport. His citing was from the yearly NFL census report.

[2]Frequently, white and black athletes are portrayed differently in the mass media. For example, Cal Ripken Jr, of the Baltimore Orioles baseball team, is seen in True Value Hardware commercials affirming the work ethic of mainstream individuals. Black athletes are seen and linked with sub- or superhuman characteristics? Gary Payton is quick like a bee, Michael Jordan can fly like a bird. These perpetuate "natural" athlete notions.

Bill Russell (former Boston Celtic great, first African American head coach in basketball) in his memoir addresses the myths and stereotypes that the media construct and reinforce. His case in point refers to a study conducted in the 1970s by a team of Miami researchers on possible bias in television sports broadcasting. They assembled a test group of elderly blind people who knew little about football, and asked them to listen to games on television. The blind people tried to guess the race of a player whenever they heard one described on the air, and their guesses turned out to be correct in an overwhelming majority of cases. When a receiver was described as having "blazing speed," they said black. When they heard about a man "who knows how to get open," they said white. A player who had "poise" and "a head on his shoulders" was white, whereas a player who was "hot," or "amazing," or "intimidating" tended to be black (cited in Russell, 1979, p. 103).

Earl Ofari Hutchinson found similar codes and themes. Hutchinson has watched every *Monday Night Football* game since 1970, starting with the Cleveland Browns game in September of that year. Over the years he has compiled words from the sports chatter of the announcers: white player (heady, good work habits, cagey, disciplined, a project, fearless, courageous, aggressive, a hustler; black player (a burner, speedster, or "can motor," moody, a head case, erratic, raw talent and doesn't live up to his potential, hears footsteps, a real animal (cited in Hutchinson, 1996, p. 55).

[3]A Home Box Office special on the African American athletic experience in America interviewed respected sport historian Gerald Early. Early pointed out during the show that in the early 1900s it was believed by many white Americans that blacks were going to die off and not survive.

Parentheses within the responses are to clarify the author's interpretation of the study. They also serve to illuminate the data for further linkage of my study to the literature on education in the context of race and sport.

References

Andrews, D. (1994). Michael Jordan: A commodity-sign of [post] Reaganite times. *Working Paper (Series 11) in Popular Cultural Studies, No. 1.* (Manchester: Manchester Institute for Popular Culture)

Ashe, A. (1993). *Days of grace.* New York: Knopf.

Coakley, J. (1994). *Sport in society: Issues and controversies.* St. Louis: Mosby.

Cole, C., & Andrews, D. (1996). Look, it's NBA showtime: Visions of race in the popular imagination. *Cultural Studies, 1,* 141–81.

Cole, C., & Denny, H. (1994). Visualizing deviance in post-Reagan America: Magic Johnson, AIDS, and the promiscuous world of professional sport. *Critical Sociology, 20,* 123–47.

Collins, C., & Cohen, D. (1993). *The African Americans.* New York: Cohen.

Davis, J. R. (1966). The Negro in American sports. In J. Davis (Ed.), *The American Negro reference book.* Englewood Cliffs, NJ: Prentice-Hall.

Edwards, H. (1969). *The revolt of the black athlete.* New York: Free Press.

Edwards, H., & Ashe, A. (1992). Videoconference on the black athlete in academia.

Harris, O. (1993). African American predominance in collegiate sport. In D. Brooks & R. Althouse (Eds.), *Racism in college athletics: The African American athlete's experience.* Morgantown, WV: Fitness Information Technology.

Harrison, C. K. (1996a). *Out there—not in there* (A reader on African American male student-athletes for the academic class African Americans in sport). Pullman, WA: Student Book Corporation.

Harrison, C. K. (1996b). Images that alter minds: Male athletes in the media. *CAHPERD Journal, 16,* 12.

Hoose, P. (1989). *Necessities: Racial barriers in American sports.* New York: Random House.

Hurt, B. (1996). The image of the black male. In R. Lapchick (Ed.), *Sport in society.* Thousand Oaks, CA: Sage.

Hutchinson, E. (1996). *The assassination of the black male image*. New York: Simon & Schuster.

Hyland, D. (1990). *Philosophy of sport*. New York: Paragon House.

James, C. (1995). Negotiating school through sports: African Canadian youth strive for academic success. *Avante, 1*: 21–34.

Kretchmar, R. (1994). *Practical philosophy of sport*. Champaign, IL: Human Kinetics.

Lapchick, R. (1991). *Five minutes to midnight*. Lanham, MD: Madison Books.

Lucas, J. A., & Smith, R. A. (1978). *Saga of American Sport*. Philadelphia: Lea & Febiger.

Murrell, A., & Curtis, E. (1994). Causal attributions of performance for black and white quarterbacks in the NFL? A look at the sports pages. *Journal of Sport and Social Issues, 18*, 224–33.

Olsen, J. (1968). *The black athlete? A shameful story*. New York: Time Life Books.

Pieterse, J. (1992). *White on black*. New Haven, CT: Yale University Press.

Rader, B. (1983). *American sports? From the age of folkgames to the age of spectators*. Englewood Cliffs, NJ: Prentice-Hall.

Rainville, R., & McCormick, E. (1977). Extent of covert racial prejudice in pro football announcers' speech. *Journalism Quarterly, 54*, 20–26.

Russell, B. (1979). *Second wind*. New York: Simon & Schuster.

Seiter, E. (1995). Different children, different dreams: Racial representation in advertising. In G. Dines & J. M. Humez (Eds.), *Gender, race and class in media: A text-reader*. Thousand Oaks, CA: Sage.

Smith, E. (1996). *Black athletes are not genetically superior*. Pacific Lutheran University News Release.

Smith, P. (1990). *Killing the spirit*. New York: Penguin Books.

Somers, D. A. (1972). *The rise of sport in New Orleans, 1850–1900*. Baton Rouge, LA: Louisiana State University Press.

Staples, R., & Jones, T. (1985). Culture, ideology, and black television images. *The Black Scholar, 16*, 10–20.

Wiggins, D. (1993). Critical events affecting racism in athletics. In D. Brooks & R. Althouse (Eds.), *Racism in college athletics: The*

African American athlete's experience. Morgantown, WV: Fitness Information Technology.

Chapter Eight

A Talk to Teachers[**]

James Baldwin

Let's begin by saying that we are living through a very dangerous time. Everyone in this room is in one way or another aware of that. We are in a revolutionary situation, no matter how unpopular that word has become in this country. The society in which we live is desperately menaced, not by Khrushchev, but from within. So any citizen of this country who figures himself as responsible—and particularly those of you who deal with the minds and hearts of young people—must be prepared to "go for broke." Or to put it another way, you must understand that in the attempt to correct so many generations of bad faith and cruelty, when it is operating not only in the classroom but in society, you will meet the most fantastic, the most brutal, and the most determined resistance. There is no point in pretending that this won't happen.

Since I am talking to schoolteachers and I am not a teacher myself, and in some ways am fairly easily intimidated, I beg you to let me leave that and go back to what I think to be the entire purpose of education in the first place. It would seem to me that when a child is born, if I'm the child's parent, it is my obligation and my high duty to civilize that child. Man is a social animal. He cannot exist without a society. A society, *in* turn, depends on certain things which everyone within that society takes for granted. Now, the crucial paradox which comforts us here is that the whole process of education occurs within a social framework and is designed to perpetuate the aims of society. Thus, for example, the boys and girls who were born during the era of the Third Reich, when educated to the purposes of the Third Reich, became barbarians. The paradox of education is precisely this—that as one begins to become conscious one begins to examine the

---

*Delivered October 16, 1963, as "The Negro Child—His Self-Image;" originally pub*The Saturday Review* December 21, 1963.

society in which he is being educated. The purpose of education, finally, is to create in a person the ability to look at the world for himself, to make his own decisions, to say to himself this is black or this is white, to decide for himself whether there is a God in heaven or not. To ask questions of the universe, and then learn to live with those questions, is the way he achieves his own identity. But no society is really anxious to have that kind of person around. What societies really, ideally, want is a citizenry which will simply obey the rules of society. If a society succeeds in this, that society is about to perish. The obligation of anyone who thinks of himself as responsible is to examine society and try to change it and to fight it—at no matter what risk. This is the only hope society has. This is the only way societies change.

Now, if what I have tried to sketch has any validity, it becomes thoroughly clear, at least to me, that any Negro who is born in this country and undergoes the American educational system runs the risk of becoming schizophrenic. On the one hand he is born in the shadow of the stars and stripes and he is assured it represents a nation which has never lost a war. He pledges allegiance to that flag which guarantees "liberty and justice for all." He is part of a country in which anyone can become president, and so forth. But on the other hand he is also assured by his country and his countrymen that he has never contributed anything to civilization—that his past is nothing more than a record of humiliations gladly endured. He is assumed by the republic that he, his father, his mother, and his ancestors were happy, shiftless, watermelon-eating darkies who loved Mr. Charlie and Miss Ann, that the value he has as a black man is proven by one thing only—his devotion to white people. If you think I am exaggerating, examine the myths which proliferate in this country about Negroes.

All this enters the child's consciousness much sooner than we as adults would like to think it does. As adults, we are easily fooled because we are so anxious to be fooled. But children are very different. Children, not yet aware that it is dangerous to look too deeply at anything, look at everything, look at each other, and draw their own conclusions. They don't have the vocabulary to express what they see, and we, their elders, know how to intimidate them very easily and very soon. But a black child, looking at the world around him, though he cannot know quite what to make of it, is aware that there is a reason why his mother works so hard, why his father is always on edge. He is aware that there is some reason why, if he sits down in the front of the bus, his father or mother slaps him and drags him to the back of the bus. He is aware that there is some terrible weight on his parents' shoulders which menaces him. And it isn't long—in fact it begins when he is in school—before he discovers the shape of his oppression.

Let us say that the child is seven years old and I am his father, and I decide to take him to the zoo, or to Madison Square Garden, or to the U.N. Building, or to any of the tremendous monuments we find all over New York. We get into a bus and we go from where I live on 131st Street and Seventh Avenue downtown through the park and we get into New York City, which is not Harlem. Now, where the boy lives—even if it is a housing project—is in an undesirable neighborhood. If he lives in one of those housing projects of which everyone in New York is so proud, he has at the front door, if not closer, the pimps, the whores, the junkies—in a word, the danger of life in the ghetto. And the child knows this, though he doesn't know why.

I still remember my first sight of New York. It was really another city when I was born—where I was born. We looked down over the Park Avenue streetcar tracks. It was Park Avenue, but I didn't know what Park Avenue meant *downtown*. The Park Avenue I grew up on, which is still standing, is dark and dirty. No one would dream of opening a Tiffany's on that Park Avenue, and when you go downtown you discover that you are literally in the white world. It is rich—or at least it looks rich. It is clean—because they collect garbage downtown. There are doormen. People walk about as though they owned where they are—and indeed they do. And it's a great shock. It's very hard to relate yourself to this. You don't know what it means. You know—you know instinctively—that none of this is for you. You know this before you are told. And who is it for and who is paying for it? And why isn't it for you?

Later on when you become a grocery boy or messenger and you try to enter one of those buildings a man says, "Go to the back door." Still later, if you happen by some odd chance to have a friend in one of those buildings, the man says, "Where's your package?" Now this by no means is the core of the matter. What I'm trying to get at is that by this time the Negro child has had, effectively, almost all the doors of opportunity slammed in his face, and there are very few things he can do about it. He can more or less accept it with an absolutely inarticulate and dangerous rage inside all the more dangerous because it is never expressed. It is precisely those silent people whom white people see every day of their lives—I mean your porter and your maid, who never say anything more than "Yes, Sir" and "No, Ma'am." They will tell you it's raining if *that* is what you want to hear, and they will tell you the sun is shining if that is what you want to hear. They really hate you—really hate you because in their eyes (and they're right) you stand between them and life. I want to come back to that in a moment. It is the most sinister of the facts, I think, which we now face.

There is something else the Negro child can do, too. Every street boy—and I was a street boy, so I know—looking at the society which has produced him, looking at the standards of that society which are not honored by anybody, looking at your churches and the government and the politicians, understands that this structure is operated for someone else's benefit—not for his. And there's no reason in it for him. If he is really cunning, really ruthless, really strong—and many of us are—he becomes a kind of criminal. He becomes a kind of criminal because that's the only way he can live. Harlem and every ghetto in this city, every ghetto in this country—is full of people who live outside the law. They wouldn't dream of calling a policeman. They wouldn't, for a moment, listen to any of those professions of which we are so proud on the Fourth of July. They have turned away from this country forever and totally. They live by their wits and really long to see the day when the entire structure comes down.

The point of all this is that black men were brought here as a source of cheap labor. They were indispensable to the economy. In order to justify the fact that men were treated as though they were animals, the white republic had to brainwash itself into believing that they were, indeed, animals and deserved to be treated like animals. Therefore it is almost impossible for any Negro child to discover anything about his actual history. The reason is that this "animal," once he suspects his own worth, once he starts believing that he is a man, has begun to attack the entire power structure. This is why America has spent such a long time keeping the Negro in his place. What I am trying to suggest to you is that it was not an accident, it was not an act of God, it was not done by well-meaning people muddling into something which they didn't understand. It was a deliberate policy hammered into place in order to make money from black flesh. And now, in 1963, because we have never faced this fact, we are in intolerable trouble.

The Reconstruction, as I read the evidence, was a bargain between the North and South to this effect: "We've liberated them from the land—and delivered them to the bosses." When we left Mississippi to come North we did not come to freedom. We came to the bottom of the labor market, and we are still there. Even the Depression of the 1930s failed to make a dent in Negroes' relationship to white workers in the labor unions. Even today, so brainwashed is this republic that people seriously ask in what they suppose to be good faith, "What does the Negro want?" I've heard a great many asinine questions in my life, but that is perhaps the most asinine and perhaps the most insulting. But the point here is that people who ask that question, thinking that they ask it in good faith, are really the victims of this conspiracy to make Negroes believe they are less than human.

In order for me to live, I decided very early that some mistake had been made somewhere. I was not a "nigger" even though you called me one. But if I was a—nigger" in your eyes, there was something about *you*—there was something *you* needed. I had to realize when I was very young that I was none of those things I was told I was. I was not, for example, happy. I never touched a watermelon for all kinds of reasons that had been invented by white people, and I knew enough about life by this time to understand that whatever you invent, whatever you project, is you? So where we are now is that a whole country of people believe I'm a "nigger," and I *don't*, and the battle's on? Because if I am not what I've been told I am, then it means that *you're* not what you thought you were *either*? And that is the crisis.

It is not really a "Negro revolution" that is upsetting the country. What is upsetting the country is a sense of its own identity. If, for example, one managed to change the curriculum in all the schools so that Negroes learned more about themselves and their real contributions to this culture, you would be liberating not only Negroes, you'd be liberating white people who know nothing about their own history. And the reason is that if you are compelled to lie about one aspect of anybody's history, you must lie about it all. If you have to lie about my real role here, if you have to pretend that I hoed all that cotton just because I loved you, then you have done something to yourself. You are mad.

Now let's go back a minute. I talked earlier about those silent people—the porter and the maid—who, as I said, don't look up at the sky if you ask them if it is raining, but look into your face. My ancestors and I were very well trained. We understood very early that this was not a Christian nation. It didn't matter what you said or how often you went to church. My father and my mother and my grandfather and my grandmother knew that Christians didn't act this way. It was as simple as that. And if that was so there was no point in dealing with white people in terms of their own moral professions, for they were not going to honor them. What one did was to turn away, smiling all the time, and tell white people what they wanted to hear. But people always accuse you of reckless talk when you say this.

All this means that there are in this country tremendous reservoirs of bitterness which have never been able to find an outlet, but may find an outlet soon. It means that well-meaning white liberals place themselves in great danger when they try to deal with Negroes as though they were missionaries. It means, in brief, that a great price is demanded to liberate all those silent people so that they can breathe for the first time and *tell* you what they think of you. And a price is demanded to liberate all those white children—some of them near forty—who have never grown up, and who never will grow up, because they have no sense of their identity.

What passes for identity in America is a series of myths about one's heroic ancestors. It's astounding to me, for example, that so many people really appear to believe that the country was founded by a band of heroes who wanted to be free. That happens not to be true. What happened was that some people left Europe because they couldn't stay there any longer and had to go someplace else to make it. That's all. They were hungry, they were poor, they were convicts. Those who were making it in England, for example, did not get on the *Mayflower*. That's how the country was settled. Not by Gary Cooper. Yet we have a whole race of people, a whole republic, who believe the myths to the point where even today they select political representatives, as far as I can tell, by how closely they resemble Gary Cooper. Now this is dangerously infantile, and it shows in every level of national life. When I was living in Europe, for example, one of the worst revelations to me was the way Americans walked around Europe buying this and buying that and insulting everybody—not even out of malice, just because they didn't know any better. Well, that is the way they have always treated me. They weren't cruel, they just didn't know you were alive. They didn't know you had any feelings.

What I am trying to suggest here is that in the doing of all this for 100 years or more, it is the American white man who has long since lost his grip on reality. In some peculiar way, having created this myth about Negroes, and the myth about his own history, he created myths about the world so that, for example, he was astounded that some people could prefer Castro, astounded that there are people in the world who don't go into hiding when they hear the word "Communism," astounded that Communism is one of the realities of the twentieth century which we will not overcome by pretending that it does not exist. The political level in this country now, on the part of people who should know better, is abysmal.

The Bible says somewhere that where there is no vision the people perish. I don't think anyone can doubt that in this country today we are menaced—intolerably menaced—by a lack of vision.

It is inconceivable that a sovereign people should continue, as we do so abjectly, to say, "I can't do anything about it. It's the government." The government is the creation of the people. It is responsible to the people. And the people are responsible for it. No American has the right to allow the present government to say, when Negro children are being bombed and hosed and shot and beaten all over the Deep South, that there is nothing we can do about it. There must have been a day in this country's life when the bombing of the children in Sunday School would have created a public uproar and endangered the life of a Governor Wallace. It happened here and there was no public uproar.

I began by saying that one of the paradoxes of education was that precisely at the point when you begin to develop a conscience, you must find yourself at war with your society. It is your responsibility to change society if you think of yourself as an educated person. And on the basis of the evidence—the moral and political evidence—one is compelled to say that this is a backward society. Now if I were a teacher in this school, or any Negro school, and I was dealing with Negro children, who were in my care only a few hours of every day and would then return to their homes and to the streets, children who have an apprehension of their future which with every hour grows grimmer and darker, I would try to teach them—I would try to make them know—that those streets, those houses, those dangers, those agonies by which they are surrounded, are criminal. I would try to make each child know that these things are the results of a criminal conspiracy to destroy him. I would teach him that if he intends to get to be a man, he must at once decide that he is stronger than this conspiracy and that he must never make his peace with it. And that one of his weapons for refusing to make his peace with it and for destroying it depends on what he decides he is worth. I would teach him that there are currently very few standards in this country which are worth a man's respect. That it is up to him to begin to change these standards for the sake of the life and the health of the country. I would suggest to him that the popular culture—as represented, for example, on television and in comic books and in movies—is based on fantasies created by very ill people, and he must be aware that these are fantasies that have nothing to do with reality. I would teach him that the press he reads is not as free as it says it is—and that he can do something about that, too. I would try to make him know that just as American history is longer, larger, more various, more beautiful, and more terrible than anything anyone has ever said about it, so is the world larger, more daring, more beautiful and more terrible, but principally larger—and that it belongs to him. I would teach him that he doesn't have to be bound by the expediencies of any given administration, any given policy, any given morality; that he has the right and the necessity to examine everything. I would try to show him that one has not learned anything about Castro when one says, "He is a Communist.? This is a way of his learning something about Castro, something about Cuba, something, in time, about the world. I would suggest to him that he is living, at the moment, in an enormous province. America is not the world and if America is going to become a nation, she must find a way—and this child must help her to find a way to use the tremendous potential and tremendous energy which this child represents. If this country does not find a way to use that energy, it will be destroyed by that energy.

Part Three

Challenges to Educational Practice

Chapter Nine

"Black Schools for Black Children": Black Males, Milwaukee, and Immersion Schools

Christopher M. Span

Introduction

Milwaukee's African American Immersion schools are perhaps the most controversial educational reform of the 1990s. They are the first public schools to utilize an African-centered approach to rectify the underachievement of African American students. Throughout their brief existence, the two schools have become both a plausible model for struggling school systems to replicate, and a center for animosity over ideological and pedagogical differences between local school officials. However, Milwaukee's African American Immersion schools are even more significant than the aforementioned statement suggests. They are a pioneering, innovative, and practical response to an ever increasing crisis in the majority of Milwaukee public schools—the persistent underachievement of African American students, in particular black male students. As such, the ultimate goals of Milwaukee's African American Immersion schools are not much different than the goals of other districts seeking to rectify the underachievement of its African American students. However, the methods utilized at the two immersion schools are different, and they directly challenge the ideological beliefs of the many actors participating or evaluating in the pilot program.

As a result, this chapter's purpose is three-fold. Drawing mostly from newspaper accounts, it first illustrates the various responses and reactions to Milwaukee's decision to incorporate the African American Immersion school concept into its public school system. As will be seen, Milwaukee's experiment echoed the national arguments waged between African-centered theorists and traditional Western-centered pedagogues. Second, this chapter summarizes the effect Milwaukee's African American Immersion schools have had on the academic achievement of their student clientele. To put it briefly, the schools have been very successful in enhancing the performance and motivation of their students, despite resistance from local opponents. Concluding this chapter is a philosophical argument for the educational values pioneered by Milwaukee's African American Immersion school experiment and for why other districts in similar situations should consider the African American Immersion school model as a practical option. However, a logical starting point is to show why Milwaukee proposed the need for African American Immersion schools.

A Critical Need—A Timely Response

In January 1990, a task force of educators, community leaders, and concerned citizens appointed by the Milwaukee Public Schools (MPS) was created to determine how the district was serving (or failing to serve) African American males. The data generated by this commission noted that approximately 58 percent of the city's 98,000 public school students were African American. It was revealed that in 1988 more than 80 percent of the 5,716 African American males attending Milwaukee high schools had a grade point average below 2.0 or C. They comprised half, or 3,565, of the 7,113 students suspended, and between 1978 and 1985, they constituted 94 percent of the students expelled (African American Male Task Force, 1990). A dispiriting reality, considering that African American males made up only 28 percent of all students in Milwaukee's public schools (Holt, 1991/92; Leake & Faltz, 1993; Leake & Leake, 1992).

Fueling these findings was the ever increasing literature, media coverage, and documented realities of the "self-destructive tendencies" of black males in American society. The "endangered" status of African American males, not just in Milwaukee but throughout the nation, was quickly becoming an all too familiar discussion topic. Bestsellers such as Johnthan Kozol's *Savage Inequalities* (1992) illustrated the plight and dilemma of growing up poor and black in urban America. Likewise, numerous scholars revealed the disproportionate number of African American male dropouts in the nation's urban school system. When the African American Male Task Force was created, black males represented over 50 percent of the nation's urban school dropouts—60 percent in Milwaukee (Task Force, 1990; Bryant, 1991; Hare, 1985; K. Johnson, 1990; Watson & Smitherman, 1991).

Additionally, scholars documented many of the negative social factors—the disproportionate number of black males in prison, the black homicide rate, unemployment, and unwed/unemployed mothers in the black community—affecting the African American community. Scholars noted that black males constituted only 6 percent of the nation's overall population, but 46 percent of the country's prison population—23 percent in Milwaukee—and more than any other group, young black males between the ages of fifteen and twenty-four were likely to die from homicide (Task Force, 1990; Watson & Smitherman, 1991). They also noted that Milwaukee had the second highest percentage of unwed mothers in the nation (behind Washington D.C.) and a myriad of single-parent unemployed households (Task Force, 1990; "Milwaukee to Try," 1990; Collison, 1988; Watson & Smitherman, 1991).

The African American Male Task Force's efforts, coupled with the negative statistics concerning the future of black male youth, shed light on the programs and practices offered in the MPS district which negatively affected not only the educational outcomes of African American male students, but all African American students. Furthermore, the group concluded that the adverse environmental conditions these learners resided and attended school in, the low teacher expectations, and the lack of societal concern over the educational achievement, attainment, and opportunity of African American children were key determinants in their academic underachievement. Consequently, the commission demanded immediate support to address, and eventually remedy, the educational underachievement of Milwaukee's African American students.

The proposed countermeasure was the establishment of two African American Immersion schools, an elementary school and a middle school, in the MPS district. The schools were the first public schools in the nation to utilize an African-centered curriculum. They were housed in two of the nineteen racially identifiable schools—schools with a 90-plus percentage of African American students—in inner-city Milwaukee, and they were immediately deemed controversial. They offered a pilot program attempting to cater to the educational needs of African American male students.

Similar to the Black Independent School model (BIS), the African American Immersion School assisted students in "acquiring competence in social skills, communication, problem solving, critical thinking, effective citizenship, self-actualization, and male and female identity development, particularly as it related to ethnicity" (Leake & Faltz, 1993, p. 383). Additionally the model attempted to reestablish the respect, responsibility, and relationship of African American people (both young and old) in terms of the development of their community and society. Altogether, Milwaukee's African American Immersion schools centered on improving the educational attainment and social opportunities of the inner-city black students by creating an atmosphere and curriculum that motivated them to excel.

Amidst the excitement and optimism there was a storm of controversy about the "appropriateness" of the African American Immersion school concept in public schooling. Milwaukee's plan to establish two such schools raised several legal and educational criticisms. Central criticisms ranged from the beliefs that schools were reestablishing segregation and promoting gender bias (because of their proponents' initial emphasis on establishing all-black, male academies), to the belief that the schools and their African-centered curricula were inherently racist. Additionally many critics—both locally and nationally—took exception to the notion that black males might need "separate schools" or "special instruction" to remedy their poor academic performance.

From the debate that ensued over the legitimacy of Milwaukee's African American Immersion schools, two distinct interpretations of the phrase "black schools for black children" emerged. At one end of the spectrum, critics maintained that the plan was nothing more than a throwback to the days of "separate but equal" segregation ("Can the Boys Be Saved?" 1990). At the opposite end, Milwaukee's African American Immersion schools were deemed "the most drastic educational approach aimed to saving the next generation of young black men" (D. Johnson, 1990, p. 1). Stuck in the middle of this debate were the participants—students, teachers, staff, and school officials—"doing the best that they could" with the limited resources, support, and time allotted. These reactions and the effects they had on the students participating in the pilot program are the focus of the following sections.

Milwaukee's African American Immersion Schools

When the MPS Board of School Directors approved the recommendations by the task force to open two African American Immersion schools, the chairman of the task force declared, "It's a celebration for the students because the board found the courage and willingness to address a critical issue" (Garofoli, 1990, p. B1). Indeed, there were many reasons for celebration. Beside the momentous fact that Milwaukee's public school system was the first to adopt the African American Immersion school model, proponents of the pilot program were guaranteed at least five years to remedy the academic underachievement of the students willing to participate in the pilot program. It had been established that they could utilize an African-centered approach in addition to the state's prescribed curriculum, and, to further assist in their endeavor, they were given greater autonomy to recruit teachers and volunteers willing to support the program's goals. Even more important, Milwaukee's African American Immersion schools were the first culture- and gender-specific programs to advance beyond many of the legal ramifications impeding various efforts attempted by other school districts nationwide.

Milwaukee was not the first city to attempt an educational reform to specifically address the underachievement of black male students. During the mid-1980s, cities such as Baltimore, Chicago, Detroit, Miami, New Orleans, and Portland also attempted to do this but were not able to attain Milwaukee's virtually unrestricted position. Chicago established private schools for African American students. Detroit established private academies for its failing black male students; however, they were soon ruled to be in violation of Title IX (Watson, 1994; Watson & Smitherman, 1991). Baltimore and Miami also developed all-black male classrooms—more specifically homerooms—that focused on the academic, psychological, and social development of the pupils (Holland, 1991). New Orleans and Portland developed alternative learning strategies and resources specifically aimed at meeting the educational needs of African American male students (Garibaldi,

1988; Green & Hammond, 1988). Like the other cities mentioned, neither New Orleans nor Portland were able to achieve the level of public and administrative support that Milwaukee initially secured. Proponents of Milwaukee's African American Immersion schools had positioned themselves to incorporate the successful programs utilized by all these other school reforms and construct a practical and proactive pedagogy applicable in predominantly African American public schools.

While public and administrative support proved to be the crucial element in the initial success of Milwaukee's African American Immersion schools, the negative statistics associated with black student achievement certainly aided proponents' arguments for the pilot program. Local administrators, the superintendent, parents, teachers, and community leaders had grown impatient with the sub-par performance of black students. The task force that proposed the establishment of the schools noted that "African American males' progress in schools appeared to be equal to that of their peers during the preschool and primary years;" however, "the same observation [could not] be made thereafter" (Task Force, 1990, p. vi).

Yet more than any other group, inner-city black Milwaukeeans, especially single black mothers, were frustrated with the district's inability to effectively provide satisfactory schooling in their communities. They linked the school-related problems of black males with the disproportionate number of African American males incarcerated, unemployed, or underemployed in their adult life. Consequently, they readily endorsed the plans for opening two African American Immersion schools. In an open forum that introduced the schools' objectives to Milwaukee's black community, one young black mother summarized the sentiment of the audience when she stated, "If they can help boys learn how to be men, I'm all for it. There's lots that a woman can't teach a boy" (D. Johnson, 1990, p. 26).

These frustrations and sentiments were incorporated in the arguments of leading advocates for the pilot program. Their disbelief in the effectiveness of the city's desegregation efforts, their support of the African-centered paradigm, and their belief that the pilot program was the initial building block needed for the restoration of the black community, all served as the rhetoric for the establishment of Milwaukee's African American Immersion schools. Proponents argued that the schools would alleviate much of the "urban miseducation" associated with the MPS district and would offer a more nurturing and congenial environment for the educational, cultural, and social development of the students (Span, 1998). Correspondingly, they insisted that increases in student performance were inevitable because of the proposed methodological, structural, and psychological modifications. Proponents were convinced that the schools would eventually serve as models that MPS would replicate and that other school districts nationwide would follow.

Immersion school advocates expressed their disbelief in the effectiveness of the city's desegregation plans. Given the limited effect desegregation had had on the majority of Milwaukee's inner-city black students, supporters of Milwaukee's African American Immersion schools contended that desegregation was not the most effective solution for these children. In 1986, when court-ordered desegregation plans ended, one task force member was convinced that Milwaukee had achieved "resegregation," not integration. Another member agreed, declaring that integration had not worked because of white flight and housing segregation (Jackson, 1990). Collectively, the task force resolved that "desegregation alone would not be sufficient" in addressing the educational performance of African American males. The task force concluded that a recognition of the educational needs these males bring to the school setting, and the ways schools structurally and functionally tend to deal with African American students was also needed (Task Force, 1990). Overall, they reiterated that less emphasis should be placed on continuing desegregation, and more on what kind of multicultural education could be given, in spite of residential patterns and boundaries.

C. Scully Stikes, a task force member and dean of Liberal Arts at Milwaukee Area Technical College, was one of the most outspoken advocates of this viewpoint. He, like most proponents of the African American Immersion school paradigm, endorsed the incorporation of an African-centered approach (i.e., the use of African and African American themes to enhance the academic performance of the student clientele) in the curricula at the pilot schools. Basing their judgment on prior research, proponents of the Milwaukee plan believed that the application of an African-centered approach would prove therapeutic in regard to the cultural and social development of local students (Bell, 1998; Gilbert & Gay, 1985; Hare, 1985; Kunjufu, 1984; Leake & Faltz, 1993). According to Stikes, this was particularly important in the overall education of black males. He argued that the institutional patterns for dealing with them had been ineffective because American society has ignored their basic cultural heritage. He concluded that "traditional schools have failed to recognize African American culture and learning styles," and that Milwaukee's African American Immersion schools would provide their students with the pride, education, and cultural knowledge needed to succeed in mainstream society. One Milwaukee Alderman, Marvin Pratt, concurred, stating, "What's missing for a lot of young people is the pride that I think an Afro-centric curriculum will foster" (Marshall, 1990, p. A1).

The idea that a culture-specific curriculum, in one form or fashion, fostered academic achievement and the overall social development of its students was not a new phenomenon; statistics have demonstrated this reality nationwide in many private Black Independent Schools (Gilbert and Gay, 1985; Gill, 1991; Hilliard, 1989, 1991/92; Shujaa, 1994). However in Milwaukee's case, it was innovative and pioneering. Milwaukee's African American Immersion schools were public not private schools, the first ever to experiment with and establish such a program. The schools were staffed with a diverse teaching force, had a conservative and conflicting school board, and a powerful and ever present teachers' union; all of these had differing (mostly negative) opinions about African-centered schooling, the legitimacy of the pilot program, and the educational innovations being advertised as "beneficial" to the student population (Span, 1998). Nevertheless, supporters of the pilot program eagerly awaited the inclusion of an African-centered approach, because they believed it had greater educational worth in predominantly African American schools than the district's prescribed Western-centered curriculum.

The argument that impelled many black Milwaukeeans to support the pilot program was the inference that the schools were able not only to rectify the academic underachievement of black males, but quite possibly capable of restoring Milwaukee's black communities. Proponents argued that it "took a village to raise a child" and called upon Milwaukee's black residents, educators, and businessmen to voluntarily assist the program. Many black Milwaukeeans saw this initiative as an effort to increase their control within their communities and over local school-based decisions and practices. Moreover, they foresaw the results, if proven positive, to be an excellent countermeasure to the negative elements—gangs, drugs, crime, teenage pregnancy, and juvenile delinquency—plaguing their communities. Without directly stating it, Milwaukee's African American Immersion schools quickly became perceived as black schools for black children *and their communities*. Many advocates firmly believed that the combined efforts of the schools' organizers would serve as the initial building blocks for the restoration of Milwaukee's black community.

Separate Schooling for Black Children

Not all Milwaukeeans agreed that, given the social, cultural, and educational conditions, black children would benefit from separate schooling. Many disapproved of the rationale or disputed the need for the city to establish the nation's first African American Immersion public schools. Despite sympathizing with proponents about the need to rectify the underachievement of African American male students, opponents of the board's decision maintained that if the schools were set up they would be reestablishing segregation. As a result, critics and proponents maintained dramatically different interpretations of the phrase "black schools for black children." Many critics viewed Milwaukee's African American Immersion schools as an "African American call for segregation" (Jackson, 1990). Moreover, adversaries of the pilot program, both locally and nationally, were unwavering in their denunciation of the motives mandating the inclusion of an African-centered approach in the schools and a male-centered theme as the primary curriculum focus.

By far the most vocal opponents of the schools were members of the local school board, the teachers' union, and affluent educators throughout greater Milwaukee. After the Board of

School Directors approved the establishment of the two experimental schools, those on the board who objected to the decision immediately offered their opinions. Board director Doris Stacy stated that the plan had "legal, educational, moral, and philosophical problems" ("Milwaukee to Try," 1990, p. 12). She firmly believed the MPS district was "institutionalizing racism" and added that the pilot program was "unconstitutional," "educationally unsound," and "morally wrong" for isolating students by race in 1990 ("African American Immersion Schools Aim to Help," 1990, p. 1; Marshal, 1990, p. A1). In her closing comments, Stacy challenged the program's logic, asking, "Will boys learn because they are separated from girls or because the classrooms are nurturing? Should white girls just be taught by white women?" ("Milwaukee to Try," 1990, p. 12) Another board director, Mary Bills, agreed with Stacy. Bills refused to support what she considered to be "racially identifiable schools," although she knew there were nineteen such schools in the MPS district, and knew the schools being discussed as probable sites for the pilot program were among them. As an alternative to the immersion school plan, she proposed earmarking 5 percent of the district's 1991–92 budget for staff development to specifically promote racial awareness strategies, after-school tutorial activities, and Saturday programs (D. Johnson, 1990).

Echoing these sentiments, some local educators called the plan a "hoax" and a "wrong-headed approach to a very complex and serious problem" ("Immersion Schools Aim to Help," 1991, p. 1; K. Johnson, 1990, p. D4). The Milwaukee teachers' union challenged the pilot program because the prerequisites authorized by the Board of School Directors for teachers who would teach at the schools infringed upon the limited personal time of its members. In order to best utilize an African-centered approach, those wanting to teach at the immersion schools were required to complete at least eighteen hours of course work in African and African American history at one of the local universities. Many teachers considered this unacceptable (Gregory, 1993a, 1993b). Additionally, local school board members refused to accommodate many of the requests of school officials well after the pilot program opened because of their disapproval of the schools' instructional methods (Span, 1998).

Milwaukee's African American Immersion schools, however, sparked an even larger debate on the national level. The National Organization for Women (NOW) and the NAACP were highly skeptical of the schools' gender and culture-specific emphasis, because they felt it challenged their lifelong commitments to equal access and integration (Brown, 1995). Concurrently, nationally recognized educators, consultants, and professionals differed over the legitimacy, style, and content proposed for the schools. Overall, the conflict associated with the Milwaukee example hinged on two main issues. First, whether the racial makeup of schools should determine the subject matter taught; and secondly, whether schools should be "specially designed" to accommodate these populations and curricula. This discord echoed the persistent arguments put forward by Western-centered, Eurocentric theorists and African-centered, multicultural theorists.

Scholars in favor of alternative or culture-specific schooling contended that Milwaukee's initiative was a positive development, given the deteriorated and politically charged infrastructure of the city's public school system. The opposition saw little educational worth in the Milwaukee plan, possibly because many could not help but view it as a segregated measure. For example, Harvard professor Charles V. Willie warned that "segregated education could send the wrong message to black students. I see nothing in this approach that will help them overcome the oppression they are experiencing from society at large" (D. Johnson, 1990, p. 26). Likewise, California's deputy superintendent Shirley Thorton called Milwaukee's plan an "unrealistic" and "segregated" approach. She hoped proponents did not think "that by pulling all the black males together [in a school] something magical would happen" (D. Johnson, 1990, p. 26).

Proponents were very much aware and disturbed that the immersion school plan had already been deemed a failure before the schools' doors opened. In response to the various criticisms pertaining to the "resegregation" of African American youth, Kenneth Holt, chair of the task force, replied: "There was no outcry to the dismal underachievement of African American students, everyone readily accepted it. We are not segregating these children, the schools as they are now are segregated and isolated" (Jackson, 1990, p. A24). Superintendent Robert Peterkin agreed. He said, "We are trying to prepare [black males] for the mainstream of society. . . . The United States of America has allowed the situation in our inner cities to grow so bad that in fact African American males right now are isolated and segregated from the remainder of society" ("Immersion Schools Aim to Help," 1990, p. 1). Joyce Mallory, who was the most outspoken board director in favor of the program, maintained that the schools were not "separatist" or "nationalistic." She continued: "The key issue is that African American males in Milwaukee and across the country are failing dismally. At least this is an effort to say that there are some structural educational changes we can make for these kids" (Worthington, 1990, p. 3).

Collectively, it seems the arguments of opponents of the pilot program reflected more the personal biases they had against the plan's programs—the African-centered approach and the black male emphasis—than the discrimination or "segregation" being promoted under the guise of alternative schooling. The fact remained that Milwaukee's inner city, where the schools were proposed, *was* a segregated community. Almost *90 percent* of the city's black population resided in only five of its twenty-four neighborhood areas (Levine & Zipp, 1993). Moreover, as aforementioned, nineteen schools in the MPS district were 90–plus percent African American, and all were in inner-city Milwaukee. Given the fact that the immersion schools were to be accommodated within two of these nineteen schools, it was virtually impossible for proponents to resegregate two schools that were already segregated. Conceivably the best summation came from a native Milwaukee columnist who stated:

> All nineteen of those schools should have been desegregated. But a federal judge more than a decade ago approved a Milwaukee desegregation plan that left those schools almost all-black. It's silly now for anyone to contend that the establishment of African American immersion programs in two of them is a segregative act. In fact, it will give the schools some special programming, that has long been the case with the system's desegregated specialty schools ("Immersion School Critics Overlook Facts," 1990, p. A10).

More Thoughts on Milwaukee Public Schools

Despite the criticisms, the negative perceptions, and the perpetual conflict that occurred after the schools opened, Milwaukee's African American Immersion schools have been very successful in rectifying the underachievement of their student clientele. In 1991, Martin Luther King Jr., Elementary School (MLK)—formerly Victor Berger Elementary—opened. It housed 560 black students, of whom approximately half were female. The majority of the students who willingly attended the elementary school were considered "at-risk." In 1993, one year after the district instituted a mandatory reading assessment test for all third graders, only 30 percent of the MLK third-grade class read at or above the national standard. Just one year later, 87 percent of the school's third-grade class read at or above the national level, an improvement of 57 percent. In 1995, 92 percent of the immersion school's third graders read at or above the national level, and this percentage has remained relatively constant ever since (Ajirotutu & Pollard, 1996; Henry, 1996). Similarly, Mathematics scores have improved 23 percent since the school's opening (Ajirotutu & Pollard, 1996; Henry, 1996; Lawrence, 1994).

King Elementary School's students have also shown a steady improvement in their writing skills. In Milwaukee, every fifth-grade student is required to provide a writing sample for institutional portfolios. The sample, produced in response to a question used throughout the district, serves to assess the approximate writing abilities of MPS students. In 1992, 63 percent of MLK's fifth-grade class passed the writing test. In 1993, 64 percent passed. A year later, 78 percent of the school's fifth-grade class passed, and in 1995, 98 percent passed. Within those four years, MLK's fifth-grade students showed a 34 percent improvement in their writing abilities (Ajirotutu & Pollard, 1996). Also, in 1993–95 MLK's attendance rate remained remarkably constant at *91* percent, no student was expelled, and every student passed to the next grade level (Ajirotutu & Pollard, 1996; Division Research and Assessment 1995–96 Report Cards, 1996; Henry, 1996). Arguably the results achieved at Milwaukee's African American Immersion elementary school are related to the programs and practices instituted. Additionally, it appears that the longer students were "immersed" in the programs offered by the schools, the better they performed academically.

Students at the African American Immersion middle school also demonstrated an improvement in their academic performance, although not to the same degree as at King Elementary. When Malcolm X Academy—formerly Fulton Middle School—opened in 1992, it did so in a storm of controversy over the legitimacy of the pilot program (Span, 1998). Unlike teachers at King Elementary School, those at Malcolm X Academy were very resistant to the pedagogical changes required. Consequently, from 1993 to 1995 the student-teacher ratio at the school was *ninety to one* in some classrooms. Malcolm X Academy had the highest teacher turnover rate in the district, and it functioned with a full-time staff of only *30 percent* of the required number (Henry, 1996).

These occurrences directly affected the academic performance of the school's students. However, more importantly they denied these students, regardless of their participation in the immersion school, the opportunity to receive a quality education, because of the political battles being waged inside and outside the school. With no opportunity to "make up" the two-plus years of lost schooling in all the political confusion, Malcolm X Academy's students were placed at a disadvantage compared to their peers. Sadly, Malcolm X Academy's students were blamed for the poor academic performance at the school, rather than the school officials who initiated the conflict. All in all, however, the Malcolm X students made significant gains. Between 1993 and 1995 the school's mean grade point average (GPA) rose steadily from 1.95 to 2.20. Also, the suspension rate decreased from 56 percent to 39 percent (Ajirotutu and Pollard, 1996; Division Research and Assessment 1995–96 Report Cards, 1996; Henry, 1996). Additionally, Malcolm X Academy's debate team has received citywide honors for their achievements. The gains made at Malcolm X Academy, however, will never equal the losses students accrued during the uncompromising conflicts that took place from 1993 to 1995.

The Educational Value of Having "Black Schools for Black Children"

Despite the reported success at both schools, many local opponents of the immersion school plan continue to maintain that the program should be eliminated. In 1995, local school board members voted to close Malcolm X Academy—although it never happened—and in 1996 these same board members proposed that both schools' African-centered curricula be scrapped (Span, 1998). Often overlooked has been the educational value the pilot program has offered to other school districts searching for feasible options in similar circumstances. Milwaukee's African American Immersion schools have given educational policy makers and practitioners a successful example of what can be achieved if the proper dedication, assistance, support, and autonomy is given to meet the needs of a targeted disadvantaged group.

Perhaps the most noticeable feature to be attributed to Milwaukee's African American Immersion schools is not just the persistent belief that all children can learn, but the belief that all children *should* be given the opportunity to learn and succeed. Given the schools' relatively brief existence so far, special attention must be paid to the motivational and academic effects each has had on its students. Milwaukee's African American Immersion schools have done what no other program had done—provided demonstrable educational gains.

Sadly, proponents of the Milwaukee plan no longer appear to be willing to accept or "salvage" the limited beneficial effects prior educational reforms such as decentralization and desegregation achieved. Moreover, few in Milwaukee are proposing alternative reforms or additional measures to combat the discouraging underachievement of the district's African American students. To quote Derrick Bell, "to push for more money and more effective plans for curriculum in all-black schools rather than exhaust ourselves and our resources on ethereal integration in mainly white suburbs" is without question a progressive step in Milwaukee (Bell, 1992, p. 63). MPS not only consolidated the limited fiscal resources available at the schools, but also expanded their fiscal base by soliciting external funds to support their programs. Milwaukee's African American Immersion schools have provided a practical and inexpensive alternative with which to confront many of the problems facing schools in Milwaukee's predominantly black communities. Thus, in essence, Milwaukee's African American Immersion schools are a testament to "black schools for black children."

Although immersion schools will probably not be the major urban school reform of the future, other schools such as Los Angeles' Marcus Garvey Academy have adopted the model. Furthermore, because of Milwaukee's initiative, many impoverished, predominantly black and Latino schools have succeeded in establishing culture-specific programs and curricula without the legal problems that usually impeded these attempts prior to Milwaukee's experiment.

Consequently, more and more public school systems across the nation are identifying and/or struggling to find practical options to rectify the academic underachievement of their black students, especially black males. The unfortunate reality is that many of these school systems "feel more at ease" using special or remedial education programs than programs utilized or suggested by immersion school proponents. Without a doubt, immersion school students are better prepared academically, and by many accounts more motivated to succeed, and this can be mostly attributed to the culture-specific and nurturing approaches utilized at the schools. Moreover, the greater sense of responsibility, control, and optimism maintained by many community residents involved with the schools' programs is undoubtedly an additional positive outcome of the immersion school program.

Conclusion

Perhaps the achievements of Milwaukee's African American Immersion schools will elevate black youths from the limited economic and educational opportunities that have restricted their social and academic access. It is ironic that the innovative practices of these schools may never be appreciated fully and hence may be relegated to the pile of other obsolete school reforms. More black communities should follow the immersion school initiative Milwaukee struggled to pioneer. But only time will tell if the education community has the tenacity to implement "black schools for black children."

References

African American immersion schools aim to help failing students. (1990, 13 June). *Christian Science Monitor*, p. 1.

African American Male Task Force, Milwaukee Public Schools. (1990). *Educating African American males: A dream deferred.* Milwaukee: Milwaukee Public Schools Publications.

Ajirotutu, C., and Pollard, D. (1996). *African American Immersion School Newsletter 1*(5), 1–18.

Bell, D. (1988). The case of the separate black school system. *Urban League Review, 11*, 136–45.

Bell, D. (1992). *Faces at the bottom of the well: The permanence of racism*. New York: Basic Books.

Brown, K. (1995). African American immersion schools: Paradoxes of race and public education. In R. Delgado (Ed.), *Critical race theory: The cutting edge* (pp. 373–86). Philadelphia: Temple University Press.

Bryant, C. (1990, 19 November). All-black school plan gets praise. *Washington Times*, p. 4 (D).

Can the boys be saved? (1990, October 15). *Newsweek, 67.*

Division and Research Assessment, *1995–96 Report Cards, District and School by School Report.*

Garibaldi, A. M. (1988). *Educating black male youth: A moral and civic imperative*. New Orleans, LA: New Orleans Public School Publications.

Garofoli, J. (1990, 27 September). 2 Milwaukee schools will target needs of black males. *Milwaukee Journal Sentinel*, p. 1 (B).

Gibbs, J. T. (1988). *Young, black and male in America: An endangered species*. Dover, MA: Auburn House.

Gilbert, S., & Gay, G. (1985). Improving the success in school of poor black children. *Phi Delta Kappan, 57*(2), 133–37.

Gill, W. (1991). *African American males: Leaving the nightmare.* Paper presented at the Annual Meeting of the University Council for Educational Administration, Minneapolis, MN, October 30–November 1, 1991.

Green, R., Franklin, C., & Hammond, N. (1988). *Increasing the achievement of black male students: The Portland Oregon Public*

Schools approach. Portland, OR: Portland Public School Publications.

Hare, B. R., & Castenell, L. A. (1985). No place to run, no place to hide: Comparative status and future prospects of black boys. In M. B. Spencer, B. K. Brookens, & W. R. Allen (Eds.), *Beginnings: The social and effective development of black children* (pp. 201–14). Hillsdale, NJ: Lawrence Erlbaum Associates.

Hare, N. (1986). Bring the black boy to manhood: The passage. *The Crisis, 92*(3), 36–47.

Henry, T. (1996, 18 December). Immersed in black history and culture. *USA Today*, p. 6 (D).

Henry, T. (1996, 18 December). Afrocentric curriculum on trial. *USA Today*, p. 6 (D).

Hilliard III, A. (Ed.). (1989). *Infusion of African and African American content in school curriculum*. Morristown, NJ: Aaron Press.

Hilliard III, A. (1991/92). Why we must pluralize the curriculum. *Educational Leadership, 49*(4), 12–14.

Holland, S. (1991). Same gender classes in Baltimore: How to avoid problems faced in Detroit/Milwaukee. *Equity and Excellence, 25*(2), 93.

Holt, K. (Dec./Jan. 1991/92). A rationale for creating African American immersion schools. *Education Leadership, 49*(4), 18.

Immersion school critics overlook facts. (1990, 23 October). *Milwaukee Journal Sentinel*, p. 10 (A).

Jackson, D. (1990, 7 October). A bold experiment in Milwaukee. *Boston Sunday Globe, 24* (A).

Johnson, D. (1990, 28 September). Milwaukee creating 2 schools for black boys. *New York Times*, p. 26.

Johnson, K. (1990, 11 October). A bold experiment for educating black males. *USA Today*, p. 4 (D).

Kozol, J. (1992). *Savage inequalities: Children in America's schools*. New York: First Harper Perennial.

Kunjufu, J. (1984). *Developing positive self-image and discipline in black children*. Chicago: African American Images.

Lawrence, C. (1994, 19 May). 3rd grade reading scores rise for MPS. *Milwaukee Journal Sentinel*, p. 1 (A).

Leake, D., & Leake B. (1992). Islands of hope: Milwaukee's African American immersion schools. *Journal of Negro Education, 61*(1), 24–29.

Leake, D., & Faltz, C. (1993). Do we need to desegregate all of our black schools? *Educational Policy, 7*(3), 370–87.

Levine, M., & Zipp, J. (1993). A city at risk. In J. Rury & F. Cassell (Eds.), *Seeds of crisis: Public schooling in Milwaukee since 1920*. Madison, WI: University of Wisconsin Press.

Marshal, S. (1990, 3 October). Milwaukee school aim: Black pride. *USA Today*, 1 (A).

Milwaukee to try schools for black boys. (1990, 8 October). *Chicago Defender*, p. 12.

MPS releases school rankings. (1995, 30 November). *The Milwaukee Journal Sentinel*, p. 6 (A).

Shujaa, M. (Ed.). (1994). *Too much schooling, too little education: A paradox of black life in white society*. Trenton, NJ: Africa World Press.

Span, C. (1998). Challenging the cycle of urban miseducation: Milwaukee's African American Immersion Schools. Unpublished master's thesis, University of Illinois at Urbana-Champaign.

Stanford, G. (1993a, 24 March). Teacher union seeks foul deal. *Milwaukee Journal Sentinel*, p. 13 (A).

Stanford, G. (1993b, 27 September). Teacher union risks alienating reform-minded. *Milwaukee Journal Sentinel*, p. 13 (A).

Watson, C. (1994). *Educating African American males: Detroit's Malcolm X Academy solution*. Paper presented at a 1994 symposium, Documenting the African American Immersion Schools: A Working Process.

Watson, C., & Smitherman, G. (1991). Educational equity and Detroit's male academies. *Equity and Excellence, 25*(2), 90–91.

Worthington, R. (1990, 20 September). Milwaukee OKs schools tailored to black males. *The Chicago Tribune*, p. 3.

Chapter Ten

Reconceptualizing Multicultural Education: Design Principles for Educating African American Males

Tyrone C. Howard

Introduction

Raising young African American males has become an increasingly complex and complicated endeavor. The challenge sounds simple, but the task is monumental. How do we raise socially conscious, academically astute, psychologically healthy, spiritually stable, and morally competent African American males in today's society? Moreover, how can we accomplish this task in a society that characterizes African American males as pathological and deviant from mainstream culture? The editors of and contributors to this book have examined this and other dilemmas from various perspectives, to understand how we, as cultural workers, can provide our sons with life-giving and life-sustaining educational environments in which to learn, grow, and contribute to today's ethnically diverse, culturally pluralistic, and interdependent world.

As a father, educator, and cultural worker for African American people I am familiar with the challenge of raising and educating young African American males. I am frequently confronted with a multitude of dilemmas that relate to this arduous task. Cultural workers concerned with improving the academic and social experiences of African American males must contemplate the following questions: How do we instill ethnic, cultural, and racial pride in our sons when mainstream imagery and rhetoric devalue and invalidate their very essence? How do we provide a holistic academic and social upbringing for our sons as they live amidst pernicious racism, hostile discrimination, and blatant exclusion? Should we accept that our sons' upbringing will never be holistic, or should we seek to establish a new paradigm which defines their experiences?

According to Paulo Freire (1970), education as the practice of freedom is to name life as one knows it. Many of our sons have not experienced education as a practice of freedom, because they have been unable to name their lived experiences in the mainstream educational arena. For many of our sons, education has not served as a conduit for educational liberation, but as a journey to academic and physical incarceration. Thus, how do we raise our sons not to be acrimonious toward a society that denigrates their personage? Our task must be to raise our sons to become social change agents at the forefront of constructing new epistemologies for the twenty-first century, where "difference" is an asset and not a stigma.

Research on Racial Attitudes

As early as the first third of the twentieth century, research by Lasker (1929) and Minard (1931) revealed that children are aware of racial differences at primitive stages of their social development; contemporary research has made similar findings (Phinney & Rotheram, 1987; Ramsey, 1987). By the age of three, most young children have internalized attitudes toward racially diverse groups. In addition, these attitudes become more negative and crystallized if deliberate intervention is not carried out (Banks, 1994; Lynch, 1987). Therefore, the need to help students develop positive attitudes and beliefs about racially diverse groups should be a primary objective of classroom teachers.

The question of how children perceive racial differences was uncovered in the research conducted by the Horowitzes (1936) and the Clarks (1939). The Horowitzes were among the first researchers to reveal the preference that preschool age African American and white children had for white dolls. The Clarks corroborated the research findings of the Horowitzes, and argued that for African American children to prefer white dolls over black dolls revealed deep-seated self-rejection. Within the past three decades there have been strong critiques of this research. According to Banks (1995), several scholars suggested that the results of the early work of the Horowitzes and the Clarks may not have revealed self-rejection among African American children, but instead the inability of African American children to distinguish between personal and group identity (Banks, 1976; Spencer, 1987; Cross, 1991).

Margaret Spencer's research (1987) suggested that African American children can have a positive self-identity, yet still show white bias as in the doll studies. She contended that these occurrences require cognitive interpretations, but the responses of African American children could reflect their desires to select the appropriate or "right" responses. Spencer argues that the findings do not connote a failure on the part of African American students to correctly identify their racial affiliation. More importantly, she argues that there is a need to conduct additional studies that examine the racial attitudes and identities of African American students themselves.

Additional research in the area of racial attitudes of young children has examined the perceptual components of racial groups. Research by Katz (1973) found that young children can more easily differentiate the faces of in-group members than they can the faces of out-group members. Therefore, Katz hypothesized that if children could differentiate the faces of out-group members this would lead to a reduction of prejudice. Katz and Zalk (1978) conducted research to test the hypothesis, utilizing four types of intervention with white students: increased positive racial contact, vicarious contact, differentiation of minority-group faces, and reinforcement condition. They discovered that vicarious contact and perceptual differences were the most effective interventions in reducing prejudice. The findings of this research are invaluable for educators who are in search of proven activities and techniques to help young children develop positive racial attitudes and perceptions.

In like manner, the work of Gordon Allport (1954) has been instrumental in understanding the nature of prejudice, and more importantly, the conditions necessary to reduce it. Allport's theory of prejudice reduction through positive interracial interaction consists of five criteria: (1) the promotion of cooperation versus competition; (2) situations in which participants experience equal status; (3) environments in which participants have shared goals; (4) contexts in which participants are given opportunities for personalized interactions; and (5) occasions when interactions are sanctioned by authority. Allport's work is important because it takes into account contextual and power issues that often hinder the reduction of prejudice, and does not assume that the mere placement of racially diverse groups together will reduce prejudice.

Given today's race-obsessed societal context, African American males are cognizant of race in their most formative years of development. For many African American males, the ways in which they come to understand their racial identities are influenced by the evaluations of significant others (White & Parham, 1990). Therefore, educators who are concerned with incorporating prejudice reduction methods and building healthy racial identity development for African American males must incorporate empowering images of African American life, history, and culture in school content. Additionally, as students mature, unreserved dialogue about race and racism can help students understand the complexities of such topics. In summary, schools must promote multicultural education.

Multicultural Education as School Reform

Teachers and cultural workers for African American males have identified and created different strategies for teaching our sons about their cultural and ethnic heritage. I have spent countless hours trying to offset the negative portrayals many youth will undoubtedly encounter of the African American male image. I have spent time teaching my own sons the importance of respecting individuals from different ethnic, cultural, and social-class backgrounds. What must be avoided in this era of the "assassination of the Black male image" (Hutchinson, 1996) is reciprocity in distortion and negative portrayal. It is important that our sons understand not to subscribe to false and distorted characterizations of others' ethnic groups, just as others have perpetuated false portraitures of them.

As African American educators, cultural workers, and mothers, many of us have created culturally rich, racially affirming home and community environments to provide our sons with a healthy understanding of who they are, their purpose, and their potential in life. However, we must also concern ourselves with what our sons confront once they leave the safe havens of our homes and communities to enter a more harsh socializing institution—U.S. schools. As an educational researcher, I am concerned with identifying and describing schooling environments that provide African American students with an equitable opportunity for academic and social success. This work is done in an attempt to replicate practices that have created culturally conscious educational environments for African American males. My research has been undergirded by the assumption that those educational environments that enable the cultural values and practices which students bring from home to be significant variables in the teaching and learning process most often create opportunities for academic success. But as cultural workers we must continue to ask: Whose values and culture are schools promoting? Furthermore, are they congruent with the student population they are serving? And if not, what are the academic and social implications for African American students?

It is imperative that schools be recognized as cultural environments that consciously and unconsciously emit values and practices that are embedded in certain social and cultural norms. Nobles, as quoted in Wynn (1992), states:

> We should be very clear that the core curriculum itself is cultural; and that the teaching methodology that we utilize in teaching the core curriculum is also cultural; and that the site leadership style is cultural, and the guidance and counsel techniques are cultural, and that the [overall] school climate is cultural, and that ultimately the aim and purpose of education itself is cultural. (p. 2)

The cultural norms in most U.S. school climates are incongruent with the cultural capital that most African American students bring from home (Boykin, 1994; Ladson-Billings, 1994; Lee, Lomotey, & Shujaa, 1990). As a result, many African American students' opportunities for school success are severely compromised because of the cultural discontinuity they experience between home and school. Subsequently, students' attempts to navigate cultural characteristics and contextual realities between the two places can result in frustration, alienation, and ultimately academic failure (Allen & Boykin, 1992; Hale-Benson, 1986).

In response to the educational inequalities and academic underachievement suffered by many students of color in U.S. schools, a series of school reform efforts have emerged over the past two decades (Asante, 1991; Banks, 1993; Haynes & Comer, 1993). One of those efforts is multicultural education.

Multicultural education is an educational reform movement, and a process whose major goal is to change the structure and cultural ethos of educational institutions (Banks, 1993, 1995; Garcia, 1982; Gay, 1988, 1994; Grant, 1977; Nieto, 1992). Banks (1995) argues that a major goal of multicultural education is to reform schools and other educational institutions in a manner that provides educational equality to students from diverse racial, ethnic, and social-class groups. In an attempt to bring clarity to the paradigm, and detail the breadth of the movement, Banks outlined five dimensions of multicultural education: (1) content integration; (2) knowledge construction; (3) prejudice reduction; (4) equity pedagogy; and (5) an empowering school culture and social structure. What follows is a discussion of how two of these dimensions, prejudice reduction and equity pedagogy, can contribute to the creation of culturally conscious learning environments for African American males.

Prejudice Reduction

Prejudice reduction is an attempt to alter the attitudes and opinions of students about cultural and ethnic groups different from their own. According to Banks (1997), it includes "lessons and activities teachers use to help students develop positive attitudes toward different racial, ethnic, and cultural groups" (p.22). A major goal of the prejudice reduction dimension is to eradicate the negative stereotypes and myths that students may possess about different cultural groups. An effective method used to offset negative or false perceptions that students have of other cultural groups is to expose them at an early age to accurate and positive images of various cultural and ethnic groups (Agnes, 1974). In addition, it is crucial to help students understand the nature of prejudice, and the ways in which it influences the viewpoints of individuals in a detrimental manner that divides people of different cultural and ethnic groups. The prejudice reduction dimension has direct relevance in creating culturally conscious schooling environments for African American males. The creation of transformed educational environments can effectively take place once teachers and students from mainstream backgrounds construct informed and nonbiased perceptions of African American people and culture.

The research that has taken place within the prejudice reduction dimension is critical because it seeks to identify ways to change the negative attitudes and beliefs that students have toward differing racial groups. Many classroom teachers state that they do not address issues about race and racial differences with their students, because of their own ignorance about racial issues and the complexities of the subject (Lark, 1990; Cannella & Reiff, 1994). Many teachers embrace the "colorblind" approach, claiming not to see color. Yet this approach has the tendency to do more harm than good for non-mainstream students (Schofeld, 1986). At a time when the U.S. has become increasingly race-conscious, and when various school programs, practices, and policies are heavily influenced by race, it is important that explicit dialogue around race become commonplace in classrooms. A responsible multicultural curriculum will include well-planned and well-conceptualized implicit and explicit prejudice reduction strategies to address the issues surrounding race, racism, power, and discrimination, and their consequences.

Equity Pedagogy

A second dimension of multicultural education that can serve as a catalyst for the creation of culturally conscious education settings for African American males is the development of an equity pedagogy. Equity pedagogy entails teachers structuring their instructional practices in a manner that helps meet the academic needs of culturally diverse students. This process includes using communication patterns, cultural norms, and methods of teaching that are culturally compatible with the students' background. Banks (1995) states that equity pedagogy "exists when teachers modify their teaching in ways that will facilitate the academic achievement of students from diverse racial, cultural, gender, and social-class groups" (p. 22). Shulman (1987) states that pedagogical content knowledge must have the capacity to "transform the content knowledge . . . into forms that are pedagogically powerful and yet adaptive to the variations in ability and background presented by the students" (p. 15). Moreover, transformative and culturally inclusive pedagogy, according to Shulman, should include:

> [K]nowledge of the most useful forms of representation of those ideas, the most powerful analogies, illustrations, examples, explanations, and demonstrations—in a word, the ways of representing and formulating the subject that make it comprehensible to others. . . . Pedagogical content knowledge also includes an understanding of what makes the learning of specific topics easy or difficult: the conceptions and preconceptions that students of different ages and backgrounds bring with them to the learning of those most frequently taught topics and lessons (Shulman, 1986, pp. 9–10).

The practice of equity pedagogy recognizes the importance of the cognitive processes and learning styles of culturally diverse students, and it attempts to find teaching styles best suited for those processes. The equity pedagogy dimension of multicultural education is an important one, because it recognizes comprehensive methods of processing information. For many African American males, linking out-of-school experiences to class content can be a simple way of improving the schooling experience (Howard, 1998).

The research on inclusive pedagogy has made significant shifts over the past thirty years. Shortly after the *Brown v. Board of Education* ruling, educators sought to identify interventions that would help offset the poverty conditions which afflicted African American students. The consensus at the time focused on the poverty of culture paradigm, which assumed that African American and other children of color were culturally deprived because of their ethnic background and socioeconomic status (Bloom, Davis, & Hess 1965; Lewis, 1965). As a result, educators looked to incorporate programs and pedagogical practices that would offset the disadvantaged conditions that prevented the academic success of culturally diverse students. A major flaw in this approach is that it perceived the culture of non-mainstream students as being deficient of purposeful values and elements, rather than these elements simply being different from European American, middle-class values. Therefore, interventions that looked to improve the educational success of culturally diverse students viewed the cultural capital of these students as negative, and interventions sought to eradicate these cultural elements. Some would argue that many contemporary approaches have not changed this approach, and still view African American students in deficit terms. However, some of the recent research on equity pedagogy has made a shift away from the cultural deficit paradigm and has attempted to embrace the values and practices of culturally diverse students, in order to view them as different from whites (Boykin, 1994; Foster, 1994; Ladson-Billings, 1994; Lee, 1995).

Au and Jordan (1981) conducted research on Native Hawaiian children and found that teachers who incorporated aspects of the student's cultural backgrounds into reading instruction witnessed higher reading achievement. Students were allowed to use a familiar language interaction style called "talk-story." Culturally congruent teaching practices included features of the student's home culture, but they did not attempt to create environments identical to those at home. Kleinfeld (1975) found results similar to Au and Jordan's with Eskimo and Indian students. She stated that teachers who were familiar with the cultural norms and communication patterns of Eskimo students created climates of emotional warmth which helped to dissipate the anxiety students had toward school. Ladson-Billings (1995) has argued that successful teachers of African American students create learning environments and use pedagogical practices that enable students to be academically successful while maintaining their cultural integrity. Her work is critical, because it attempts to destroy the fallacy that African American students who excel academically have abandoned their cultural heritage and as a result "act White" (Ogbu & Fordham, 1986).

In parallel, Michelle Foster's research (1994) has outlined five key attributes of effective black teachers. While Foster's research has paid attention to black teachers and students, the attributes that she has identified could equally be applied to other cultural groups and retain its effectiveness. Foster states that culturally sensitive teachers (1) display cultural solidarity, which includes teachers having a strong sense of identity within the communities they teach; (2) link classroom content to students' experiences, which involves bringing community experiences into the classroom; (3) focus on the whole child, as teachers seek to foster not only the academic growth of students but their social and emotional development as well; (4) use familiar cultural patterns, which entails the recognition and validation of cultural norms and values; and (5) incorporate culturally compatible communication patterns.

An important element in the equity pedagogy paradigm is paying attention to the social cues which influence the learning process. Learning occurs within the context of social relationships; therefore teachers who understand social variables familiar to the student's cultural capital have a major advantage in engaging students in the learning process. Heath's ethnographic research (1983) on the communication patterns of students in a small community highlights the important role of understanding community context and norms as a prelude to school success. For many African American males, sports, rap, and hiphop culture in general serve as forums for athletic and artistic expression and creativity. These genres are attractive to many African American males because they do not stifle their core cultural qualities. The challenge for cultural workers, particularly in education, is to find ways to make schools a forum in which African American males can maintain their cultural identity and ingenuity in the pursuit of academic excellence.

An additional component that is related to the research on equity pedagogy is the research that has examined the learning styles and cognitive processes of culturally diverse students (Hale-Benson, 1982; Irvine & York, 1995; Shade, 1982, 1986, 1989). The research on cognitive processes helps to inform classroom teachers on how to construct teaching styles in ways which complement the manner in which children interpret and process new information. Shade (1989) and Hale-Benson (1986) have argued that African American students are at a disadvantage in most school settings because they prefer learning environments with multiple stimuli, that are people-centered, and that encourage kinesthetic and active instructional activities. The learning environments in most U.S. schools are not arranged in such a manner as to nurture these learning modalities, and this is one of the reasons for the disproportionate school failure of many African American students (Lee, Lomotey, & Shujaa, 1990). While the research on learning styles can be construed as essentializing ethnic groups, it has attempted to identify central tendencies observed in culturally diverse groups, and not to label all members of a particular ethnic group as certain types of learners. More importantly, this research suggests that teachers should utilize a multitude of pedagogical practices in their classroom settings, to grant all students an equal opportunity for academic success, as well as to promote metacognition.

Design Principles for Classroom Practice

In order to transform schools in a manner that meets the academic and social needs of African American males, a blueprint is needed for educators to understand appropriate curricular and pedagogical interventions that will offer new directions and positive outcomes. Prejudice reduction and equity pedagogy represent broad conceptual dimensions, offering potential for cultural workers who are concerned with improving the educational experience of African American students. However, specific design principles may be of greater value to cultural workers in the pursuit of day-to-day strategies that can enhance the teaching and learning process. Below, I have provided four design principles that are related to the prejudice reduction and equity pedagogy dimensions.

1. Ethnic Identity Development: One of the integral components of reducing prejudice is for individuals to have a healthy level of ethnic and racial identity. African American males need healthy constructions of their self-image as black males, in order to counterbalance the preponderance of negative portrayals. The internalization of a negative self-concept is a variable that can contribute to the academic underachievement of African American students (White & Parham, 1990). Thus, the development of a healthy self-concept for them has social and academic implications. The introduction of historical and cultural literature that provides positive accounts of African American people and culture is an important first step in developing well-rounded depictions of African American men.

2. Explicit dialogue about race/racism: An essential step toward reducing prejudice is providing a forum in which African American males can dialogue explicitly about issues related to race and racism. African American males are one of the largest targeted groups of racism in this country. Thus, a fundamental element of their identity revolves around race. Educational environments must be able to create avenues within the teaching and learning process that enable African American males to bring their cultural capital and lived experiences to the table, in ways which do not disguise the role that race plays for them on a day-to-day basis.

3. Culturally Consistent Communicative Competencies: African American discourse patterns have been characterized as nonlegitimate, substandard, and impoverished methods of communicating (Wofford, 1979). As a result, African American students who use such discourse patterns have been unfairly categorized by many teachers as cognitively deficient and culturally deprived (Jackson, 1981). Teachers need to be able to acknowledge the important role that communication plays in academic development (Gutierrez & Stone, 1997; Lee, 1995). Teachers can structure discourse patterns, conversation styles, phrases, person-to-person interactions, and vocabulary in ways consistent with the communication modes their students use at home. Culturally consistent communicative competencies can include (1) teachers recognizing the verbal propensities of many African American students; (2) making proverbs, analogies, and sayings an integral part of classroom discourse norms; (3) respecting, and not denigrating, the use of Black English Vernacular; (4) having an awareness and understanding of nonverbal communication skills; and (5) being comfortable with the wide range and unique characteristics of African American interaction styles.

4. Culturally Congruent Value Orientation: A culturally congruent value orientation allows teachers to make deliberate attempts to link their students' lives, values, and experiences outside the classroom with their experiences inside the classroom. A culturally congruent value orientation attempts to offset the hegemonic mainstream psyche that is prevalent in many classrooms (Boykin, 1994; Lee, Lomotey, & Shujaa, 1990). As a result, communicating, expressing, being, and succeeding are done in a manner that does not cause students to compromise their cultural competence. Embedded within these concepts are implicit and explicit messages and values taught to African American students by people concerned with helping African Americans in general. This principle is predicated on the notion that students' cultural capital should undergird teachers' instructional practices and the classroom ethos (Lee, 1995). Bourdieu (1977) refers to cultural capital as the set of values, customs, and knowledge that families transmit to their children in order to reproduce existing cultural and class membership. A culturally congruent value orientation means that teachers attempt to replicate various aspects of students' home lives in the classroom to create cultural continuity between home and school.

Conclusion

Multicultural education as a means of educational transformation goes beyond the idea of adding ethnic content to the curriculum. A reconceptualization of multicultural education is one that attempts to alter the racial attitudes that teachers bring to their classrooms. Racial and cultural attitudes devoid of mischaracterization offer African American males a significant opportunity for success-producing academic environments. Central to this idea of multicultural education is the construction of a school ethos that empowers African American students academically, socially, and psychologically. This idea seeks to establish a culture that deliberately promotes intergroup relations committed to preparing students to participate in the building of a pluralistic and interdependent society. The role that cultural workers play in the holistic development of African American males carries great importance. Not only must our efforts be spent creating quality interactions with our sons for their academic and social advancement, but equitable time must be spent transforming school settings to become surrogate cultural centers for them in our absence.

References

Agnes, M. (1974). Influences of reading on the racial attitudes of adolescent girls. *Catholic Educational Review, 45*, 415–20.

Allen, B. A., & Boykin, A. W. (1992). African American children and the educational process: Alleviating cultural discontinuity through prescriptive pedagogy. *School Psychology Review, 21*(4), 586–96.

Allport, G. W. (1954). *The nature of prejudice*. Cambridge, MA: Addison-Wesley.

Asante, M. K. (1991). The Afrocentric idea in education. *Journal of Negro Education, 60*(2), 170–80.

Au, K., & Jordan, C. (1981). Teaching reading to Hawaiian children: Finding a culturally appropriate solution. In H. Trueba, G. Gutherie, & K. Au (Eds.), *Culture and the bilingual classroom: Studies in classroom ethnography* (pp. 139–52). Rowley, MA: Newbury.

Banks, C. A. M., & Banks, J. A. (1995). Equity pedagogy: An essential component of multicultural education. *Theory into Practice, 34*(3), 152–58.

Banks, J. A. (1993). Multicultural education: Development, dimensions, and challenges. *Phi Delta Kappan*.

Banks, J. A. (1994). *Multiethnic education: Theory and practice* (3rd ed.). Boston: Allyn & Bacon.

Banks, J. A. (1995). Multicultural education: Historical development, dimensions, and practice. In J. A. Banks & C. A. M. Banks (Eds.), *Handbook of Research on multicultural education* (pp. 3–24). New York: Macmillan.

Banks, J. A. (1997). *Teaching strategies for ethnic studies* (6th ed.). Boston: Allyn & Bacon.

Banks, W. C. (1976). White preferences in blacks: A paradigm in search of a phenomenon. *Psychological Bulletin, 83*, 1170–86.

Bloom, B. S., Davis, A., & Hess, R. (1965). *Compensatory education for cultural deprivation*. New York: Holt.

Boykin, A. W. (1994). Harvesting talent and culture: African American children and educational reform. In R. Rossi (Ed.), *Schools and students at risk* (pp. 116–38).

Cannella, G. S. & Reiff, J. C. (1994). Preparing teachers for cultural diversity: Constructivist orientations. *Action in Teacher Education, 16*(3), 37–45.

Clark, K. B., & M. P. (1939). The development of consciousness of self and the emergence of racial identification in Negro preschool children. *Journal of Social Psychology, 10*, 591–99.

Comer, J. P. (1980). *School power*. New York: Free Press.

Cross, W. E. Jr. (1991). *Shades of Black: Diversity in African American identity*. Philadelphia: Temple University Press.

Foster, M. (1994). Effective Black teachers: A literature review. In E. R. Hollins, J. E. King, & W. C. Hayman (Eds.), *Teaching diverse populations: Formulating a knowledge base* (pp. 225–41). New York: State University of New York Press.

Freire, P. (1970). *Pedagogy of the oppressed*. New York: Continuum.

Garcia, R. L. (1982). *Teaching in a pluralistic society: Concepts, models, strategies*. New York: Harper & Row.

Gay, G. (1988). Designing relevant curricula for diverse learners. *Education and Urban Society, 20*, 327–40.

Gay, G. (1994). *At the essence of learning: Multicultural education*. West Lafayette, IN: Kappa Delta Pi.

Grant, C. A. (1973). Black studies materials do make a difference. *The Journal of Educational Research, 66*(9), 400–4.

Grant, C. A. (1977). *Multicultural education: Commitments, issues, and applications*. Washington, DC: Association for Supervision and Curriculum Development.

Gutierrez, K., & Stone, L. D. (1997). A cultural-historical view of learning and the learning disabilities: Participation in a community of learners. *Learning Disabilities Research & Practice, 12*(2), 123–31.

Hale-Benson, J. (1986). *Black children: Their roots, culture, and learning styles*. Baltimore, MD: The Johns Hopkins University Press.

Haynes, N., & Comer, J. (1993). The Yale school development program: Process, outcomes, and policy implications. *Urban Education, 28*(2), 166–99.

Heath, S. B. (1983). *Ways with words: Language, life and work in communities and classrooms*. New York: Cambridge University Press.

Horowitz, E. L. (1936). The development of attitude toward the Negro. In *Archives of Psychology* (No. 104). New York: Columbia University.

Howard, T. C. (1998). *Pedagogical practices and ideological constructions of effective teachers of African American students.* Unpublished dissertation, University of Washington, Seattle.

Hutchison, E. O. (1996). *Assassination of the black male image.* New York: Simon & Schuster.

Irvine, J. J., & York, D. E. (1995). Learning styles and culturally diverse students: A literature review. In J. A. Banks & C. A. M. Banks (Eds.), *The handbook of research on multicultural education* (pp. 484–97). New York: Macmillan.

Jackson, J. (1981). Some psychosocial factors affecting learning to read and reading for disadvantaged black children. *The Negro Educational Review, 32*(2), 18–26.

Katz, P. A. (1973). Perception of racial cues in preschool children: A new look. *Developmental Psychology, 8*, 295–99.

Katz, P. A., & Zalk, S. R. (1978). Modification of children's racial attitudes. *Developmental Psychology, 14*, 447–61.

Kleinfeld, J. (1975). Effective teachers of Eskimo and Indian students. *School Review, 83*, 301–44.

Ladson-Billings, G. (1994). *The dreamkeepers. Successful teachers of African American students.* San Francisco: Jossey-Bass.

Ladson-Billings, G. (1995). Toward a theory of culturally relevant pedagogy. *American Educational Research Journal, 32*, 465–91.

Larke, P. J. (1990). Cultural diversity awareness inventory: Assessing the sensitivity of preservice teachers. *Action in Teacher Education, 12*(3), 23–29.

Lasker, B. (1929). *Race attitudes in children.* New York: Holt, Rinehart & Winston.

Lee, C. D. (1995). Signifying as a scaffold for literary interpretation. *Journal of Black Psychology, 21*(4), 357–81.

Lee, C. D., Lomotey, K., & Shujaa, M. (1990). How shall we sing our sacred song in a strange land? *Journal of Education, 172*(2), 42–61.

Lewis, O. (1965). *La vida: A Puerto Rican family in the culture of poverty—San Juan and New York.* New York: Random House.

Lynch, J. (1987). *Prejudice reduction in the schools.* New York: Nichols.

Minard, R. D. (1931). *Race attitudes of Iowa children.* Iowa City: University of Iowa Press.

Nieto, S. (1992). *Affirming diversity: The sociopolitical context of multicultural education.* New York: Longman.

Ogbu, J., & Fordham, S. (1986). Black students' school success: Coping with the "burden of acting white." *Urban Review, 18*(3), 176–206.

Phinney, J. S., & Rotheram, M. J. (1987). *Children's ethnic socialization: Pluralism and development.* Beverly Hills, CA: Sage.

Ramirez, M, & Castenada, A. (1974). *Cultural democracy, bicognitive development, and education.* New York: Academic Press.

Ramsey, P. G. (1987). Young children's thinking about ethnic differences. In J. S. Phinney & M. J. Rotheram (Eds.), *Children's ethnic socialization: Pluralism and development* (pp. 56–72). Beverly Hills, CA: Sage.

Schofeld, J. W. (1986). Causes and consequences of the colorblind perspective. In J. F. Dovidio and S. L. Gaertner (Eds.), *Prejudice, discrimination and racism* (pp. 231–53). New York: Academic Press.

Shade, B. J. (1982). Afro-American cognitive: A variable in school success? *Review of Educational Research, 52*(2), 219–44.

Shade, B. J. (1986). Is there an Afro-American cognitive style? *The Journal of Black Psychology, 13,* 3–16.

Shade, B. J. (Ed.). (1989). *Culture, style and the educative process.* Springfield, IL: Charles C. Thomas.

Shulman, L. S. (1986). Those who understand: Knowledge growth in teaching. *Educational Researcher, 15*(2), 4–14.

Shulman, L. S. (1987). Knowledge and teaching: Foundations of the new reform. *Harvard Educational Review 57*(1), 1–22.

Spencer, M. B. (1987). Black children's ethnic identity formation: Risk and resilience of caste-like minorities. In J. S. Phinney & M. J. Rotherman (Eds.), *Children's ethnic socialization: Pluralism and development* (pp. 103–16). Beverly Hills, CA: Sage.

Swisher, K., & Deyhle, D. (1989). The styles of learning are different, but the teaching is just the same. *Journal of American Indian Education* [Special Issue], 1–13.

White, J. L., & Parham, T. A. (1990). *The psychology of blacks: An African American perspective*. Englewood Cliffs, NJ: Prentice Hall.

Wofford, J. (1979). Ebonics: A legitimate system of oral communication. *Journal of Black Studies, 9*(4), 367–82.

Wynn, M. (1992). Empowering African American males to succeed. A ten-step approach for parents and teachers. Pasadena, CA: Rising Sun Publishing.

Chapter Eleven

Cultural Guardianship: A Model for Supporting Gay~African American Boys/Men

Michael Mobley

Multiculturalism has been characterized as the "fourth force" in the field of counseling (Cheatham & Steward, 1990; Pedersen, 1990). It is believed that the first three theoretical forces, Psychoanalytic, Humanist, and Behaviorist, did not address the issue of culture in the counseling process. Multicultural counseling has been defined as "a situation in which two or more persons with different ways of perceiving their social environment are brought together in a helping relationship" (Pedersen, 1988; p. viii). Indeed, the infusion of culture into counseling parallels the growing multiracial and multiethnic population of the United States.

The cultural groups targeted for inclusion in the multicultural movement have been debated. The question arises: Does multiculturalism include only racial and ethnic groups, or are other distinct cultural groups such as women, gay men, lesbian women, and bisexual men and women to be included? Locke (1990) and Lee & Richardson (1991) strongly advocate a race/ethnic-oriented multiculturalism. These researchers call attention to the history of slavery in the United States and present forms of discrimination and prejudice toward racial and ethnic members of society as their rationale for exclusivity. However, Fukuyama (1990) and Pope (1995) promote an inclusive approach which acknowledges women, gay, lesbian, and bisexual individuals, persons with disabilities, and the elderly in their multicultural orientation. The inclusive approach recognizes the shared experience of oppression across various cultural groups (Freire, 1993). This author supports and promotes definitions of multiculturalism, that is, the general as well as culture-specific depending on situational context.

The diverse multicultural pluralism in society is evident on college and university campuses. Concerted efforts are directed toward integrating a multicultural perspective into programming efforts, personnel and staff representation, course content, and policies and procedures governing institutions of higher education. Indeed, educators are being advised, trained, and charged to be culturally appropriate in their service to all students in higher education. Cheatham (1991) notes that "There is no easy resolution of the complex task of how to ensure cultural pluralism on U.S. campuses. There is faith that the issue will yield to the concerted efforts of principled, committed educators—both those responsible for the curricula and those responsible for the co-curricula" (pp. 34–35).

It is commendable that diverse cultural groups are being acknowledged, and afforded rights and privileges of support and service based on their unique cultural heritage. However, a uniform cultural group-oriented focus has been adopted, such that racial and ethnic members are viewed in separation from women, gay, lesbian, and bisexual individuals, and/or individuals with disabilities. This collective, mass approach to identifying cultural groups denies and overshadows individuals who identify with more than one of the "selected," protected categories of culture. For example, a heterosexual male African American student with a disability may not experience affirmation of his gender, race/ethnicity, and physical abilities simultaneously. In fact, we often do not permit the close examination of race and sexual orientation. Race in America is a divisive fault line (West, 1994; Hacker, 1992). Sexual orientation, that is, gay, lesbian, and bisexual identities, is an equally divisive fault line. On the sociopolitical landscape, these two cultural markers, race and sexual orientation, are not often addressed simultaneously.

In this chapter my goal is to directly focus on race and sexual orientation. The unique cultural group I will address is Gay~African American Boys/Men (hereafter "G~AAB/M"). My intention is to give careful consideration to this culturally distinct population, G~AAB/M, because often the voices and experiences of this group are unheard. A review of the social science literature demonstrates that very few scholarly inquiries have sought to examine G~AAB/M as a distinct cultural group (Adams & Kimmel, 1997; Icard, 1986 and 1996; Johnson, 1981; Loiacano, 1993; Monterio & Fuqua, 1994; Peplau, Cochran, & Mays, 1997; Wall & Washington, 1991). The majority of studies tend to examine African American men and the issue of HIV/AIDS (Dowd, 1994; Peterson, 1997; Peterson, Folkman, & Bakeman, 1996; Roberts, 1995). Indeed, the existing research tends to collapse all racial/ethnic minorities within a gay, lesbian, and bisexual culture, opposed to maintaining individually distinct cultural groups of racial/ethnic gays, lesbians, or bisexuals (Greene, 1994 and 1997).

Consequently, this chapter will be devoted to G~AAB/M. The sociocultural and psychological influences on G~AAB/M will be examined, and implications for educating them in higher education will be discussed. The first objective of this chapter is to offer you an increased level of awareness and sensitivity as well as knowledge about G~AAB/M. The second objective is to have readers reflect on their own race and sexual orientation and their interactions with G~AAB/M in education, particularly in colleges and universities.

The symbol "~" has been used between the words "Gay" and "African American" to signify a critical self-identification process within this culturally distinct population. The "~" indicates that the primary and secondary facets of cultural identity among G~AAB/M may vary from individual to individual. Johnson (1981) interviewed two groups of G~AAB/M: both those who affirmed that their racial identity was more salient than their sexual orientation identity and those who affirmed the reverse. That is to suggest that "African American, gay males" more readily identified with African American culture, community and causes such as civil rights. Whereas "gay, African American males" more readily identified with the larger Euro-American gay culture, community, and causes such as gay rights. Thus, in this chapter the phrase "Gay~African American Boys/Men," or "G~AAB/M," attempts to alert the reader to the power of self-identification and subsequent social and political affiliations.

Cultural Identity Development Models: Race and Sexual Orientation

To fully understand the complexity of G~AAB/M, we must grasp the highly socially influenced processes of racial and sexual identity development. G~AAB/M are challenged to integrate both the racial and the sexual orientation components of their cultural identity. Indeed, current social science literature offers an extremely limited perspective on this developmental process among G~AAB/M (Barber & Mobley, 1999; Icard, 1996). It is my opinion that understanding the dual cultural identities of G~AAB/M is critical. As indicated earlier, the issues of race and sexual orientation are divisive fault lines in America. If an individual does not belong to the dominant group in either of these categories, race or sexual orientation, he may be subject to various forms of prejudice, harassment, discrimination, and/or violence (Loiacano, 1993). Consequently, for a G~AAB/M there is an increased likelihood of being the target of a hate crime. He is forced to watch "both of his backs."

There are several minority and racial identity development models that help us understand the process of embracing one's racial identity within a racist society (Atkinson, Morten, & Sue, 1998; Cross, 1995; Helms, 1990 and 1996). Helms' model delineates a nonlinear developmental process wherein an individual gains increased self-awareness and knowledge about his African American (black) identity in relation to the dominant racial group in society, whites. In her model she identifies cognitive, affective, and behavioral responses likely to be exhibited by African Americans (blacks) in relation to whites. Recently, Helms (1996) has referred to the notion of culturally characteristic response patterns as "ego statuses." That is, every individual represents a composite set of "ego statuses" across his or her racial cultural identity. Helms emphasizes that each of these ego statuses is related to a specific form of information-processing strategy, that is, the way "people encode, analyze, react to, and retrieve racial information" (p. 155). Furthermore, she notes that observable behaviors or "schemata" may be associated with each ego status. In the African American (black) identity model there are five unique ego statuses: Conformity, Dissonance, Immersion/Emersion, Internalization, and Integrative Awareness (Helms, 1996). The highly contextual process of racial identity development includes an initial period in which an African American male may not necessarily regard his race as being salient. He may view himself as being human, and similar to all others in his environment including whites. At some juncture, racial salience develops; a high value of being connected to other

African Americans, recognizing the realities of being "Black in America," dominates perspective taking; and a devaluing of whites and white culture characterizes the African American male's ego status. In the final ego status category, racial salience exists in connection with the acceptance of some white cultural group members and perspectives. The African American male in this ego status is able to recognize both the positive and the negative aspects of any individual. He attempts to evaluate every individual based upon his/her actions, regardless of racial background or other cultural facets of identity (i.e., gender, sexual orientation, or religious/spiritual affiliation).

In regard to sexual orientation identity development, several researchers have proposed models to explain this phenomenon (Cass, 1979; 1996; Coleman, 1982; McCarn & Fassinger, 1996; Troiden, 1989). One of the most widely referenced models is that of Vienne Cass. In Cass's model, two forces, significant others' expectations and societal norms, are embedded within a gay male's interpersonal congruency theory. Cass (1979) posits that stability and change in human behavior are dependent on the congruency or incongruency that exists within an individual's interpersonal environment.

Within this theory, the state of congruency represents an acceptable and comfortable way of being in the world. An individual experiences stability in his life during a state of congruency. Conversely, the state of incongruency represents an unacceptable and uncomfortable way of being in the world. An individual experiences instability in his life during a state of incongruency. The states of congruency and incongruency (Cass, 1979) are related to, and indicative of, the ways in which an individual experiences his gay identity. Cass contends that the state of incongruency serves as a catalyst to move an individual toward resolving experienced cognitive, affective, and/or behavioral dissonance related to his gay identity. Successful resolution of incongruency results in progression and growth, while unsuccessful resolution leads to potential identity foreclosure, that is, the individual's gay identity development process may be postponed.

In Cass's model, there are six stages an individual may experience in gaining self-understanding of his/her sexual orientation identity development: Identity Confusion, Identity Comparison, Identity Tolerance, Identity Acceptance, Identity Pride, and Identity Synthesis.

1. Identity Confusion: The individual begins to question his sexual orientation. However, he experiences confusion because this new perception of himself as gay is incongruent with his previous perception of himself as heterosexual (especially given the ongoing and enduring heterosexist and homophobic messages promoted in society).

2. Identity Comparison: At this time, a young man may begin to externally explore and compare himself with others to determine his sexual orientation. While in this stage, gay males tend to seek out gay reading material, identify with other gay males in their environment, and attempt to understand why they "feel different" from their peers.

3. Identity Tolerance: In this stage, a gay male establishes increased contact with the gay community. Yet he still presents himself as being heterosexual in non-gay environments. This form of identity management has been referred to as "passing" or in some cases, "being in the closet."

4. Identity Acceptance: Being more comfortable with his sexual orientation, the gay male begins to embrace this aspect of his personal, cultural identity. Often this is the stage when gay men begin to "come out" to significant others in their life, particularly family members and close heterosexual friends. They may have already "come out" to known and suspected gay and lesbian individuals in their social network.

5. Identity Pride: Gay men feel proud about their gay identity, and begin to seek activities and environments that will nurture and support their sexual orientation identity. The emotional joy about being gay sometimes coexists with intense anger toward heterosexuals who are not accepting of gay males.

6. Identity Synthesis: A gay man is willing to disclose the nature of his sexual orientation to anyone, and simultaneously to deal with the range of positive to negative reactions this may elicit from others. At this time, having a gay identity is perceived as being just one other aspect of his entire personal, cultural identity. The awareness and observation of heterosexism and homophobia still

makes him angry, but this feeling is not as intense as during the identity pride stage.

Cass's model may be characterized as being culturally biased. The sexual orientation identity development process she delineates speaks primarily to the experiences of white gay men and lesbian women. It does not specifically address the unique experiences of non-white gay men and lesbian women, in particular G~AAB/M. Consequently, I believe that we must be cautious in utilizing Cass's model in understanding the cultural development process of a gay identity among African American men (Barber & Mobley, 1999). Again, within a predominantly heterosexual white society, G~AAB/M have two unique challenges to surmount.

Acceptance and Affirmation

> And that is a real fear that I have. I fear losing sanity, and so maybe that is the reason why I scrutinize people with such care. Because I do depend upon others' perceptions of me for validation, and I have been hurt so much by that in the past. Because, I mean, living in an environment where there's been so many things that have told me I was freaky, I was crazy, I was stupid. And how much I had to fight against that, and struggle. I had just kind of forgotten how much I fought to remain sane. I lived in a world which wanted to tell me that I wasn't. And that was a real battle. (Larry, in Loiacano, 1989)

Gay~African American male students may seek to gain acceptance and affirmation among several campus community populations: the African American community, the gay, lesbian, bisexual, and transgendered (GLBT) community, and the GLBT community of color. The specific community a Gay~African American male student seeks to call home may be determined by his self-identification process and/or by the particular ego statuses associated with both his race and his sexual orientation. Recognizing that, for some G~AAB/M, race is the most salient aspect of their cultural identity, a G~AAB/M may seek solace within the larger African American community and forsake alliances with the GLBT community. On the other hand, men who identify their sexual orientation as being more salient may seek to interact with the gay community, whether it is predominantly white or not. Finally, there are boys/men who may recognize a strong need for the integration of both their sexual orientation and their racial identities; they may seek to affiliate with their brothers and sisters within the gay and the African American community.

Invisible and Visible Cultural Identities

As students within higher education, G~AAB/M may recognize that they possess cultural identities which are devalued by many students, staff, and faculty in the predominantly white academy. Indeed, many university and college campuses promote and reflect a strong hegemonic, white male, majority, heterosexual orientation in the life and heart of the institutions, both inside and outside the classroom. Thus, the level of acceptance, comfort, and sense of integration experienced by G~AAB/M will be affected by their visible cultural identity (race) as well as their invisible cultural identity (sexual orientation).

Note these student comments:

> My blackness is what you see first. I can cover up my being gay. (Anonymous, quoted in Johnson, 1981)
>
> Being Black and being homosexual, one forms a double consciousness of being oppressed. By forming a consciousness of being Black, I gradually came to form a consciousness of what it is to be gay and oppressed too. (Lionel Cuffie, founder of Rutgers Student Homophile League)
>
> I probably can avoid gay detection. It's obvious that I'm Black. Being Black is the bottom line. People know that about me from hearing me talk or seeing me. I'm Black even when I'm not sexual. (Anonymous, quoted in Johnson, 1981)

From students' testament, race is a primary social influence characteristic that directly impacts how African American males are experienced in higher education. Many stereotypes and myths exist about "black males," such that many non-blacks (and perhaps some blacks) may inappropriately and falsely attribute to and project collective behavioral and cultural response patterns onto an individual black male. He may not be afforded an opportunity to present his uniquely individual personality because he is typecast through his racial reference group. Unfortunately, many African American males in higher education, especially in the earlier ego statuses of racial identity, may feel pressure to defy the stereotypes and myths instead of simply being themselves. The ability to effectively manage and negotiate "race matters" (West, 1994) within the university and college environment is not an easy task for young African American men whether they are gay or heterosexual.

Nor is the ability to carefully and selectively share an invisible cultural identity (such as a gay sexual identity) to others (friends, faculty, or others) in higher education a simple task. Coming out is a particularly vulnerable move for a G~AAB/M for several reasons. First, he risks being rejected by the larger university community members, particularly in the African American community. Second, he may risk shattering the stereotype of hypermasculinity often associated with "black men." Consequently, his gender role identity will be questioned and potentially come under fire. Third, his internal and psychological ego strength will be challenged, as he manages and negotiates being perceived as a "gay man." Finally, again, depending on the individual's racial identity development, he may forfeit support from his racial reference group.

It is critical to note that this cultural/social influence process of acknowledging a unique racial and sexual orientation identity among men is not without its challenges within historically black colleges and universities (HBCUs). For an African American male, the collective identity of race shared with brothers and sisters in higher education may serve as a lifeline. Indeed, the reasons African American males decide to attend HBCUs may be related to their racial identity development process. Undoubtedly, a certain level of self-awareness and understanding about race and racial issues in society has been reached by many African American males attending HBCUs. However, these same men may have given very little thought or attention to their sexual orientation, particularly if they have characteristically assumed a heterosexual identity prior to college. The ability to manage and negotiate a gay identity within a HBCU may prove more challenging if a G~AAB/M assumes the stereotypical belief that members of the African American community are more homophobic than Euro-Americans (Boykin, 1996). Indeed, there exists a formidable task of establishing support and protection within HBCUs for G~AAB/M, given the few openly acknowledged and/or official HBCU gay, lesbian, and bisexual student groups and organizations. To date, there has been strong opposition to the establishment of such organizations on black college campuses. Thus, the tasks and challenges associated with creating a healthy supportive network and safe space on college campus (whether predominantly black or white) for G~AAB/M may appear insurmountable.

Cultural Guardianship: A Model for Supporting G~AAB/M in Higher Education

It is a challenge to nurture and sustain G~AAB/M in higher education. In general, African American males as individuals may be regarded as the least-valued and least likely to survive among racial/ethnic groups (Parham & McDavis, 1987). As educators, we have roles and responsibilities as cultural guardians to enhance and advance both the professional and the personal development of all our students (Mobley, 1999), including those G~AAB/M within our care. The degree to which we may effectively educate, nurture, and "guard" G~AAB/M in higher education rests upon our ability to critically examine aspects of our own cultural identities. An increased understanding of ourselves as cultural beings will increase our ability to recognize and distinguish intersections of commonalities as well as differences. This intersectionality hinges upon our ability to assess without bias or prejudice how we are similar to and/or different from the Gay~African American male students we are entrusted to enrich educationally. More elegantly stated:

> As with so many issues of race and sexual orientation, there is an inclination among many individuals to apply stereotypes to entire groups. Interestingly, where there is, as I shall call it, an *intersection of commonalities*, it usually focuses on gender, race, or sexual orientation. For most people, any *intersection of differences* also focuses on gender, race, or sexual orientation." (Mobley, 1998, p. 175)

I propose that, to be dutiful cultural guardians, we must carefully examine our own cultural identities of race and sexual orientation (inevitably, also gender, although this is not explored in this chapter). I argue that how we understand our own racial identity development (black/African American, white/Euro-American, Asian/Asian American, Chicano/Hispanic/Latino,

Native American), and the dominating ego status(es) perspective, affects how we respond to G~AAB/M. Nevertheless, how we understand our own sexual orientation identity development (heterosexual, bisexual, gay, or lesbian) and its related ego status(es) also impacts this significant interpersonal student-educator relationship.

The primary objective of the Cultural Guardianship Model in support of G~AAB/M is for educators to gain increased awareness, sensitivity, and knowledge with regard to their own racial/sexual orientation cultural heritage, as well as the racial/sexual orientation cultural heritage of their students. A second and equally important objective is for educators to increase their range of skills in interacting with G~AAB/M students. The Cultural Guardianship Model, defined in the context of race and sexual orientation, has three components: (1) learning about oneself; (2) learning about G~AAB/M; and (3) learning about how one relates and interacts with G~AAB/M (Bowman, 1996; Mobley, 1999). In the first component, the energy and attention is dedicated to the educator learning more about his or her own racial and sexual orientation identity. In the second component, time and focus are concentrated on educators learning about the cultural background, sociopolitical influences, and psychosocial factors affecting G~AAB/M. In the final component, an educator reflects on how she/he relates to G~AAB/M based upon her/his own racial/sexual orientation identity development.

Learning About Oneself: A Guided Activity on Racial and Sexual Orientation Awareness

The presentation of racial and sexual orientation identity development models assists educators in more fully understanding the dynamic functioning of G~AAB/M. However, it is also important that educators reflect on their own racial/ethnic and sexual orientation identity. Both of these cultural facets of your identity influence your worldview and therefore how you relate to G~AAB/M. I encourage educators to think about and respond to the following questions:

1. What is your racial/ethnic background? How have the cultural values, norms, and perspectives associated with your racial/ethnic family/community influenced your understanding of

G~AAB/M? Does your racial/ethnic cultural community hold positive or negative attitudes toward gay, lesbians, and bisexuals in general? Does your racial/ethnic community "see" G~AAB/M? Or are all gays, lesbians, and bisexuals assumed to be non-black? In genuinely reflecting on and responding to these questions, it is my hope that your self-assessment of your racial/ethnic identity may impact your understanding and interactions with G~AAB/M. All too often many individuals, as a result of our heterosexist/ homophobic and racist socialization process, are quite uncomfortable with and prejudicial toward gay men in general, and African American gay men in particular.

2. What is your sexual orientation status? How did you come to learn about your sexual orientation, especially if you identify as being heterosexual? What social influences and experiences helped you to discover your sexual orientation? Having a heterosexual identity, how did you learn about the values, norms, and customs associated with this sexual orientation status? Did your parents, teachers, relatives, and/or close neighborhood friends teach you?

3. For heterosexuals: How have you learned to respond to gays, particularly G~AAB/M? Have you ever experienced same-sex attractions? How would you feel if another man/woman of the same sex expressed intimate emotional feelings toward you? Are you comfortable responding to this advance? Do you feel that heterosexual orientation is the only viable sexual orientation identity? Such that being gay, lesbian, or bisexual does not matter? What have you learned about the way you should respond to gays?

4. For White gays, lesbians, and bisexuals: How do you understand and experience G~AAB/M? Do you perceive the unique commonalities as well as differences G~AAB/M may experience being a part of the larger "white gay community"? Are you conscious of how heterosexual privilege may be afforded to some African American boys/men who are intimately involved with other boys/men, because these boys/men are presumed to be "straight" due to their skin color or racial status? Do you recognize your own racist attitudes, behaviors, and feelings, developed as a result of our prejudicial socialization process? Many Gay~African American males have reported being denied

entrance to gay clubs and bars solely because of the color of their skin. Are you aware of this practice? Do you understand the effects of such practices on the life experiences of G~AAB/M? Finally, what specific actions have you undertaken to eliminate racism within the gay community, in society in general, and within yourself?

Learning about G~AAB/M: More Queries and Comments

As an educator, regardless of your discipline or field of study, how much have you learned about G~AAB/M during your formal educational journey? Do you recall studying or reading about the experiences of G~AAB/M? Do you recall socializing and interacting with G~AAB/M at some time during your formal educational journey? Or do you recall ridiculing or making disparaging remarks about boys/men whom you perceived to be "queers," "faggots," or "sissies"? Often, we know very little about the life experiences of G~AAB/M. The mainstream culture tends to suppress the existence of this unique cultural group. In addition, sometimes members of this group themselves tend to remain deeply embedded in the closet, thereby hiding from the general population, not to mention their own racial community group.

As an educator, I strongly encourage you to shatter the walls of ignorance and expand the boundaries of knowledge about G~AAB/M. In this chapter, several references have been cited that will assist you in learning more about G~AAB/M. As you seek to increase your understanding, it may be helpful to expose oneself to African American Gay themed literature, movies, and/or documentaries. Writers such as James Baldwin, E. Lynn Harris, Audre Lorde, Toni Morrison, Essex Hemphill, Marlon Riggs, Keith Boykin, B. Michael Hunter, Shawn Stewart Ruff, and others have articulated the joys and struggles of being "black and gay" in America. There are movies like *Tongues Untied* and *Looking for Langston* which depict graphic images of the cultural essence of living as a G~AAB/M. These various media provide ample opportunities for you as an educator to increase your cultural awareness, sensitivity, understanding, and knowledge about G~AAB/M. It is highly recommended that you immerse yourself in discovering their unique experiences. This is a journey that you need not travel alone; invite a colleague and/or friend to join you. This may broaden and further enrich your learning process.

Finally, the most powerful means of learning about G~AAB/M involves establishing communication and dialogue with G~AAB/M in your own community. Do you know African American men who are intimately involved with other men? Is there an open acknowledgment that a particular African American male is gay? Or do you and others simply presume that he is? Without violating personal liberties and privacy, there may be two or three men who are openly gay or truly known to be gay that you may be able to befriend. It is critically important that you disclose your genuine interest in learning more about G~AAB/M. As you begin to uncover and discover specific information about these men's experiences, remember not to stereotype but simply appreciate their unique representation of being gay. The Cultural Guardianship Model encourages educators to explore the commonalities and differences within this unique cultural group, and to acknowledge that not all G~AAB/M are the same.

Interactions and Relationships: Forming Alliances with G~AAB/M

As a direct consequence of learning about G~AAB/M through research, literature, films, documentaries, and interpersonal interactions, educators are more likely to develop the critical skills necessary for interacting with and relating to this group. An important function of effectively interacting with others is being able to listen with empathy. Empathic listening requires a deep level of understanding and sensitivity to the life experiences of another. As a result of increasing your understanding and knowledge about G~AAB/M, educators are primed to be supportive and understanding listeners.

In forming alliances with G~AAB/M you become an "Ally" who accepts and respects this G~AAB/M while being inclusive of his multiple cultural identities. As many of you may know, it is critical in racial/ethnic mentoring relationships between faculty and students for African American students feel supported in their identity as racial being. The experience on college and university campuses is mediate by African American students' skin color, especially on predominately White institutions but also

HBCUs as well. This is equally true for those African American male students who are gay. Their cultural affirmation on campus impinges on finding "safe spaces" wherein they may openly acknowledge this often invisible facet of cultural identity. Indeed, as an "Ally" you afford G~AAB/M a "safe space" with you in being open to provide advising, instruction, mentoring, and professional development.

In this capacity as an "Ally" you also benefit. Your ability to respond and relate to the needs of G~AAB/M students increases and expands as a result of each individual alliance you form. Your own racial and sexual orientation identity will be enhanced. The critical points of "commonalities" and "intersections" across race and sexual orientation manifest themselves in genuine ways that may challenge and influence your cultural worldview. Furthermore, you now have the ability to act as a resource or cultural broker for other faculty within your program/department. In demonstrating your support as a Cultural Guardian, you role-model for your colleagues and potentially inspire them to forge similar relationships with G~AAB/M.

Concluding Thoughts

Every cultural group has its own set of values, norms, jargon, behaviors, and attitudes that reflects their common experience. G~AAB/M are no different. Having increased your knowledge about G~AAB/M, you will have a new vocabulary and possibly a new cognitive capacity for engaging in dialogue and communication. You may now understand the social dilemmas experienced as a consequence of being gay. You may now understand the complex struggle of integrating an African American identity with a gay sexual orientation identity. You may now understand the burden and intense frustration experienced by G~AAB/M as a result of being the victims of racial discrimination from both the dominant, hegemonic, Euro-constructed society and the predominantly "white gay community." You may now understand the joy and happiness experienced in long-term same-sex relationships. You may now understand the intense pleasure of being an openly gay parent within one's community. Cultural Guardianship makes it possible for educators to "now understand."

Many G~AAB/M would appreciate the opportunity to interact with and relate to others who more fully understand and accept their unique multiple cultural identities. As an educator, you are in a position to demonstrate your support and your openness to furthering the educational journey of G~AAB/M. You are in a unique position to both affirm and accord educational privileges and personal pride by fostering healthy educator-student relationships with G~AAB/M. I hope that as a result of reading this chapter, you are willing to accept the challenge of being a cultural guardian for G~AAB/M within your institution. Are you willing to extend a hand in support of G~AAB/M? Are you willing to be a cultural guardian?

References

Adams, C. L., & Kimmel, D. C. (1997). Exploring the lives of older African American gay men. In B. Greene (Ed.), *Ethnic and cultural diversity among lesbians and gay men* (pp.132–51). Thousand Oaks: CA, SAGE.

Atkinson, D. R., Morten, G., & Sue, D. W. (1998). *Counseling American minorities: A cross-cultural perspective* (4th ed.). Dubuque, IA: Wm. C. Brown.

Barber, J., & Mobley, M. (1999). Counseling Gay Adolescents. In A. Horne & M. Kesilica (Eds.), *Handbook for counseling boys and adolescent males*. Newbury Park, CA: Sage.

Boykin, K. (1996). One more river to cross: *Black and gay in America*. New York: Doubleday.

Bowman, V. E. (1996). Counselor self-awareness and ethnic self-knowledge as a critical component of multicultural training. In J. L. DeLucia-Waack (Ed.), *Multicultural counseling competencies: Implications for training and practice*. Alexandria, VA: Association for Counselor Education and Supervision.

Cass, V. C. (1979). Homosexual identity formation: A theoretical model. *Journal of Homosexuality, 4*(3), 219–35.

Cass, V. (1996). Sexual orientation identity formation: A western phenomenon. In R. Cabaj & T. Stein (Eds.), *Textbook of homosexuality and mental health* (pp. 227–52). Washington, DC: American Psychiatric Press, Inc.

Cheatham, H. E. & Stewart, J. B. (1990). *Black families: Interdisciplinary perspectives*. New Brunswick, NJ: Transaction Publishers.

Cheatham, H. E. (1991). *Cultural pluralism on campus*. Alexandria, VA: American College Personnel Association.

Coleman, E. (1982). Developmental stages of the coming out process. *Journal of Homosexuality, 7*(2–3), 31–43.

Cross, W. (1995). The psychology of nigrescence: Revising the cross model. In J. G. Ponterotto, M. Casas, L. A. Suzuki, & C. M. Alexander (Eds.), *Handbook of multicultural counseling* (pp. 93–122). Thousand Oaks, CA: SAGE.

Dowd, S. A. (1994). African American gay men & HIV and AIDS: Therapeutic challenges. In S. A. Cadwell, R. A. Burnham, &

M. Forstein (Eds.), *Therapists on the front line: Psychotherapy with gay men in the age of AIDS* (pp. 317–37). Washington, DC: American Psychiatric Press, Inc.

Freire, P. (1993). *Pedagogy of the city*. New York: The Continuum Publishing Company.

Fukuyama, M. A. (1990). Taking a universal approach to multicultural counseling. *Counselor Education and Supervision, 30*(1), 6–17.

Greene, B. (1994). Ethnic-Minority lesbians and gay men: Mental health and treatment issues. *Journal of Consulting and Clinical Psychology, 62*(2), 243–51.

Greene, B. (1997). *Ethnic and cultural diversity among lesbians and gay men*. Thousand Oaks, CA: SAGE.

Hacker, A. (1992). *Two nations: Black and white, separate, hostile, unequal*. New York: Ballantine Books.

Helms, J. E. (1990). *Black and white racial identity: Theory, research, and practice*. New York: Greenwood Press.

Helms, J. E. (1996). Towards a methodology for measuring and assessing racial as distinguished from ethnic identity. In G. Sodowsky & J. Impara (Eds.), *Multicultural assessment in counseling and clinical psychology* (pp. 143–92).

Icard, L. D. (1986). Black gay men and conflicting social identities: Sexual orientation versus racial identity. *Journal of Social Work and Human Sexuality, 4*, 83–93.

Icard, L. D. (1996). Assessing the psychological well-being of African American Gays: A multidimensional perspective. In J. F. Longres (Ed.), *Men of Color: A context for service to homosexually active men* (pp. 25–50). Binghamton, NY: Harrington Park Press.

Johnson, J. M. (1981). *Influence of assimilation on the psychological adjustment of Black homosexual men* (Doctoral dissertation). Dissertation Abstracts International, 42, 4620B. (Order No. DA8201500).

Lee, C. C., & Richardson, B. L. (1991). Promise and pitfalls of multicultural counseling. In Lee & Richardson (Eds.), *Multicultural issues in counseling: New approaches to diversity* (pp. 3–9). Alexandria, VA: American Association for Counseling and Development.

Locke, D. C. (1990). *A not so provincial view of multicultural counseling. Counselor Education and Supervision, 30*(1), 18–25.

Loiacano, D. K. (1989). *Gay identity issues among Black Americans: Racism, homophobia, and the need for validation. Journal of Counseling and Development, 68,* 21–25.

Loiacano, D. K. (1993). Gay identity issues among black Americans. In L. Garnets & D. Kimmel (Eds.), *Psychological perspectives on lesbian and gay male experiences* (pp. 364–75). New York: Columbia University Press.

McCarn, S. R., & Fassinger R. E. (1996). Revisioning sexual minority identity formation: A new model of lesbian identity and its implications. *Counseling Psychologists, 24*(3), 508–34.

Mobley, M. (with Cheatham, H. E.). (1999). R. A. C. E. – Racial Affirmation and Counselor Educators. In M. Kesilica (Ed.), *Race in counselor education*. Alexandria, VA: American Association for Counseling and Development.

Mobley, M. (with Levey, M.). (1998). Lesbian, gay, and bisexual students of color. In Levey, Blanco, and Jones (Eds.), *How to succeed on a majority campus: A guide for minority students* (pp. 171–197). Belmont, CA: Wadsworth Publishing Company.

Monterio, K. P., & Fuqua, V. (1994). *African American gay youth: One form of manhood. The High School Journal, 77*(1–2), 20–36.

Parham, T. A., & McDavis, R. J. (1987). Black men, an endangered species: Who's really pulling the trigger? *Journal of Counseling and Development, 66,* 24–27.

Pedersen, P. B. (1990). The multicultural perspective as a fourth force in counseling. *Journal of Mental Health Counseling, 12(*1), 93–95.

Pedersen, P. B. (1988). *Handbook for developing multicultural awareness*. Alexandria, VA: American Association for Counseling and Development.

Peplau, L. A., Cochran, S. D., & Mays, V. M. (1997). A national study of the intimate relationships of African American lesbians and gay men: A look at commitment, satisfaction, sexual behavior, and HIV disease. In B. Greene (Ed.), *Ethnic and cultural diversity among lesbians and gay men* (pp.11–38). Thousand Oaks, CA: SAGE.

Peterson, J. L. (1997). AIDS-related risks and same-sex behaviors among African American men. M. P. Levine & P. M. Nardi (Eds.), *In changing times: Gay men and lesbians encounter*

HIV/AIDS (pp. 283–301). Chicago, IL: The University of Chicago Press.

Peterson J. L., Folkman, S., & Bakeman, R. (1996). Stress, coping, HIV status, psychological resources, and depressive mood in African American gay, bisexual, and heterosexual men. *American Journal of Community Psychology, 24*(4), 461–87.

Pope, M. (1995). The "salad bowl" is big enough for us all: An argument for the inclusion of lesbians and gay men in any definition of multiculturalism. *Journal of Counseling and Development, 73*(3), 301–4.

Roberts, T. L. (1995). African American gay males with HIV/AIDS: Building upon cultural capacities to survive. In G. A. Lloyd & M. Kuszelewicz (Eds.), *HIV disease: Lesbians, gays, and the social services*, (pp. 75–87). New York: Harrington Park Press.

Troiden, R. R. (1989). *The formation of homosexual identities. Journal of Homosexuality, 17*(1–2), 43–73.

Wall, V. A., & Washington, J. (1991). Understanding gay and lesbian students of color. In N. J. Evans and V. A. Wall (Eds.), *Beyond tolerance: Gays, lesbians, and bisexuals on campus* (pp. 67–78). Alexandria, VA: American College Personnel Association.

West, C. (1994). *Race matters*. New York: Vintage Books.

Chapter Twelve

When "At Promise" Black Males Meet the "At Risk" School System: Chaos!

Vernon C. Polite

Introduction

This chapter examines the social context of schooling of a cohort of 115 African American males who attended Metropolitan High School (MHS) between 1986 and 1989.[1] Drawing upon elements of chaos theory, a construct emerging from the field of quantum physics (Gleick, 1987; Prigogine & Stengers, 1984; Zukav, 1979), it explores the systematic methods of schooling avoidance behaviors invoked by these students. Two central theoretical assumptions associated with chaos theory are relevant to this exploration. The first assumption is that seemingly minor, remote, and isolated conditions or changes within or outside a system can have profound consequences upon it. The second is that a phenomenon is best understood through an examination of the interrelation of its various components rather than by a focus on one or more of its component parts (Griffiths, Hart, & Blair, 1991). By highlighting the ecology of resistance to schooling at one inner-city public high school, this chapter attempts to show how actions, policies, and procedures, viewed at the time as innocuous and insignificant, resulted in poor academic preparation and a generally chaotic school environment that adversely affected African American males. The relationships between the various central components responsible for the education of African American males at MHS thus emerge as critically important.

Chaos Theory and Education

Chaos theory gained prominence as quantum physicists failed to predict with accuracy the position and momentum of particles or the dramatic structural changes that occurred as molecular matter evolved from minuscule to massive proportions (Gleick, 1987). During the past two decades, many researchers in disciplines other than Physics, particularly the social sciences, have focused on the applicability to their fields of study of the theoretical assumptions and concepts associated with chaos theory. Edward Lorenz, a meteorologist at the Massachusetts Institute of Technology, endeavored to predict changes in the atmosphere, utilizing a computer program that simulated a weather system (Gleick, 1987). Based on these findings, Lorenz proclaimed the existence of a "butterfly effect," whereby the minutest atmospheric event, the fluttering of a butterfly's wings, for example, could result in drastic and even catastrophic weather events hemispheres away (Gleick, 1987). Freedman (1992) argues that the essence of business management today is making sense out of chaotic and/or potentially chaotic organizations. According to Hayles (1990), researchers who examine chaos theory argue that it is best understood in terms of the nonlinear relationship between order and disorder.

Urban educationalists have clearly noted that schools and school systems that serve large percentages of African American males are often beleaguered by widespread chaos and academic underachievement (Davis & Jordan, 1994; Fine, 1991; Garibaldi, 1992; Kozol, 1991; Leake & Leake, 1992; Polite, 1993a, 1993b). That many urban school districts serving African American students are unprepared to address the widespread incidence of school failure among African American males is also evident. However, most theories of school failure address aspects of the problem but not the system as a whole. The use of chaos theory as a framework for explaining the effects of the U.S. educational system on African American males thus seems promising. Chaos theory seems particularly helpful in that it provides a holistic framework for explaining the impact of pervasive and possibly harmful patterns of institutional, group, and individual behaviors embedded within disordered school systems. This holistic approach would necessitate, as Griffiths et al. (1991) argue, that "all events deserve attention and monitoring" (p. 440). As they further contend, "If we do not think holistically, we may not account for relationships among elements. In fact, we may ignore some elements because they are too small" (p. 440).

Blair (1993) has applied the six theoretical concepts associated with chaos theory to educational systems. Inferring a *butterfly effect* with regard to the academic underachievement of

African American males, for example, Blair's findings imply that widespread disruption in schools serving large numbers of these males can be linked to a seemingly insignificant event: namely, the failure to properly guide individual potentially able African American males into higher level Mathematics and Science courses during their early years of schooling. A second aspect of chaos theory, *the onset of turbulence,* is closely linked to the butterfly effect and is often difficult to discern. In systems that minimize the importance of and fail to address the microevents that coalesce to yield a butterfly effect, this turbulence generally manifests itself as unanticipated disruptions in day-to-day school functioning, such as violence on school campuses or severe financial crises within districts. This turbulence is followed by *dissipative structures* and *random shocks,* two constructs that can be specifically related to the nonlinear nature of chaos-ridden schools and school districts. Corresponding activities in the school system context are the repeated minor or major disruptive events, policies, and social interactions, both internal and external to the system, that wreak havoc in the system's ability to function smoothly and effectively. These disruptions are most often unpredictable and devastating, and they generally preclude the possibility of the district regaining its original state.

Blair next extrapolates the concept of *strange attractors* from chaos theory, to refer to the central components of a system that seem to be the focal points from which disastrous events evolve. For example, a nonresponsive school board could serve as such a component, in that it directly or indirectly reshapes the school system by its policies and actions. Blair further suggests that *recursive symmetries* are created between the various levels and components interacting in a chaotic system. In other words, the culture of troubled school districts, such as that of the Metropolitan City schools, evolves from a host of explicit and implicit curriculum designs, policies, and rules that repeat and reinforce patterns of anti-intellectual and anti-schooling behaviors. Lastly, Blair relates the chaos theory concept of *nonlinear feedback mechanisms* to educational dilemmas. She notes that normal feedback mechanisms generally allow a system to gain accurate information regarding its output, which can be used to alter practices that work to the system's detriment and to improve operations. However, in chaotic systems, Blair maintains, feedback mechanisms do not follow the normal pattern. Instead, the most negative information about a system is continually recycled back into it and used, not to help improve circumstances within it, but to maintain chaotic functioning. For example, a local media story about a group of African American males arrested for trafficking in a large quantity of drugs five years after leaving MHS noted that the young men's criminal activities began when they were in their second year of high school. Such information, because it links the school to criminal activity, suggests a causal relationship that negatively influences public perceptions of the educational process at MHS, and impedes efforts to improve conditions at the school.

This examination of the quality of education available to African American males at MHS begins with a consideration of the significant changes that occurred at the school between 1970 and 1990. It continues with an assessment of how those changes altered the educational opportunities for African American students, males in particular. Although the design of the original study (Polite, 1991) and follow-up analyses (Polite, 1993a, 1993b) did not draw upon the tenets of chaos theory, this secondary analysis clearly demonstrates its usefulness as a theoretical construct that appears helpful for educators who seek explanations for the conditions of schooling facing most African Americans and other disadvantaged groups in troubled schools.

The Case of School Avoidance at MHS

The Setting

The Metropolitan Public School District is located in the predominantly African American midwestern suburban town of Metropolitan City, one of many middle-income communities in the United States that is contiguous to a core city or situated within the first or second geographical ring surrounding a core city (Culver, 1982; Farley, 1983; Grier & Grier, 1983; Polite, 1993a, 1993b; Stahura, 1983). Metropolitan City is approximately three square miles in size and is located adjacent to one of the nation's major urban industrial centers. Its core city, not unlike other older and primarily African American cities across the country (Massey

& Denton, 1988), is encircled by scores of incorporated municipalities.

MHS was built with all the amenities of an upper socioeconomic level community high school of the late 1950s. Complete with a radio station, planetarium, television station, theater, and deep-diving and Olympic-sized swimming pools, the school's programs were fashioned to serve a "known" white student population. Indeed, the administrators who designed MHS actually designed it with their own children in mind, as many of their sons and daughters attended the school and its feeder schools.

In the early 1970s, among the more than 90 percent white students and teachers at MHS, the majority was Jewish. Subsequent to the migration of African Americans out of the core city into the surrounding suburbs, about one hundred of MHS's students, or slightly less than 9 percent of the total student body, were African American. These students did not actually reside within the Metropolitan City limits, but lived in a lower socioeconomic level township that was included in the school's attendance area. Because the township was approximately two miles away, they were most often bussed to MHS. As early as the 1950s, a strong yet often turbulent and perplexed relationship had been established between African Americans and Jews in communities like those surrounding MHS. The African Americans who settled in many eastern and midwestern urban cities followed the migration patterns of Jews, for the simple reason that Jews commonly rented and sold property to African Americans in areas where other whites would not (Stevenson, 1988). African Americans began moving directly into predominantly Jewish Metropolitan City during the mid-1970s. Consequently, while the Metropolitan City school district gained an average of ninety African American students each year, it lost approximately the same number of white students each year between 1970 and 1990.[2]

Although small in number in 1970, MHS's African American students early expressed their anger over discrimination and alienation at the school. They staged a walkout and demanded social and curricular changes acknowledging African American history and culture. Specifically, they demanded African American representation on all student organizations, a series of courses in African American studies, Black History Month activities, and the hiring of African American teachers. The students were granted their demands by the school's administration. In return for these concessions, however, they were required to sign an agreement with the principal "to conduct themselves in an exemplary manner and to abide by all the rules, regulations, and policies of the school." In his remarks to the student body at an assembly held to discuss the walkout and the agreements, the principal concluded with the following statement:

> I would also say that we have a great school that turns out great scholars and students who achieve and succeed in the colleges and universities and in the vocations of their choices to a greater degree than other schools. This is a tribute to a fine student body and to one of the finest staffs of teachers I have ever worked with.

The student walkout was followed by riots involving racial violence in both 1970 and 1974. Several white students were assaulted during these incidents. The riots resulted in the local school board holding several highly emotional and well-publicized disciplinary hearings. The state board of education sent representatives to monitor these hearings and ensure that the decisions reached were unbiased. Several African American males were expelled, and many others were placed on long-term suspension as a result of the hearings.

In 1970, MHS was reputed to be one of the best secondary schools in the state. However, within a relatively short period of time, twenty years, the school changed drastically in terms of its students' socioeconomic status, achievement orientation, and attitudes toward schooling. The most dramatic change, however, was in the racial makeup of the school. By the close of the 1980s, the MHS student population was predominantly African American. It was also ranked as one of the lowest-achieving schools in the state. While in 1970 the school was seen as a haven of highly personalized classroom, extracurricular, and co-curricular interactions between teachers and students, by 1980 it was controlled by layers of rules and structures designed to control student behavior, primarily that of African American males.

The Sample

The findings discussed in this chapter were culled from longitudinal research centered on a cohort of 115 African American males who were members of the 1989 MHS graduating class (Polite, 1991). The progress of these students, and of the school system as a whole, was tracked over a three-year period from January 1987 (the middle of the students' second year of high school) through December 1989 (following their expected graduation date of June 1989). A follow-up study to examine the school-to-work transition of these males was conducted during Summer 1992, when the cohort had reached an average age of twenty-one years (Polite, 1993a, 1993b).[3]

The history of African American males at MHS has been marred by social issues of alienation, political impotence, and student resistance to schooling (Polite, 1993a, 1993b). Though this group of students made up only 39 percent of the 1,000–plus enrollment at the school in late 1986, they were grossly overrepresented with respect to the school's disciplinary processes. For example, African American male MHS students made up 100 percent of those charged with on-site weapons violations and assaults on teachers, 95 percent of those charged with drug-related violations, 66 percent of students punished for fighting on campus, and 67 percent of students suspended for disorderly conduct in class. Among the 115 African American males participating in the present study, only 60 (52 percent) actually graduated from MHS; one-quarter (25 percent) were dropped from the school's roster for nonattendance, and only 4 out of 115 (3 percent) scored high enough on the American College Test (ACT) college entrance exams to gain acceptance at a four-year college. By the late 1980s, African American males in the suburban, middle-class MHS school community, like their counterparts in impoverished inner-city school districts, were the least likely to complete school, enroll in college, or secure adequate employment.

The Study

My research made full use of established qualitative research strategies such as those described by Bogdan and Biklen (1992). Included among these strategies were six hundred hours of on-site observation. Additionally, as an African American high school administrator, I was required to attend and frequently did attend African American–sponsored cultural and social activities in the school community. I was a participant-observer in that I was both a researcher and an administrative employee of the school district. This difficult dual role offered one clear advantage: access to the whole system, its policies, and procedures—a central assumption associated with chaos theory. Another strategic aspect of my study involved a total of 242 semistructured interviews conducted with 65 African American males in the class of 1989 (138 interviews), 35 MHS teachers and staff (55 interviews), and 35 parents of students in the cohort (49 interviews). Beyond that, I analyzed official and unofficial documents such as students' transcripts; class rosters; report cards; attendance, suspension, and expulsion reports; and related school board documents.

Avoidance in Black and White

The data gleaned from my observations, interviews, and the above-listed sources reveal that, with the exception of the minimum graduation requirements, African American males at MHS generally had total control over course selection in their academic programs. Unfortunately, however, not only did they have total control, they most often made choices that neither prepared them for college nor for work.

Not unlike the students examined in Powell, Farrar, and Cohen's *The Shopping Mall High School* (1985), the African American males at MHS understood the graduation requirements, yet they built their high school program around a melange of meaningless electives. The comments of one of the study respondents, Shahid, were typical regarding the course selection process:

Polite: How did you select your courses in high school?

Shahid: Just basically by the requirements that they [school officials] had and the electives. Whatever was the easiest, where I didn't have to go through so much trouble, that's the electives that I picked.

Polite: Do you think a lot of students did that?

Shahid: Of course. We all did.

Polite: So they avoided the harder sciences and Math courses?

Shahid: Yeah.

Polite: Do you regret that now [three years following high school]?

Shahid: Pretty much. Once I went to community college, my Algebra wasn't good, my Math skills weren't good, my English skills were okay. As far as Science and History, I hardly knew anything.

Polite: What were some of the courses you took [in high school] that were just a waste of your time?

Shahid: They were basically Home Economics, a little of Child Development, gym. The swimming requirement, that was fine. I think I took gym almost every year. Nobody told me, "Why don't you take this or that?" So, I took that.

Polite: Generally speaking, how involved were your parents in the school?

Shahid: They really couldn't get involved too much in the beginning because they both worked, plus I have other brothers and sisters. So, me and my sisters had to take responsibility for them [younger siblings], too. (Polite, interview)

At first glance, the course selection process described above seems straightforward: African American males simply by-passed the more challenging courses available at MHS. However, upon closer scrutiny, the process is actually quite complicated, in that it involved much more than this, but also spoke to the role and function of school personnel and parents as accomplices in the miseducation of these African American males. Thus, the parents could best be described as self-effacing or passive participants. The following comments from Mrs. Taylor were typical of the African American parents whom I interviewed:

Taylor: There's so many things being said about MHS and those teachers and counselors that I just don't know. A lot of people are thinking of pulling their kids out of there, from what I heard. You know, because they [other parents] said the kids are not learning anything [at MHS]. I don't know, I have no proof. I'm just going by what other parents are saying, and it's not good talk. *And that bothers me* [italics added].

Polite: Tell me what happens when you visit the school to speak with the counselors, principal, or the teachers.

Taylor: Mr. Polite, I don't know what to ask those teachers up at that school.

Polite: Just how involved are you in your son's education?

Taylor: Look, Mr. Polite, my husband and I moved out here when the boys were in elementary school because we thought that the school system was better than in the city. But sometimes, I think that we made a big mistake. My sons are in the tenth and eleventh grades at MHS and I feel that this is my greatest challenge. Most of [their] teachers seem to have concluded that the majority of the black boys come from one mold: beyond help. There are very few teachers [at MHS] who treat the black boys as individuals and try to work with them accordingly. As parents, we can't know everything that's going on up at that school, especially now with all those courses the kids take. I have a high school education and a pretty good job, but I still don't understand what they are preparing my son to do in life. I thought that the counselors were supposed to help the kids. *That's their job* [italics added]. (Polite, interview)

The parents of MHS's African American male students were clearly aware that there were problems at the school, yet they refrained from direct involvement, opting instead to blame the school for their sons' academic failures. Most of these adults earnestly believed that the school was responsible for ensuring that their sons received a quality education. As a result, few attended school activities, and their lack of involvement led the school's teachers and administrators to adopt a deficit view of African American parents. Mrs. Smith was one of the more active parents at MHS. Her comments on parental involvement were particularly telling:

Polite: Mrs. Smith, I am interested in knowing more about parental involvement at MHS. Could you talk about parental involvement?

Smith: We didn't have that. I don't know how it is now, but no, we did not have that. Conferences, I felt, were pretty good, mainly because the parents *had to go there to get the report cards* [italics added]. But then, on the other hand, if they didn't go, I think it was mailed out or they could get it later on. But now as far as the PTA [parent-teacher association], I tried being active with the PTA as well as with the booster clubs. And I ended up spending really more time with the booster club. And it was just a case where even the parents who had kids who were playing basketball or football and whatever, they did not come to the games, nor did they come to the special recognition events where the guys and young

> ladies received their letters, or trophies, or whatever. They [parents] were not there. So I feel many times that the support was not there. Now, it could have been that they were working, or whatever reason, but the support was definitely not there. My youngest boy now attends a private school and it is required that parents participate, so that's where I spend my time now. (Interview)

Peer pressure was evidently a contributing factor that discouraged the more able African American males at MHS from engaging in academic pursuits. Many of my student respondents reported that they chose nonacademic courses to allow them more time to spend cutting classes with their friends. The father of one of the respondents offered what was perhaps the most candid explanation of the adverse effects of peer pressure on black male academic achievement:

> I used to tell my wife about the peer pressure all the time. [Our son's] friends became more important than family. It's something that you can't put your hands on really, but it was there. The love for his friends superseded everything. All these guys really loved each other like brothers. *School was a game* [italics added]. They played a game and they lost. I don't know whether Mike Williams's parents are on your list, but Mike was a strong negative influence on my son and other boys in the neighborhood. But in my son's case, he had everything that you could visibly see. I took him to basketball, football, any type of practice he wanted to go to. He ate well. He dressed well. And up until seventh or eighth grade, he was motivated as far as going to school because he enjoyed it. He got to high school, and there were a lot of things going on that I wasn't aware of. I was taking [some college] classes myself and my attention was diverted to that. I'd take him to school, and evidently he wasn't staying in school. I'd drop him off at school, and pick him up from school, and meanwhile, he wasn't in school. (Interview)

For many of MHS's African American males, negative peer pressure included association with the school's drug subculture. By 1992, three years after their 1989 graduation from high school, 8 of the 115-member MHS cohort were arrested for trafficking large quantities of drugs. I visited three of the eight incarcerated students in prison during the summer of 1992. The three confided to me that their drug dealings began during their second year of high school. They also reflected that their high school careers were negatively affected by their drug activities.

An obvious change has occurred in the texture of the relationships between MHS's teachers and students since the 1970s. Whereas teacher-student relations at MHS prior to the 1970s were based on collegial, highly personal interactions, those of the late 1980s were, in the opinion of the typical African American male respondent in my study, impersonal and highly specialized. As the MHS school population gradually changed, and as the school experienced major changes in its academic output, the roster of teachers and administrators remained largely unchanged: mostly white and Jewish. There were five African American and seventy white teachers employed at the school in the mid-1980s. Nearly half of the teachers were nearing retirement. Of the fourteen new teachers who were hired between 1986 and 1988, only I was an African American. The average teacher had taught at the school since the early 1970s (which, at the time of this study, amounted to a minimum of sixteen years, experience) and maintained strong interpersonal relationships with his or her coworkers. In fact, the majority of the teachers had known each other since their high school years in the core city. Nearly 70 percent were long-time residents of Metropolitan City; thus, the students who attended school were most often their own sons, daughters, and neighbors. They attended the same temples and churches as their students and their students' families, and interacted regularly with them in religious and social activities outside of school.

A typical expression of the difference in teachers' relationships with their students between the earlier years and the mid-1980s was offered by one white teacher, Mrs. Shapiro, who had worked in the Metropolitan City school district for more than twenty-five years:

> First of all, it was the population, and it was mainly a white population. And the kids were more motivated. And slowly the population *changed* [italics added], and things just sort of evolved from there. Well, when I hear a lot of people, unfortunately, they compare how it was then and how the kids are now. And it really is too bad because I do see a difference in test scores. And we still have some real terrific kids, but we don't have as many. But I see teachers get upset, really get upset. And I think this is what they want [pause] they want to retire because it isn't like it used to be. (Interview)

My interviews with longstanding MHS school personnel revealed the existence of an implicit "hands off" philosophy of schooling among these teachers and counselors, who maintained that parents and students had the sole authority to make choices regarding course selection. This philosophy was reinforced over time, as school personnel became increasingly fearful of inappropriately tracking the mounting numbers of African American students entering the school. As parental involvement in MHS activities declined, the veteran MHS teachers commonly blamed the new students' parents and home value systems for the lack of academic engagement on the part of African American males. This view was shared by the school's few African American teachers. For example, Mrs. Washington, an African American who had taught at the school for more than ten years, offered the following comments:

> There is no sense of direction. The kids [in the earlier years] seemed to care more about grades, about learning, about achievement, about college, about their future. Our students now seem to be lost. . . . I don't think that there is anything going on at home that makes the connection between study habits and the value of an education and value of furthering one's education by going to college. I don't think there is much of a concern or a caring situation at home for many of them. (Interview)

Above all other factors which surfaced throughout this study, none was more pervasive than the issue of teachers as caring individuals. Though the change in the general makeup of the student body over twenty years was most blatantly reflected in the quality of instruction, the African American males were most concerned with the fact that more often than not teachers simply did not demonstrate caring. According to one student respondent named Rakeem:

> A few of the teachers cared, but most didn't. For example, Mr. Smith and teachers like that didn't care what you do. You sit in class and do your work, you passed. He really didn't put any effort towards it. He will say, "come back later on," and he won't be there or they [teachers] would pass you [give the student a passing grade] and you know that you weren't suppose to pass or they just give you somethin' easy to do that you already would know. (Interview)

The message, explicit or implicit, conveyed to these students was "whether you perform or you don't, I don't care." As one African American teacher at MHS noted, "The feeling of disinterest seems to increase with each passing year."

Efforts to encourage academic excellence for African American males at MHS were nonexistent. Jermaine was one of the few academically and athletically outstanding students in the cohort. Fortunately, he graduated with honors and went on to attend a historically black college to study business. His reflection on his relationship with his high school Chemistry teacher was particularly telling:

> I may have liked Chemistry had I liked the teacher, but I didn't really care for the teacher and I already didn't like Science, and he just made it two negatives. The first card marking I got an "A" in Chemistry. He and I were discussing the second card marking and whether I would continue with part two of the Chemistry course. I made the mistake of telling the teacher that I didn't plan on taking Chemistry. He didn't try to help me see the importance of the class. He just gave me a "B" for the second card marking. (Interview)

Teachers, counselors, and other staff repeatedly confirmed African American male students' perceptions of being "pushed out" of school. One counselor offered her thoughts on why so many of the African American males were seen wandering about the school during the school day, apparently uninvolved in the learning process. Her comments are also related to the issue of caring:

> Counselor: I think that a lot of teachers don't get into their teaching and they're always looking for ways to get rid of some of these students. It's a terrible thing to say, but I feel that they are always trying to get rid of them.
>
> Polite: Is it that they can't handle them or they don't like them or they have problems with them or themselves or . . . ?
>
> Counselor: *They . . . just . . . don't . . . care. . . . They just don't . . . care* [italics added]. It's like those teachers who come in every day and have a book assignment, and as long as they [students] sit and be quiet, they could be doing anything. There is not a lot of interaction between the teachers and students here anymore. (Interview)

Not all, but far too many teachers demonstrated little or no care for the African American males at MHS. A few teachers, particularly some in the school's business department, informed me that they experienced very different, positive relationships with their African American male students. However, increased social distancing between the teachers and students at MHS was an identifiable factor associated with the patterns of schooling avoidance and the poor overall educational outcomes for the school's African American males. The majority of these students reacted by ceasing to care about school or school personnel, becoming disruptive, and putting forth very little energy in the area of academics. Their reactions contributed to making the school climate a chaotic one. Physical fights and class disruptions were commonplace. More than 1,100 three-day suspensions were meted out per year, mostly to African American male students. A steady increase in school-site violence, most of it involving African American males, was noted. More and more, teachers were threatened and assaulted.

It is possible to consider the education of African American males at MHS as a complex avoidance process involving parents, teachers, administrators, and the students themselves. The table below gives the number of courses in Mathematics and Science completed by African American males at MHS:

Courses Completed in Traditional Mathematics and Sciences by African American Male Students in MHS's Class of 1989 (N= 107)*

Academic Courses	*Number Completed*	*Percent Completed*
Algebra	36	34%
Algebra 2	31	29%
Geometry 1	21	20%
Geometry 2	14	13%
Chemistry 1	10	9%
Chemistry 2	7	7%
Physics 1	6	6%
Physics 2	4	4%

* *The original number of 115 was reduced by 8 to reflect those students who transferred to other schools due to a change in residence.*

Although the school offered the same higher level Mathematics and Science courses in the 1980s that were available in the early 1970s, few African American males enrolled in them. Corresponding shifts away from the higher level courses in English, Social Studies, and foreign languages are evident as well.

Although the student body included less than 9 percent white students, enrollment in the upper-level courses was nearly 100 percent white. A close examination of students' records revealed that less than 15 percent of the African American males selected higher-level courses in Mathematics, Science, and Social Studies. The vast majority, 85 percent, selected only those courses required to graduate. For example, the school required two full years of Mathematics as a prerequisite for graduation. Consequently, the overwhelming majority of African American males at MHS commonly enrolled in one year of basic Mathematics and one year of pre-Algebra, thereby minimally satisfying this requirement. Considering that upper-level Mathematics and Science courses are generally considered "gatekeeper" courses for college entrance, and tend to drive a school's curriculum, the avoidance of these courses by a large segment of the student population is significant. More significant still is the finding that nearly half the African American males at MHS between 1986 and 1989 dropped out of school and did not receive a diploma.

Rethinking the Chaos of Schooling

Although the school avoidance framework solidly explains much of what happened and is happening to African American males at MHS, additional research could serve to confirm these findings. Central concepts of chaos theory can be drawn upon to explain the schooling avoidance patterns that have adversely affected these students. At the outset, it appears that the major concepts associated with chaos theory are clearly applicable. As mentioned earlier, however, the original data obtained from my 1991 and 1993 studies were not collected with chaos theory in mind as the guiding theoretical framework. This approach emerged as a result of my secondary analysis of the data. There remains a need for further research at MHS or similar schools for which chaos theory can serve as the theory driving the research.

The gradual change, over a period of twenty years, in the racial makeup of MHS from predominantly white (including Jewish) in the early 1970s to predominantly African American, caught many of the school's teachers and administrators by surprise. Thus, metaphorically speaking along the lines of chaos theory, the flap of a butterfly's wing in India—e.g., the enrollment of a few African American students back in 1970—resulted in catastrophic weather conditions in Florida—e.g., the widespread, chronic school failure of African American males by the 1990s. The riots of the early in 1970s were among the first evidence of turmoil at MHS, and marked the onset of turbulence. The disciplinary hearings that followed the student protests of the 1970s, and the subsequent suspension of large numbers of African American male students, brought widespread negative publicity and turmoil to a district and school that formerly were known for their outstanding student achievement. Turbulence erupted regularly in the form of class disruptions and fights involving both black and white students, but primarily African American males. On one occasion, for example, an African American male student was refused admittance to a disciplinary detention session. After much loud banging on the door by the student, the supervising teacher opened the door. The student then pointed a toy gun in the teacher's face and fired a plastic disk, striking the teacher just below the eye. The teacher, thinking the gun was real, panicked and reacted hysterically. Word of the incident caused widespread fear among the teachers.

Several indications correspond to the dissipating structures referred to in chaos theory, including the findings that (1) the parents of African American male students at MHS effaced themselves and abandoned their role in the education of their sons; (2) the students themselves were pressured by their peers to resist schooling; (3) the teachers and counselors failed to demonstrate caring; and (4) the administrators failed to display instructional leadership. These findings are also evidence of the nonlinear relationships among the key components of the MHS environment. Taken individually, any one of those factors might be considered unimportant or even negligible. When closely and collectively examined, it becomes apparent that deeply embedded patterns of behavior and relationships among the various elements had a dissipating effect on the nature and structure of schooling at MHS. The "shocks" (a chaos theory term) caused by declining academic outcomes were less random than predictable, given the academically dysfunctional conditions and relationships established among and between MHS's students, parents, counselors, and teachers. Less predictable and far more random were the widespread incidents of violence and school disruptions.

This case study of MHS revealed the existence of several strange attractors or focal points from which major events evolved. The African American male students' rejection of insensitive teachers seem to have been central to much of the chaos at MHS. Indeed, the teachers were a constant focal point of turmoil. Regarding the presence of recursive symmetries, in the case of MHS, repeated patterns of interactions among key players in a system emerge as extremely important. The teachers' consistent failure to care about or effectively teach their African American male students is a dynamic component of this. For example, the school's only Chemistry teacher was absolutely hated by African American students. During a three-year period in the late 1980s, not one African American student received a grade higher than "C" from this teacher. Consequently, very few of these students opted to take Chemistry, which precluded the possibility of their taking higher-level science courses. Ironically, the school's only auto mechanics teacher never passed an African American male student in the three years this cohort was attending MHS; however, many African American males elected to take his course.

Since the 1970s, MHS's academic output and overall school climate with respect to African American males has been progressively more dismal, volatile, and chaotic, such that it should come as no surprise that nearly 25 percent of the African American males in the class of 1989 were arrested before their graduation in June 1989. News of this type was constantly fed back into the school and community from the police department, which is located directly across the street from MHS. Thus, the continual information exchange between police personnel and school administrators was a negative feedback mechanism that no doubt contributed to the dismal image of the school held by so many.

Conclusion

The use of traditional qualitative research methods was essential to the emergence of an understanding of the depth of interrelationships between the central components at MHS: the school's African American male students, school personnel, and parents. Additionally, appraisal of the data obtained from this study within the framework of chaos theory contributed greatly to this understanding. In the absence of such a conceptual framework and methodology, the findings presented in this chapter would likely have appeared shallow.

As the present study reveals, however, chaos theory holds promise as an effective construct to explain, holistically, the ecological circumstances related to the education of African American males. It affords committed researchers an effective tool, but requires an extended research window and special research conditions. A central tenet of chaos theory is that the central components must be thoroughly and closely scrutinized. Therefore, researchers who seek to engage it as a conceptual framework in efforts to explain schooling avoidance and school failure must also be "insiders," with broad access to the various central components of the system under study. Moreover, they should expect to engage in an extremely rigorous process.

The present study represents a unique and risky approach to qualitative research in that I, the investigator, served as both an administrator and a researcher in the system under study. While this double-consciousness allowed me fuller access to students, teachers, administrators, parents, and records, it posed countless and highly perplexing role conflicts and ethical dilemmas. For example, there were occasions when I observed African American males engaging in behaviors that violated the school's code of conduct. In the traditional role of an administrator, I would be expected to discipline those involved. However, as a researcher, I found that such events provided insights into the contextual issues operative at the study site; thus, my inclination was to let them run their course. On other occasions, my position as an African American administrator researching the interactions of African American male students and their predominantly white teachers created tension between me and the teachers. The fact that numerous individuals, both African American and non-African American, teachers, administrators, students, and parents alike confirmed my findings as valid was particularly significant for me as a researcher.[4] Clearly, there are inherent research dilemmas as researchers negotiate their roles within the system. The potential for role and ethical conflicts that can compromise the integrity of such investigations is significant.

In recent years, a number of school improvement plans have been developed and implemented at MHS under the direction of a new superintendent and a new principal. Both have adopted, as a special focus, an emphasis on improving the academic outcomes of African American males. However, it remains true that one of the most disconcerting dilemmas facing urban educationalists today is the lack of effective strategies for changing the poor educational and social outcomes of the African American males who attend public schools across the nation. This chapter has highlighted the recursive patterns of schooling avoidance which collectively resulted in widespread underpreparation for a cohort of African American males and a climate of seemingly unexplainable chaos at one public high school. In the case of MHS, there emerged clear patterns of avoidance—a method in the madness.

Endnotes

[1]All names associated with the school, its students, faculty, and parents have been changed to protect their anonymity.

[2]The author gratefully acknowledges the financial support provided by the Spencer Foundation of Chicago for the completion of this follow-up research.

[3]My in-depth interviews with adults, both black and white, confirmed that the white residents moved out of the district as a result of their improved socioeconomic status, concern for the declining quality of education, and fear of student racial unrest at school. The most obvious change, the racial makeup of the school, was clear to teachers, parents, and students alike.

[4]Five African American males in the class of 1989 cohort; the superintendent of schools for the MHS district (an orthodox Jew); the associate superintendent (a non-Jewish white male); the principal of MHS (a non-Jewish white male); two members of the local board of education (one orthodox Jewish male and one non-Jewish white male); the area council president of the MHS parent-teacher association (an African American woman); and six tenured teachers (five Jewish females and one African American female).

References

Blair, B. G. (1993). What does chaos theory have to offer educational administration? *Journal of School Leadership, 3*, 579–96.

Bogdan, R., & Biklen, S. (1992). *Qualitative research.* Boston: Allyn & Bacon.

Culver, L. (1982). Changing settlement patterns of black Americans, 1970–1980. *Journal of Urban Affairs, 4*, 29–48.

Davis, J. E., & Jordan, W. J. (1994). The effects of school context, structure, and experiences on African American males in middle and high schools. *Journal of Negro Education, 63*(4), 570–87.

Farley, J. (1983). Metropolitan housing segregation in the 1980s: The St. Louis case. *Urban Affairs Quarterly, 18*, 247–59.

Fine, M. (1991). *Framing dropouts: Notes on the politics of urban public high school.* Albany: State University of New York Press.

Freedman, D. H. (1992). Is management still a science? *Harvard Business Review, 70*, 26–38.

Garibaldi, A. M. (1992). Educating and motivating African American males to succeed. *Journal of Negro Education, 61*(1), 12–18.

Gleick, J. (1987). *Chaos: Making a new science.* New York: Penguin.

Grier, G., & Grier, E. (1983). *Black suburbanization in the 1970s.* Bethesda, MD: Grier Partnership.

Griffiths, D. E., Hart, A. W., & Blair, B. G. (1991). Still another approach to administration: Chaos theory. *Educational Administration Quarterly, 27*(3), 430–51.

Hayles, N. K. (1990). *Chaos bound: Orderly disorder in contemporary literature and science.* Ithaca, NY: Cornell University Press.

Kozol, J. (1991). *Savage inequalities: Children in America's schools.* New York: Crown Publishers.

Leake, D. O., & Leake, B. L. (1992). Islands of hope: Milwaukee's African American immersion schools. *Journal of Negro Education, 61*(1), 4–11.

Massey, D. S., & Denton, N. A. (1988). Suburbanization and segregation in U.S. metropolitan areas. *American Journal of Sociology, 94*(3), 592–626.

Polite, V. C. (1991). *All dressed up with no place to go: A critical ethnography of African-American male students in an urban high school.* (UMI Dissertation Abstracts, 5032, 91–29–487)

Polite, V. C. (1993a). If only we knew then what we know now: Foiled opportunities to learn in suburbia. *Journal of Negro Education, 62*(3), 337–54.

Polite, V. C. (1993b). Reproduction and resistance: An analysis of African American males' responses to schooling. In M. Shujaa (Ed.), *Too much schooling, too little education: A paradox of black life in white societies* (pp. 183–202). Trenton, NJ: African World Press.

Powell, A., Farrar, E., & Cohen, D. (1985). *The shopping mall high school.* Boston: Houghton Mifflin.

Prigogine, I., & Stengers, I. (1984). *Order out of chaos: Man's new dialogue with nature.* New York: Bantam Books.

Stahura, J. M. (1983). Determinants of change in the distribution of blacks across the suburbs. *Sociological Quarterly, 24,* 421–33.

Stevenson, M. F. Jr. (1988). *Points of departure, acts of resolve: Black-Jewish relations in Detroit, 1937–1962.* Unpublished doctoral dissertation, University of Michigan, Ann Arbor.

Zukav, G. (1979). *The dancing of the Wu Li masters: An overview of the new physics.* Toronto, Canada: Bantam Books.

Part Four

The Commencement

Chapter Thirteen

Prophets of Power in the Professoriate: A Sermon for Cultural Workers

M. Christopher Brown

Disclaimer: For the benefit of the churched, unchurched, religious, and non-theist, it is necessary for me to speak briefly to the subtitle, "A Sermon for Cultural Workers.[1] Many identify the word sermon with its primary definition—a religious speech or conversation. However, the word sermon also refers to any speech on public conduct or duty. What follows is a marriage between my personal voice and scholarly discourse. It is also important for me to acknowledge the homiletic outline which will be utilized. One of the standard texts on homiletics is William Evans' *How to Prepare Sermons and Gospel Addresses*. However, any true teacher/preacher/prophet knows that no text can dictate personal style. Thus the following sermon is outlined in my own pulpit voice.

The Opening Commentary

Good evening. I am delighted to have this opportunity to share my thoughts with you. It is good to be in a room filled with so many teachers, and possibly cultural workers. I know that some of you are here tonight by choice and others by delegation. I commend those of you who have already chosen to be cultural workers. However to those of you who join us for the purposes of criticism, fulfilling a course credit requirement, and/or as a condition of employment, I declare that schools can build a new social order (Counts, 1932).

There is a dark veil over the future of our youth, especially African American youth (black males in particular). The veil is the burden of miseducation. "Miseducation results from being trained rather than educated" (Akbar, 1982, p. 2). School has become a place where the only lessons that many learn are how to walk in straight lines, sit quietly in rows, and raise their hands to request the performance of their bodily functions. Education and schooling have become preparation for prison at best, and societal misappropriation (i.e., poverty, homelessness, hopelessness, and despair) at worst. Consequently, a significant amount of time in colleges and universities needs to be spent "unlearning" primary and secondary school training. Sadly, many institutions neglect this duty.

I stopped by tonight to tell you that there is a better way. Colleges can teach students how to maximize the human potential which might otherwise be wasted. Those of us assembled can reform, transform, and revolutionize the academic enterprise. The first step is for each and every one of us to recognize our responsibility, acknowledge our potential, and engage in the cultural work of empowerment. Therefore let us hear a "Word" on educational change, and the possibilities for African American youth and the nation's youth in general.

The Text

I would like to take my text from one of the sacred writings of old. In olden times, many prophets arose to foretell those things which would occur in the life of a nation-state. Among those ancient sages was the prophet Joel. His prophecies were so apocalyptic and canonical that they have been memorialized in a book bearing his name. I believe that in his words there is a message for those of us who dare call ourselves teachers, educators, and professors.

In the Book of Joel, chapter two, verse twenty four, we find these words written: "And it shall come to pass afterward, that I will pour out my spirit upon all flesh; and your sons and your daughters shall prophesy, and your old men shall dream dreams, your young men shall see visions." (Joel 2:24, King James Version)

If I can hold your attention for just a little while, I would like to preach from the subject PROPHETS OF POWER IN THE PROFESSORIATE. Again, Prophets of Power in the Professoriate.

The Situational Context

Have you seen them? They are our children. They are wide-eyed, eager, anxious, and ambivalent. They are children who wait and watch for us to teach and touch their lives. They are children who arrive on college campuses barely eighteen. They are children who too soon become adults facing the pressures of sex and sexuality, alcohol and drug proliferation, class schedules and intellectual rigor, as well as recreation and personal development.

They are children fresh from their parents' homes, seeking and searching for identity, place, and direction.

The above are not the sum total of the maturational tests and trials confronting today's college students, particularly those from marginalized groups. African American students and other students of color must encounter racism and xenophobia. Native Americans must endure mascots which desecrate their spiritual symbols and iconography. Gay, lesbian, and bisexual students must endure campus-sponsored functions woven with gilded threads of heterosexism and homophobia. Just recently, I saw a brochure for one university's freshman orientation that included a session on "Dating: Male-Female Campus Relations." Imagine the challenges and experiences facing students who intersect the margins of race, sex, gender, sexuality, physical ability, and/or economic disadvantage.

It is not enough to say euphemistically that kids will be kids, until we have teachers who can explain what adulthood is really all about. Professors must ask themselves can we help? or will we hinder the students? Likewise, do we even know or understand the work of a college professor? Be careful Mr./Mrs. I-Know-What-Students-Need. I asked the question whether or not you knew how to help them—aid, assist, or guide. I did not inquire of your ability to tell them what to do—mandate, dictate, or manipulate.

Khalil Gibran (1923) was not just talking to parents when he spoke of children. He could have just as easily been speaking to college professors. In his book *The Prophet* it is easy to replace the word "student" with "children." If the great Lebanese poet were speaking tonight, he would say to you:

> Your [students] are not your [students].
> They are the sons and the daughters of Life's longing for itself.
> They come through you but they are not from you,
> And though they are with you yet they belong not to you.
> You may give them your love but not your thoughts,
> For they have their own thoughts.
> You may house their bodies but not their souls,
> For their souls dwell in the house of tomorrow,
> Which you cannot visit not even in your dreams.
> You may strive to be like them, but seek not to make them like you.
> For life goes backward nor tarries with yesterday. (p.17)

How many times have we heard our colleagues romanticizing, saying that students are not like they were yesterday? How many times have we heard our colleagues say, "When I was in school things were different"? The students who enter our college classrooms are not there to imitate us. The students who enter our college classrooms are not there to be indoctrinated with our narrow, self-centered guideposts for life. Students come to the university to engage in critical thinking and liberal learning, and to learn how to exercise their mental capacities.

I see the blank stares and looks of bewilderment. You are pondering my call for empowerment with Gibran's declaration on youth. You are saying, "Mr. Rev. Dr. Teacher/Preacher/Prophet Man, we think you have contradicted yourself." There is no contradiction; there is a correlative. Faculty must assist students as they navigate the labyrinth of college, but faculty must not chart their course. Each student must find his/her way serendipitously. It is our job to remove or place warning signs near those pitfalls and detours which may harm or hinder student progress. We must not walk the maze for them, but must cheer them on as they embark upon the course of life, living, and destiny. We must tell them that they can, they will, and they *must* attain. We must be Prophets of Power in the Professoriate.

The Scriptural Exegesis

What does the prophet Joel have to say about the professorial quest to be Prophets of Power? In the Book of Joel, the prophet announced that the day would come when men and women would both prophesy, that the seniors would dream, and that the young would envision. This is a powerful prophesy for faculty. This prophesy gives hope to what we can and must do to aid and empower our youth. The text issues a challenge to faculty to teach, preach, and prophesy.

It could be said that teaching is what faculty say to students regarding the disciplinary subject matter relevant to their collegiate majors. Preaching is what faculty proclaim to students and others (intentionally or unintentionally) about the role, purpose, and function of education. Prophesying is how faculty inspire students by assuring them that some "thing" is coming which is greater than their current condition or position. Hence, prophecy is an act of empowerment. Empowerment, as we have already discussed, must be included among the primary activities performed by college professors. Professors must be Prophets of Power.

You say, "Well now Mr. Rev. Dr. Teacher/Preacher/Prophet Man, if I am correct, prophesying is sacred and professoring is secular." That is both correct and incorrect. The sacred and secular are not polar, but polarized. The words prophet and professor are not opposites, they are just contextualized differently. The Latin etymology of the words is similar. Prophet comes from "propheta," meaning to speak. Professor comes from "profiteri," meaning to acknowledge or affirm. Neither word as originally utilized denoted sacredness or secularity. However, both words call for the individual to verbalize, and as such may be interchanged.

Patricia Williams (1991), in *The Alchemy of Race and Rights,* says that "the school created a dense atmosphere that muted [her] voice to inaudibility" (p. 55). Faculty have been hoodwinked into being intellectually silent about educational change and social justice. Faculty no longer write or speak from the passion of their voices. Their thoughts and musings are filtered through research methods, citations to prior scholarship, and accreditation guidelines on instructional content. The audacity of the professorial presence has been diminished by a system that disempowers faculty, and therefore disempowers students. Faculty must reclaim their voices and boldly announce their authentic and unfiltered thoughts and experiences (Brown, forthcoming).

College professors should prophesy good things regarding a new social order, free from the stresses and strains of inequality in educational attainment because of race, sex, gender, economics, and/or other condition. Simultaneously, faculty must prophesy the end of the current hegemonic regime that gives primacy to whiteness, class, caste, maleness, heterosexuality, militarism, imperialism, and privilege. They must craft a language that engenders equity, empowers the marginalized, and elevates social justice. Geneva Smitherman (1991) asserts that "language . . . play[s] a dominant role in the formation of ideology, consciousness, and class relations," and therefore that "consciousness and ideology are largely the products of . . . the sociolinguistic construction of reality" (p. 117).

Language can change reality. When we say to our students, "You do not understand," we simultaneously construct the reality (real or perceived) that we do understand. "Powerful political statements [are] registered through the designatory terms by which individuals reference themselves and other . . . people" (Harper, 1996, p. 54). The words that professors teach, preach, and prophesy to their students can and will become "self-fulfilling prophesies"; hence the term (Merton, 1968). A self-fulfilling prophecy leads to behavior that makes the prophecy become true. What are the self-fulfilling prophesies that faculty currently plant in their students' cognitive schemata? Have faculty prophesied good things or bad? This is a question that we must each ask ourselves, because what is now clear is that all faculty have prophesied (knowingly or unknowingly) through their teaching.

Americans, particularly those of African descent, have a rich history in the traditions of teaching and preaching (Lightfoot, 1988). We have heard John Dewey teach about the need for pragmatic and experiential schooling. We have heard Martin Luther King preach about equality and justice in society. We have heard Thurgood Marshall both teach and preach about quality schools for all children. The time has now come for faculty/cultural workers to teach, preach, and prophesy new dreams and visions.

Currently social reform is being brokered by politicians (e.g., Newt Gingrich, Linda Chavez), economists (e.g., Thomas Sowell, Milton Friedman), and ideologues (e.g., Diane Ravitch, Wardell Connerly). College faculty must return to their "profession." Faculty must engage in the work of building a cohesive culture. To those who promote conservativism in education, I ask, is the current system worth conserving? This nation and our world need prophets of power. Men and women with a "Word" for our times. Prophets like George Counts who asked, "Dare the school build a new social order?" (Counts, 1932; Prophets like Patti Lather who assert that there is a place for "feminist research and pedagogy with/in the postmodern" (Lather, 1991). Prophets like Paulo Freire who proclaimed that the educational system was infested with a "pedagogy of the oppressed" (Freire, 1970). Prophets like

Patricia Hill Collins who advance "black feminist thought" (Collins, 1990). Prophets like Cornel West who stand firm and unabashedly teach, preach, and profess that "race matters" (West, 1993). We need Prophets of Power in the Professoriate.

Prophets—persons preaching, prophesying prophecies. Power—from the Greek word "dynamikos," meaning explosive, productive activity. Professoriate—in the university, the classroom of society. We need prophetic professors preaching and prophesying self-fulfilling prophecies that are explosive, dynamic, and productive in the university—our societal classroom. We need Prophets of Power in the Professoriate.

The Three-point Lesson

The "Word"

Let us turn now to the three prerequisites needed to be a prophet of power. The first thing that a prophet of power must have is a "Word." What is the "Word" Is it merely that thing which is spoken by a teacher/preacher/prophet? Is the "Word" merely the combination of speech symbols and sounds? Is the "Word" a set of linguistic forms which are both written and spoken? No, no, no; the "Word" has got to be more than that. All of this talk about touching and changing lives. All of this pontification about self-fulfilling prophecies. All of this translating Latin and Greek. The "Word" has to be more than written or spoken linguistic forms.

Charles Lawrence (1995) says that the "Word" is an "articulation and validation of our common experience. It is a vocation of struggle against dehumanization, a practice of raising questions about the reasons for oppression, an inheritance of passion and hope" (Lawrence, p. 336). I think we have it now. The "Word" is the sum total of our lived experiences (real, vicarious, and intellectual) translated into useful lessons of empowerment. The "Word" is the seed for liberation, emancipation, and education. The "Word" is the key that unlocks the mental and cognitive shackles of human potential. The "Word" is the thing that says to poor children that they can be economically stable. The "Word" is the thing that says to black and brown children that their skin is not the entirety of their humanity or their possibilities. I know about the "Word."

You ask what do I know about the "Word"? I know that I heard it and believed, and changed my social condition and statistical projection. Me—the Mr. Rev. Dr. Teacher/Preacher/Prophet Man. I grew up as a child of the "Word." I grew up with prophecies which said I could become something greater than my "at-riskness." Growing up in a single-parent home, just me and my mother believing the "Word." Living out a working-class existence with a middle-class dream; believing the "Word." I was energetic and optimistic about the "Word," so the school system labeled me hyperactive and placed me in a classroom for the emotionally handicapped (EH). Educational statistics suggest that my academic trajectory should have ended there, but there were teachers like Velma Brown (no kin) and Mozelle Myers who preached and prophesied the "Word" over me. Self-fulfilling prophetic "Words" about my giftedness. I left that class and went on to graduate from high school with honors, ranked number eight in the senior class. My class rank and positionality were the manifestations of self-fulfilling prophecies regarding my ability to achieve.

The "Word" is lively and did not stop at North Charleston High School. I went to college where I heard the "Word" preached every day from every corner of the campus. South Carolina State University is a small, rural, underfunded black college located in the town of Orangeburg, but the campus is filled with teacher/preacher/prophets. Prophets like Roy Simms, Martha Jean Heggins, Terrence Cummings, Maceo Nance, Frances Mack, Carl Carpenter, and Connie Shivers, who teach, preach, and prophesy every day to poor, black students (like me) that they could do anything they desired, if they worked hard enough. I graduated from South Carolina State cum laude; another prophecy self-fulfilled.

On the "Word" of those Orangeburg prophets I went on to the University of Kentucky with $1500, eight boxes, and a dream. I encountered John Harris, Reginald Alston, Ed Sagan, and Virginia Nordin who kept giving me the "Word." In less than a year I graduated with a written thesis, a Master's degree, and an understanding that I too must begin preaching and teaching the "Word." The Kentucky prophets sent me off to Penn State, where Cathy Lyons, Bernard Bell, Bob Hendrickson, Estela Bensimon,

Henry Giroux, Joe Kincheloe, and a host of other scholars prophesied to me about the "Word" and its role in social change. Three years later, on August 9, 1997, at the age of twenty-five, I graduated with my Ph.D. in Higher Education with a cognate in Jurisprudence and Political Theory. Not bad for the poor little black boy in an EH classroom, from a single parent home in South Carolina, who was labeled "at-risk." It is not anything so great that I have done, but the "Word" that teachers and educators continued to teach, preach, and prophesy about my potential and possibilities. I now preach the "Word."

Vincent Harding (1981) asks us in his book, *There Is a River*, a very probing question about the "Word." He asks, "What is the role of the . . . spoken word, the preached word, the written word, the published word . . . ?" (p. 82: The answer is empowerment. The "Word" is designed to inspire students/individuals to transform their current conditions into new realities. The "Word" is intended to be an illuminating light that shines bright upon the road of possibility, entreating all who will to walk therein so that they may study, learn, and grow.

Faculty must learn the "Word" if they are to be Prophets of Power. They must continuously work toward decolonizing their own minds and the minds of their students. Faculty must rethink hegemonic assumptions, and reconceptualize privilege and power. Prophets of Power are not racist. Prophets of Power are not sexist. Prophets of Power are not homophobic. Prophets of Power are not classist or elitist. Prophets of Power do not slight those with limited physical ability. Prophets of Power are open, honest, and authentic. Prophets of Power both imbibe and embody the "Word" which they teach, preach, and prophesy.

College professors must speak the "Word," read the "Word," spread the "Word," and live the "Word." It is only through the "Word" of empowerment that we can ever touch lives. Only the "Word" can transform the world. The "Word" is truth. Faculty must know the truth, for it can and will make them and their students free. Proverbs, eighteenth chapter, twenty-first verse, announces that "Death and life are in the power of the tongue."

Dreams and Visions

The second prerequisite for Prophets of Power in the Professoriate is dreams and visions. Dreams are abstract creations of the imagination. Visions are concrete creations of the imagination. Dreams and visions are both necessary, but they serve two distinct purposes. For Prophets of Power, dreams are the guiding principles and philosophies which are the essence of cultural work. Visions on the other hand are the policies and practices which are concrete manifestations of cultural work (e.g., publications, programs, initiatives).

Charles Lawrence (1995) says that "dreamers, be they prophets, politicians, or philosophers, challenge established understandings" (p. 350). Dreams and visions reconfigure the academic, social, and political spaces which are critical to teaching/preaching/prophesying. One of the fundamental travails for cultural workers is to "break with the hegemonic modes of seeing, thinking, and being that block our capacity to see ourselves oppositionally, to imagine, describe, and invent ourselves in ways that are liberatory" (hooks, 1992, p. 2). Faculty must work to free themselves so that they can free their students, colleagues, and others.

The challenge is for each professor to have the dream that every school (and ultimately the world) can be a better place. Prophets of Power must dream and believe that students can live better lives in a reconstructed social order. They must dream that the power of the "Word" can change and mend lives which are decimated and distressed by the pernicious effects of the present society. However it is not enough to dream; faculty must also envision. Envisioning is the act of building and establishing. Professors must write books and articles that articulate a new plan for society. Faculty must work with policy makers to draft guidelines which when implemented provide for a better today and tomorrow. It is not enough to provide orange juice; we must grow orange trees. Cultural workers must know that the work that is done today will promote and reproduce transformative work (both academic and social) in perpetuity.

In both dreams and visions, Prophets of Power must create "counter-spaces" which allow social justice to flourish. Counter-spaces allow those empowered by the "Word" to participate in the dismantling of the hegemonic structure, and assist in the erection of societal paragons of liberty and equity. The creation of counter-spaces is designed to facilitate individual access to transformative cultural work, and to permit all persons to "reclaim public space for the public good" (Kelley, 1997, p. 156). Dreams and visions are the conduits by which cultural workers establish, maintain, and advance counter-spaces. Dreams and visions are the principal tools of teacher/preacher/prophets in the university and society.

Some years ago I visited the National Civil Rights Museum in Memphis, Tennessee. Those of you who have been there know that the museum is adjoined to the Lorraine Motel, which was the site of the tragic assassination of Dr. Martin Luther King. On a bronze tablet outside the hotel, in the alleged assailant's line of fire, is a most bemusing scriptural quote. The tablet reads: "And they said one to another, Behold, this dreamer cometh. Come now therefore, and let us slay him, and cast him into some pit, and we will say, Some evil beast hath devoured him: and we shall see what will become of his dreams" (Genesis 37:19–20).

Are you a dreamer? Do you have empowering visions? Do your dreams and visions challenge the system? Do your dreams and visions resurrect fear, loathing, and opposition within the dominant power structure? Do they wish to silence your dream? Are your dreams premised on social justice? Are you envisioning policies, practices, and publications which advance cultural work and the "Word"? What is your dream? What is your vision?

Practicing What We Preach

Let me hurry on, lest I hold you too long. The third and final prerequisite for Prophets of Power is that faculty must practice what they preach. I know too many of my so-called fellow teacher/preacher/prophets who espouse dreams and advance visions which they neither believe nor practice. There are faculty members who write about erecting villages of dissimilarity, yet they reside in self-constructed, isolated enclaves of homogeneity. There are professors who proclaim allegiance to transformative democratic social theory, but will vote against giving tenure to colleagues who do paradigm-shifting work on social reconstruction, critical race theory, feminist discourse, and/or postcolonial studies (see *Taboo: The Journal of Culture and Education*, Spring 1997).

One of the major problems with current academic prophecy is that too many of the potential prophets of power are hypocrites. Too many professors say and write one thing, but believe another. Too many professors are "liberal" in the most derogatory sense of the word. These are the faculty who advance liberalism with the same consistency as a fairweather friend. Derrick Bell (1987) points out that it behooves cultural workers to be cognizant of his theory of interest convergence. He argues that the dominant power structure never yields power or products in the interest of social justice alone. Bell argues that any time the dominant group "liberally" advances the interest of marginalized people, the dominant group has some unstated interest of its own. Hence, the dominant group is only liberal when there is something to be gained which makes it more dominant.

As Prophets of Power, professors cannot teach/preach/prophesy that which they neither believe nor practice. Prophets of Power must provide living lessons for social change. Prophets of Power must stand before demagogues, pedagogues, and ideologues and denounce the partisan, privileged, prejudiced assumptions rooted in conservative principles, policies, and practices. Faculty must be the torchbearers for better schools and a better world. The challenge of torchbearing, though daunting, it is not impossible. It is easy to light the way to transformative societal change if all you have to do is live. It is easier for faculty to practice what they preach than to pretend.

Years ago, when I was an undergraduate in college, my Aunt Keren spoke a "Word" to me which I will never forget. My mother and aunt would come and pick me up at the end of nearly every semester. As I departed campus one holiday season, we were in the car talking about my semester's activities as a teacher education major and self-proclaimed public speaker. At the end of my soliloquy, my aunt interjected the "Word" which resonates daily in my mind. She said, "The most important lessons that you will ever teach will be to the people standing in the wings." I have lived to discover the truth in her "Word" to me. There are people with whom I have never spoken or interacted, but whose lives I touch by my living example. There are people who will never take a class under my instruction who are taught by my daily engagements in cultural work and social reconstruction. Such ought to be the case for all Prophets of Power in the academy.

Is it evident to students or colleagues that you are engaged in cultural work without your telling them? Does your everyday life preach volumes, or do you have to point to your sporadic and minuscule instances of social reconstruction? R. Eugene Rice (1996), a scholar-in-residence at the American Association for Higher Education, says that "what is needed is a broader, more coherent conception of the scholarly work of faculty" (p. 2). In response to Rice's request for innovative professional performance, there are three things which Prophets of Power must do. They must engage in academic midwifing, role molding, and frientoring with their students. Simply put, professors performing under the cultural work rubric must be academic midwives, assisting in bringing to life the sleeping potential and possibilities of their students. Prophets of Power must role mold by actively helping students construct themselves and their cognitive dexterity in ways which will maximize the student's potential. Finally, frientoring requires teacher/preacher/prophets to create safe spaces in which faculty and students can engage in nonhierarchical discourse and advising (Brown, forthcoming; Brown, Davis, & McClendon, 1999).

The Invitation to Discipleship

Much has been said tonight about educational change and our professorial responsibility to effect that change. Education is the only occupation in which there is no penalty for performance failure. Doctors are sued for malpractice. Lawyers are disbarred. Financial brokers have their licenses revoked. What should society require as penance for faculty who are neglectful of their duties as cultural workers? Maybe no atonement will be needed if all faculty become Prophets of Power. Those of us here tonight can show our faculty colleagues a better way. Can you be a Prophet of Power in the Professoriate? Will you be one? The world is in need of faculty who will be Prophets of Power. We need faculty engaged in the cultural work of teaching/preaching/prophesying. Teaching is cultural work (Freire, 1998).

Our classrooms are crowded with the underprepared and the miseducated. In many institutions of higher learning, professors have become babysitters for the uninterested. Lack of interest is a luxury of the oppressor. Marginalized groups must be interested and empowered if they are to have liberty, justice, and equity. The poor, oppressed, and dispossessed are in need of teacher/preacher/prophets who will prophesy the "Word" according to their experience. There is a better world which is not, but could be, with the aid of Prophets of Power. The power to change our condition and subsequently the world is living in each of us.

Will you be a disciple of change? Will you be a cultural worker? Is there one who will be a Prophet of Power? Is there one who is willing to teach, preach, and prophesy the "Word"? The "Word" is power. The "Word" is transformative. The "Word" helps enact dreams and visions. It is the "Word" that must be preached and practiced.

Is there one? Who will be a Prophet of Power in the Professoriate? Will you be a Prophet of Power?

References

Akbar, N. (1982). *From miseducation to education*. Jersey City, NJ: New Mind Productions.

Bell, D. (1987). Introduction to Gil Kujovich's equal opportunity in higher education and the black college: The era of separate but equal. *Minnesota Law Review*, 72(1), 23–27.

Brown, M. C. (forthcoming). Involvement with students: How much can I give? In M. Garcia (Ed.), *Microcosms of diversity: Succeeding in an academic career as a faculty of color*. Westport, CT: Greenwood Press.

Brown, M. C., Davis, G. L., and McClendon, S. A. (1999). Mentoring graduate students of color: Myths, models, and modes. *Peabody Journal of Education, 74*, 105-18.

Collins, P. H. (1990). *Black feminist thought: Knowledge, consciousness, and the politics of empowerment*. Boston: Unwin Hyman.

Counts, G. S. (1932). *Dare the school build a new social order?* New York: John Day.

Evans, W. (no date). *How to prepare sermons and gospel addresses*. Chicago: Moody Press.

Freire, P. (1970). *Pedagogy of the oppressed*. New York: Continuum.

Freire, P. (1998). *Teachers as Cultural Workers*. Boulder, CO: Westview.

Gibran, K. (1923). *The Prophet*. New York: Alfred A. Knopf.

Harding, V. (1981). *There is a river*. New York: Vintage.

Harper, P. B. (1996). *Are We Not Men? Masculine anxiety and the problem of African-American identity*. New York: Oxford University Press.

hooks, b. (1992). *Black looks: Race and representation*. Boston: South End Press.

Kelley, R. D. G. (1997). *Yo' mama's disfunktional? Fighting the culture wars in urban America*. Boston: Beacon Press.

Lather, P. (1991). *Getting smart: Feminist research and pedagogy with/in the postmodern*. New York: Routledge.

Lawrence, C. R. (1995). The word and the river: Pedagogy as scholarship as struggle. In K. Crenshaw et al. (Eds.), *Critical race theory: The key writings that formed the movement*. New York: The New Press.

Lightfoot, S. L. (1988). *Balm in Gilead: Journey of a healer*. New York: Addison-Wesley.

Merton, R. K. (1968). *Social theory and social structure* (2nd ed.). New York: Free Press.

Rice, R. E. (1996). *Making a place for the new American scholar.* Washington, DC: American Association for Higher Education.

Smitherman, G. (1991). "What is Africa to Me?" Language, Ideology, and African American. *American Speech, 61* (2), 115–32.

West, C. (1993). *Race matters*. Boston: Beacon.

Williams, P. J. (1991). *The alchemy of race and rights*. Cambridge, MA: Harvard University Press.

Contributors

M. Christopher Brown II, a former American Educational Research Association/Spencer Foundation Research Fellow, is an assistant professor of Higher Education in the Department of Educational Organization and Leadership at the University of Illinois at Urbana-Champaign. His research investigates the systemic and structural challenges to effective and efficient functioning in postsecondary institutions. This system of inquiry attempts to make visible the hidden voices of race and power in the law, policy, history, and governance surrounding and within colleges and universities. Dr. Brown is the author of *The Quest to Define Collegiate Desegregation: Black Colleges, Title VI Compliance, and Post-Adams Litigation* (1999), as well as numerous articles and book chapters. Currently, he is revisiting the philosophy of social reconstruction, in order to outline its usefulness as a research methodology and a framework for policy analysis. Undaunted in his belief that schools can build a new social order, Dr. Brown is hoping that his new work on social reconstruction will help radical educators and critical theorists realize their aims as cultural workers and change agents. Dr. Brown holds a Ph.D. in Higher Education with cognates in Political Theory and Jurisprudence from the Pennsylvania State University.

James Earl Davis is a visiting scholar in the Institute for Research on Women and Gender (1998–99) at the University of Michigan-Ann Arbor, on leave from the University of Delaware where he is an associate professor in the School of Education. At the University of Delaware, he is also a faculty affiliate in the Center for Community Development and Family Policy in the College of Urban Affairs and Public Policy. He received his Ph.D. in Social Policy and Evaluation from Cornell University and completed a post-doctoral research fellowship in the Division of Education Policy at the Educational Testing Service in Princeton, New Jersey. A former National Academy of Education/Spencer Foundation Postdoctoral Fellow, Dr. Davis' research and teaching are in the areas of sociology of education, program evaluation, educational assessment, and public policy. His current research focuses on masculinities in schools and the social and educational experiences of African American boys/men. He is coeditor (with Vernon Polite) of *African American Males in School and Society: Practices and Policies for Effective Education* (1999).

James Baldwin was a renowned literary figure and social critic in both African American and American culture. His article "A Talk to Teachers," originally published in the December 21, 1963 issue of *The Saturday Review*, appears in a collection of his nonfiction work, *The Price of the Ticket* (1985).

Karl Bell is an advising specialist at Missouri Western State College and a graduate student at the University of Missouri-Kansas City. His research is centered on how "literacies of power" intersect with race in educational environments.

Garrett Albert Duncan specializes in conducting research that problematizes race and positionality in urban school settings. He holds an assistant professorship in both the Department of Education and the African and African American Studies program at Washington University in St. Louis. He recently guest edited (with Michele Foster) a special issue of *The Journal of Negro Education* (1996).

C. Keith Harrison is an assistant professor in the Division of Kinesiology, Department of Sports Management and Communication, at the University of Michigan. He is also is founder and director of the Paul Robeson Research Center for Academic and Athletic Prowess. His research interests include race relations and sport, images of athletes in advertising, and ethnic athletic identity.

Tyrone C. Howard is an assistant professor of Teaching and Learning in the College of Education at the Ohio State University. His research interests include curricular and instructional reform, and the education of African American students.

Michael Mobley is an assistant professor of Counseling Psychology at the University of Missouri-Columbia. Dr. Mobley is currently working on constructing a model for counseling gay, lesbian, and transgendered persons of color.

William Eric Perkins is the author of the widely acclaimed book, *Droppin' Science: Critical Essays on Rap Music and Hiphop Culture* (1996)? Dr. Perkins is a former assistant dean of the W.E.B. DuBois College House at the University of Pennsylvania.

Vernon C. Polite is associate professor of Educational Administration at the Catholic University of America. Dr. Polite's research focuses on urban school leadership, race, class, and gender issues, and qualitative research strategies. He has recently published (with James E. Davis) *African American Males in School and Society: Practices and Policies for Effective Education*.

Christopher M. Span is a doctoral student in the Department of Educational Policy Studies at the University of Illinois, Urbana-Champaign. His Master's thesis on Milwaukee's immersion schools has produced several publications and presentations.

Edward Underwood is head of the Department of Urban Leadership and Policy Studies in the School of Education at the University of Missouri-Kansas City. Professor Underwood specializes in designing strategies for classroom teachers to integrate cultural diversity into urban school curricula.

COUNTERPOINTS

Studies in the Postmodern Theory of Education

General Editors
Joe L. Kincheloe & Shirley R. Steinberg

Counterpoints publishes the most compelling and imaginative books being written in education today. Grounded on the theoretical advances in criticalism, feminism, and postmodernism in the last two decades of the twentieth century, Counterpoints engages the meaning of these innovations in various forms of educational expression. Committed to the proposition that theoretical literature should be accessible to a variety of audiences, the series insists that its authors avoid esoteric and jargonistic languages that transform educational scholarship into an elite discourse for the initiated. Scholarly work matters only to the degree it affects consciousness and practice at multiple sites. Counterpoints' editorial policy is based on these principles and the ability of scholars to break new ground, to open new conversations, to go where educators have never gone before.

For additional information about this series or for the submission of manuscripts, please contact:

Joe L. Kincheloe & Shirley R. Steinberg
637 West Foster Avenue
State College, PA 16801

To order other books in this series, please contact our Customer Service Department at: